"[A] compelling narrative . . . An elevated manner of address and a rich vocabulary at odds with his impoverished state and deadbeat friends make Mr. Eighner a quirky guide into the homeless condition as he plunges on, through Miracle Miles, desert flea markets, and dusty truck stops, surviving en route the complex architecture of highway access ramps, subzero temperatures, psychotic companions, and an amazing encounter with the Texas welfare system."
—*The Wall Street Journal*

"Eighner's account of his life on the streets is great writing, factual and declarative like George Orwell's *Down and Out in Paris and London*, personal and affecting like *The Diary of Anne Frank*. And he is funny. . . . I found myself remembering its visceral details in my dreams."
—*L.A. Style*

"Strongly recommended . . . His unique voice [is] part naive innocence, part eccentric fool. Remarkable."
—*Library Journal*

"Lars Eighner has written a remarkable book, and introduced us to an unforgettably singular character—himself. His elegant, courtly language and wry sense of humor play a perfect counterpoint to the grubby misadventures he recounts. Comparisons to Defoe's *Robinson Crusoe* and Hamsun's *Hunger*—as well as, of course, Orwell and Ackerly—leap to mind. Eighner is a witty and informative commentator (he knows a lot of odd, interesting stuff), and an astute, economical portraitist of various grifters, scroungers, pathological liars, and Good Samaritans who cross his path. This book will become a classic of down-and-out literature. But beyond that, Eighner belongs with the classical personal essayists, who can compel our attention on any subject, because of the idiosyncratic suppleness and sanity of his voice."
—Phillip Lopate

W9-CON-315

"An unaffected, absorbing narrative. Eighner fills his pages with vivid descriptions, perceptive observations, humor, and a writing style that carries the reader easily and almost painlessly over troublesome issues."   —*Booklist*

"In spare, unsensational and often elegant prose, Eighner tells how it was possible for him to live from what he gleaned in Dumpsters. . . . [He's] a clearheaded observer of the world."
                                                              —*Publishers Weekly*

Also by Lars Eighner

Bayou Boy and Other Stories
BMOC

Travels
with
Lizbeth

THREE YEARS ON THE ROAD
AND ON THE STREETS

Lars Eighner

St. Martin's Griffin
New York

www.stmartins.com

Parts of the introduction and chapters 1 and 2 and brief passages of several of the essays appeared in somewhat different form as "Travels with Lizbeth" in *The Threepenny Review*, Winter 1991.

"On Dumpster Diving" first appeared in *The Threepenny Review*, Fall 1991, and was first published in book form in *The Pushcart Prize XVII* (Pushcart Press, 1992).

"Phlebitis" first appeared in *The Threepenny Review*, Spring 1992.

"Daniel" first appeared in *The Threepenny Review*, Winter 1993.

The Library of Congress Cataloging-in-Publication Data is available upon request.

ISBN 978-1-250-03625-4 (trade paperback)
ISBN 978-1-4668-3644-0 (e-book)

St. Martin's Griffin books may be purchased for educational, business, or promotional use. For information on bulk purchases, please contact Macmillan Corporate and Premium Sales Department at 1-800-221-7945, extension 5442, or write specialmarkets@macmillan.com.

First St. Martin's Griffin Edition: December 2013

10 9 8 7 6 5 4 3 2 1

To Cliff Hexamer, Steven Saylor, Wendy Lesser, and, of course, Lizbeth

CONTENTS

INTRODUCTION

When I began this account I was living under a shower curtain in a stand of bamboo in a public park. I did not undertake to write about homelessness, but wrote what I knew, as an artist paints a still life, not because he is especially fond of fruit, but because the subject is readily at hand.

In the summer of 1989, when I was in the bamboo, I supposed interest in homelessness had peaked in the presidential election of the previous year. Moreover, I thought my experiences with homelessness were atypical.

I still think my experiences were atypical, but I have come to disbelieve in typical homelessness. I had some advantages and some disadvantages and I chose the course that seemed most likely to provide the survival of myself and my dog Lizbeth on the most comfortable terms of which our situation would admit.

I did not often associate with other homeless people. I avoided the homeless shelters and hobo jungles. I did not attempt to survive on the streets of a very large city, but made my way for the most part in a liberal and affluent area of an overgrown college town. Although I often despaired of improving my material situation, I seldom lacked for a feeling of self-worth or a sense of mission. On the other hand, I spent most of my time in Texas, where a general contempt for the poor is reflected in a useless, vestigial social welfare system. I handicapped myself by adopting from the first a policy of not stealing and not begging on the streets. And, of course, I would not be parted from Lizbeth. I do not pretend to speak for the homeless. I think no one could speak for all the various people who have in common the condition of being homeless. I do not know many of the homeless, but of the condition of being homeless I know something, and that is part of what I have written about.

In truth, becoming homeless was a long process that I can date only arbitrarily. I had been without a reliable income for about a year before I left the shack I had been living in. For about five months after I left the shack I traveled and imposed on friends and strangers, so that I spent only part of the time on the streets. Moreover, throughout that first period I believed I had one prospect or another of improving my situation and I did not regard myself as truly homeless.

When I had the opportunity to get off the street for a week or a month or even for only a night, I did so; my object was not to explore homelessness but to get off the street. I have recounted these events in the ordinary narrative manner, but have only summarized the events of my longer stopovers. Eventually I became homeless enough to suit anyone's definition. In spite of the challenges that homelessness presented, the chief characteristic of my experience of homelessness was tedium. The days and nights that Lizbeth and I were literally without a roof over our heads, although by far the majority of the more than two years encompassed here, are represented by relatively few examples. One of those days was so much like each of the others that to call any of them typical would be an understatement. Our immediate needs I met with more or less trouble, but once that was done I could do no more. Day after day I could aspire, within reason, to nothing more than survival. Although the planets wandered among the stars and the moon waxed and waned, the identical naked barrenness of existence was exposed to me, day in and day out. I do not think I could write a narrative that would quite capture the unrelenting ennui of homelessness, but if I were to write it, no one could bear to read it. I spare myself as much as the reader in not attempting to recall so many empty hours. Every life has trivial occurrences, pointless episodes, and unresolved mysteries, but a homeless life has these and virtually nothing else. I have found it best in some parts to abandon a strictly chronological account and to treat in essay form experiences that relate to a single subject although they occurred in disparate times and places.

I have changed the names of people and of institutions throughout this account. I know my perspective did not often reveal the best side of people. When it did, I think I best return the favor by respecting the privacy of those who helped me. At any rate, I thought to name some and not name others would imply a criticism of those not named that, in some cases, I did not intend.

Any homeless life entails certain dangers and discomforts. I have tried not to make too much of these, for I suppose people who have always lived in comfort will imagine the worst. In fact, my homelessness involved far more mundane annoyances and petty irritations than terrors and pains.

Sometimes I escaped into daydreams à la Walter Mitty. I amused myself at night by studying the stars, and by day I read cast-off astronomy, paleontology, and philosophy books. No one will ever know if I become senile. Since childhood I have had the tendency to be absentminded, abstracted, and off in another world. Thus, I not so much became accustomed to minor physical discomforts as I often failed to notice them. Perhaps this was not all to the good, for had I been less abstracted I might have been driven to measures that would have altered my situation in one way or another.

I must say something of Lizbeth.

She seemed not to suffer much, so long as we had a bedroll for her to lie upon. She liked softness and warm places. She seemed to be compensated for all the discomforts of our new life by being constantly near me.

Although as a puppy she had shown an aptitude for amusing herself, she loves human attention and like Browning's duchess she is pleased indiscriminately whencesoever it comes. In this she frustrates herself because she seeks attention by barking in a way that people who know little of dogs interpret as threatening. In the ultimate she prefers to sleep at her master's feet, but being constantly at leash-length from anyone would please her. With few exceptions, this was a great adventure for her.

For my part, I must admit, the romantic and timeless aspects of a man and a dog seeking their sustenance together, relying on each other's special abilities for survival, and accompanied by the ghosts of all such pairs that have hunted together since man and wolf were first allied—that was not lost on me.

I often write or say *we*, meaning Lizbeth and I. Some people find this peculiar, but I fail to see why. I do not say *we planned, we hoped,* or *we thought,* because I do not think that way. I do say *we walked, we camped,* and *we slept.* I do not anthropomorphize Lizbeth in my mind or in my words.

While it is perfectly evident to me when Lizbeth is happy, bored, tired, or thirsty, I do not write clever things she is supposed to have thought. I do talk to her and say to her some things I think are witty, but I certainly do not suppose that she apprehends anything more than I am paying attention to her and whatever she may gather from my tone of voice.

My point is that the relationship between me and Lizbeth is that of man and dog. That I have made some sacrifices to avoid abandoning her or having her put to death in her youth seems to me entirely within the proper scheme of the relationship of man and dog—my proper performance under an ancient interspecies contract.

Lizbeth had her disadvantages. I could not go some places with her. Usually I had no safe place to leave her. Individuals and institutions who might have helped me alone could not consider the two of us. She is not an especially bright dog, and even so I regret not having trained her to the extent of her abilities in her youth. I often averted disaster only by anticipating her behavior, which is to say, I suppose, she has trained me. I was never confronted with a choice between Lizbeth and some permanent, significant advantage. I might have given her up to obtain a few days lodging here or there, but then I would have been back on the streets without the advantages of having her. I do not mind admitting that I love my dog. But anyone who has had to sleep by the side of the road in some wild place may appreciate that an extra pair of keen ears, a good nose, and sharp teeth on a loud, ferocious ally of unquestionable loyalty have a certain value that transcends mere sentiment. If she did not save my life, and I am not so sure she did not, she did prove herself worth having many times over. My loyalty to her may seem touching to some people, and others may take it as evidence of my irrationality, but it always had, too, the aspect of preserving a valuable asset.

I am indebted to Steven Saylor, who collected and preserved parts of this account while I was in no position to keep things as fragile as ink and paper, to Wendy Lesser of *The Threepenny Review*, whose early interest in this work encouraged me to complete it, and of course to the many people who helped us while we were on the streets, some of whom did more good than they knew.

Lars Eighner
Austin, Texas
Autumn 1992

Travels
with
Lizbeth

ONE

Austin to Tucson: Hitting the Road

Billy inelegantly brought his little black Scirocco about and drove back toward Austin. That car was Billy's shibboleth; he never learned to pronounce its name although he was frequently corrected by parts dealers, his mechanic, and me. Never mind. In Billy's mind it was a Porsche and that was the way he drove it.

There we were, Lizbeth the bitch and I, with a pile of gear I could carry only a few yards at a time, by the side of the road in what seemed to me to be a desolate area. I had not been to the desert yet.

At that moment I had my first doubts that moving to California was the best idea I had ever had and that my plans were entirely adequate.

My plans, so far as they went, were in three parts.

My friend Rufus was in prison in Las Vegas on a charge of "gross and public lewdness"—a picturesque title for a crime, I thought. He had propositioned a minor, but as it was known that the minor was a prostitute, Rufus had been allowed to plead to the lesser charge. He was due to be released soon—exactly when, I was not sure—and he had mentioned in writing that I might visit him and his benefactor, an older man I had never met, at their home in La Puente, California.

I could see from my map that La Puente was not so far from Los Angeles. Rufus always seemed happy to see me and owed me some hospitality. But as I stood by the side of the road it occurred to me that Rufus had nothing of his own and perhaps his companion, who owed me nothing, would not be so happy to see me.

The second part of my plan was to obtain a position with one of the gay men's magazines that had bought my short stories. I had been writing short stories for the gay men's market for about five years. A collection of my stories had been published and had been a critical success. One of the magazines in Southern California had recently advertised in its own pages for an assistant editor, and thinking myself exceptionally qualified for such work, I had sent a résumé. That periodical had not had time to respond, but I took the fact of the advertisement as evidence that the demand for literary talent was brisk in the Los Angeles area.

By the side of the road I reflected on my lack of experience in layout, copy fitting, and all the other aspects of magazine work, except copy- and proofreading. But I was just as willing to start in the mail room.

My third thought was to seek a position working with PWAs (people with AIDS). For this I had fifteen years of related work experience. I had kept books and filed tax forms for a nonprofit eleemosynary corporation, I had maintained medical records, I had stalked the elusive third-party payment, I had wrestled with budgets and written parts of proposals, I had tiptoed—not always successfully—through the minefield of alternative agency collective decision-making, I had directed a suicide-prevention and drug-crisis center, I had carried bedpans and changed linens on occupied beds, and I had ruthlessly manipulated other agencies into providing the services they were supposed to provide for my clients. I thought if there were any order in the universe at all, I had been provided with this particular combination of skills and experience to be of some use in the AIDS crisis.

The only drawback I could see here was that in Southern California such work would probably entail lots of sensitivity training, encounter groups, and similar things that always make me want to throw up.

Perhaps the idea of moving to California was not so wonderful after all, but remaining in Austin certainly offered no better prospects.

By exploiting the formalities of the eviction process, I might have remained in the little shack on Avenue B a few weeks longer. But I had been without a job for almost a year. The shack had changed hands in the height of Austin's real estate boom. My new landlord had taken out an enormous loan to acquire the property and was in no position to extend me any more credit.

I had resigned from the state lunatic asylum under threat of being fired. I had always been in trouble at the asylum, for the humane published policies of the institution conflict with the abusive habits of some of the staff, and I often found myself in an unpopular position. But in the event, I was in trouble for complaining of being assigned to vegetative patients who had been warehoused at the institution since birth. That was not the work I had been hired to do and I found it emetic.

I sought work elsewhere. I knew I could do many things that might turn a profit for anyone who would employ me. But I had no documentary evidence of my skills. I had made a point of attending staff-development classes at the asylum. Those classes qualified me for more advanced positions at the asylum but provided me with no credentials that would be accepted elsewhere. My previous experience had been with a so-called alternative agency that did not believe in documents of any sort. What I knew of computers and electronics I had learned as a hobbyist. I had qualified as a first-class radio-television engineer, but my FCC license had not proved useful when I first got it and had long since lapsed. I knew I could write, but whenever I learned of a position for a staff writer, the position required a college degree, which I did not have.

I went to the state unemployment commission. In past years when I had been unemployed the commission had provided me with inappropriate referrals. Now it was too swamped to do even that. The bust had hit Austin. Only those who claimed unemployment compensation could see a counselor. I did not qualify for unemployment compensation because I had resigned my last position, and it would have been the same if I had been fired for cause. Since I was not a drain on the state fund, I would not get any help in looking for a job.

As for public assistance, it is like credit—easier to get if you have had it before. That you have qualified for one sort of benefit is often taken as evidence that you are eligible for another. Documents from one agency are accepted as proof of need at another agency. But as I had never received any form of public assistance before, I had no documents. When I was asked to provide documents to prove I had no income, I could not do so. I still do not know how to prove lack of income.

The private charities had organized a clearing house, originally under the direction of the Catholic Church and still dominated by it. There I was told plainly that having neglected to produce children I could not support, I was disqualified for any benefit. Single men, I was told, were persons of sacred worth, but if only I could come up with a few mewling little wretches, illegitimate would do, then something might be done for me.

Sadly I had neglected to become addicted to drugs or alcohol and had not committed a serious crime. Rehabilitation was out of the question. But some hope was held out if I were to become maimed before funds ran out in that category.

Wherever I went I noticed an enormously fat blond woman, at least twice my size, with two screaming, undernourished brats. She fared better than I at the public and private agencies; they could hardly do enough for her. The waifs were about three and five years of age. The peculiar thing was they were never the same children. She had a different pair with her every day. So I must assume she had at least sixteen children under the age of six, and I can hardly begrudge her all the assistance she received.

I continued to write and to send my stories to the gay magazines that had bought them in the past. I had not yet learned to write when I was uninspired, and at three cents a word, paid six to eight months after I had finished a story, I could not make a living, though I sold all the stories I wrote.

Nearly every block in Hyde Park, as my neighborhood in Austin was called, had at least one foreclosure sign. The banks and the savings and loans were beginning to go belly up. The bust might not have been so bad if it had not been for the boom. Once, Austin had many old roomy houses that were inhabited by musicians and artists, students, punks, and latter-day hippies. The rents were low and such households stayed afloat so long as the law of averages prevented all of the occupants being out of work at once. Years before I had survived in Austin on a low income by living in such places. But during the boom many of these old houses were replaced with condos. When the bust hit, the condos went into receivership and housed no one.

As I watched the vacant condos deteriorate I understood the depression stories, stories that always seemed incredible to me, of people waiting in lines for thin soup while food rotted on the docks.

Going to California seemed to me to be something I could do, and I wanted to do something rather than to wait for the sheriff to come to put my things on the street. As I stood by the side of the road, weighing the uncertainties, I wondered whether the urge to do something had not led me to do the wrong thing.

While I had my second thoughts about our traveling to California, Lizbeth became fascinated by the sheep.

The eastern extreme of the Edwards plateau, where Billy had let us out, consists of small rolling limestone hills with grasses, low shrubs, and even the occasional tree. While hardly the picture of fertility, such land can support life as we know it, to wit: sheep, deer, and less-fortunate cattle.

I walked Lizbeth to the fence. The sheep did not tarry. Nonetheless Lizbeth found many smellworthy things and I did not hurry her. I took off my heavy jacket. Billy and I had agreed that I should get an early start, but in the way such things go with Billy, it was afternoon when he dropped Lizbeth and me by the road. Although the date was January 20, 1988, the sky was bright and clear and the temperature would reach into the eighties.

I counted the change in my pocket: less than a quarter, mostly in pennies. I smoked one of Billy's cigarettes. I arranged the gear and tightened the straps. I knew I was overpacked. Having never been to the desert before, I discarded the three-liter plastic Coke bottle filled with water which fit nowhere because Billy had suggested it at the last moment. I did have a canteen.

I made Lizbeth sit up on things where she could be seen. Then there was nothing to do except to begin hitchhiking. My sign read: TO L.A. WITH DOG. I did not want people to stop and then decline to take Lizbeth when they discovered her.

The problem was to get to the interstate.

Interstate 10, which goes to Los Angeles, runs northwest from San Antonio. We were on Highway 290, which to the east of Austin is a major highway joining the state's largest city to its capital, but to the west, where we were, goes 143 miles to meet the interstate in the middle of nowhere. There is little traffic and most of it is local. A local in a pickup with farm plates gave us a ride of less than five miles. Lizbeth rode in the cab. We were let out on a curve, just over a rise, so anyone going our way could not see us until he was as good as past us.

I had a large, square backpack that contained close to twenty-five pounds of dog food and some other odds and ends. Tied to the bottom of the pack was a bedroll consisting of a large comforter and several blankets wrapped around a hospital scrub suit and a large, heavy caftan that had been made for me by the former housemate who had brought Lizbeth, as a puppy, into the shack on Avenue B. The backpack would have been a load for me in any event, but the lack of a frame made it all the more unwieldy. I could only get the pack on my back by reclining on it, hooking my arms through the straps, and thrashing my limbs like a supine cockroach to right myself.

Besides the backpack there was also a rollbag in a trendy color that I found with several like it in a Dumpster behind a gift shop, the lot having been discarded, I soon discovered, because their nylon zippers were wholly inadequate. In addition, I had hooked another, smaller bookbag through the handles of the rollbag. I had also the heavy pea jacket I had been wearing, which I laid along the length of the rollbag.

Thus the most efficient way to move a few hundred yards was to leapfrog the various pieces of luggage a few score yards at a time until everything was past the first highway sign, which I supposed had been placed with some regard for its visibility. The move being made, it was still many hours until we got another ride. This was Wednesday and on a weekday most of the local traffic was single women, whom one never expects to stop. Late enough in the afternoon that he had already got off work in Austin, an electrician in a pickup stopped and again Lizbeth rode in the cab.

In this part of Texas it is often difficult to distinguish unreformed hippies from country types of about the same age, and indeed they are often the same. This driver had a great bushy red beard and recalled hitchhiking with a dog in the late Sixties, particularly in the Pacific Northwest. Perhaps this was the first ride Lizbeth got for us. The driver offered me a part of a tiny roach and was surprised I did not smoke marijuana.

I had shaved closely that morning and had been given for the trip an excellent short haircut by a former companion who was a professional hairdresser. Perhaps anyone of my obvious age and station was to be presumed to smoke marijuana. I had forced myself to smoke it for a number of years, but I always found it dysphoric and at last learned to refuse it in spite of the social consequences. The driver went a few miles out of his way to leave us in Johnson City.

We were let out at a Circle K, one of a chain of convenience stores found throughout the Southwest. The clerk let me water Lizbeth from the tap at the side of the building. I refreshed myself at the same time.

Eventually a semitrailer stopped and I gathered up my gear, but the driver meant only to go into the store. Having got the gear together, I decided to walk to the outskirts of town. Sunset was approaching and several carloads of local youth had already yelled insults at me. I could see from the increasing speed-limit signs that I was near the edge of town. I hoped to find an inconspicuous spot to lay out the bedroll.

We had gone only a few blocks when a young couple in an old car offered us a ride. They whispered among themselves as if there were some reason besides ordinary etiquette not to invite me to join the party. From the way the male spoke, hardly able to pack enough words into a sentence, I would guess the reason was meth-amphetamines.

They are popular drugs in Central Texas and the labs are often located in the country because the synthesis is very smelly. However that may be, this ride put Lizbeth and me far enough out in the country that I might lay out the bedroll without fear of being disturbed. I sat on the gear and wrote a postcard in the last moments of twilight.

Then Lizbeth got us the first ride I am sure she was responsible for. A man, perhaps in his fifties, said he had passed us and seen the dog and come back for us. He drove us to his home in Fredricksburg. His wife, he told me, worked in a veterinary clinic in Austin and they both rather fancied dogs. This last I might have concluded for myself. They had, it turned out, four house dogs of various sizes and many yard dogs.

Lizbeth does not suffer other dogs to come near me, but this problem was evidently not new to my hosts for they had an improvised system of runs and gates so that Lizbeth could be accommodated and fed by herself.

This couple lived with the aged female parent of one of them. She reminded me of all the wives of my granduncles in that it was impossible to tell whether she was becoming senile or simply had always been a nitwit. My granduncles, I have always supposed, chose fluff-brained flappers in reaction to my grandaunts-by-blood, who were intelligent and levelheaded, if not domineering and obstinate. I was given dinner of chicken à la king of a sort, based on Miracle Whip. I remarked on how beautiful Fredricksburg is, speaking from memory because I had hardly seen any of it in the dark. I related the story of my grandmother's Germans.

In the first part of the nineteenth century, an association of German princes in hopes of eliminating poverty deported large numbers of poor people, some of them to the Texas coast. Although this was supposed to be colonization, in fact the people were more or less dumped on the shore, sometimes by shipwreck, but inadequately provisioned at best. Malaria was then very common on the Texas coast and the immigrant population was decimated many times over. The Germans moved inland and settled in various parts of Central Texas. Fredricksburg was one of these settlements. This much of the story any native knows. Few, however, know of the orphan colony. A large band of children removed afoot from the coast to Fredricksburg, but there is no historical record of how they made their way.

The research was done before I could remember, but a central fact of my childhood, aside from the boxes of bond paper, typewriter erasers, eraser shields, and the upright Underwood, was my grandmother's composition of her book-length narrative poem that told how the children may have made it and then followed them up to the outbreak of the Civil War. Grandmother was no hearts-and-flowers old-lady poet, and some parts of her work were thought too racy for me when I was younger. I never read the manuscript when I was older. But I became perfectly familiar with the historic bones of the plot.

I should say this was my maternal grandmother, who, so far as I know, had no particular reason to choose this subject except that it seemed to her a good one. My own surname, if it is German, has no Texas connection.

Unfortunately my hosts, although they listened to my story patiently enough, were not natives and could not amplify any of the details. They agreed that Fredricksburg is beautiful—the oldest stone buildings being picturesque and pristine not so much for restoration as for maintenance. The gentleman agreed to drive us to the interstate. By the time we left, Lizbeth was frantic. She had never been away from her puppyhood home before and the separation from me and the presence of all the other dogs left her in a dither. She jumped from the backseat into my lap and licked me wherever she could reach until we were let out.

I thought we were let out at the junction of Highway 290 and I-10, sixty-three miles to the west of Fredricksburg. But in fact we had been taken twenty-three miles due south where I-10 passes through Comfort, Texas. The difference on I-10 was one mile more than the Pythagorean sixty-seven miles, but at least we had made it to the road that went right through to L.A. We might even get a ride all the way. But not that night.

No cars were using the entrance ramp. We walked along the ramp, but when we reached the highway there were no lights and the night was dark and moonless. We could not be seen. I was tired. I had not slept much the night before. The frontage road was above our heads and on it was a well-lit auto dealership. Beyond that was darkness and perhaps a place to sleep. With some difficulty Lizbeth and I scaled the grassy incline to the frontage road. Here was a guard rail. Lizbeth would not go under it, nor could she jump over it. To lift her over the rail I had to remove the backpack or else its weight would have dumped me over.

Past the auto dealership on the frontage road we found a curious little grassy spot. Even in the morning I could not make out what it was. It was landscaped. A gravel road looped around it but did not go off anywhere. I did not really care what it was except that it seemed unlikely we would be disturbed there for the rest of the night. I laid out the bedroll, put on the heavy caftan, and crawled in.

Naturally Lizbeth crawled into the bedroll too, but she found it too cold at her usual station behind my knees. She got under the caftan and wiggled up until her nose just stuck out of the neckhole. This might have been cozy enough except that she detected the security guard at the auto dealership whenever he made his rounds. She barked.

As concealment seemed to me the most logical first strategy in providing for our safety, I was concerned that I could hardly control Lizbeth, although the guard never came closer to us than a couple of hundred yards. Discovery where we were might not have been so bad, but I thought surely we would come to times that our survival would depend upon Lizbeth's not giving away our position. I got little sleep. We were up at first light. After the burst of hope and energy that comes with dawn, my mood sharply declined. Getting the pack on my back had been a struggle when I first tried it. Now moving at all was becoming difficult.

Lizbeth would not eat. I dumped most of her food. Twenty-five pounds was more than she would eat in a month. Of course she would not eat that morning because she had gorged herself the night before in Fredricksburg—our hosts had mixed meat in with her food. She would not be hungry enough to eat plain, dry dog food for a day or two, although she would be happy to have any little scrap of human food she could get. I knew her eating habits as well then as I know them now. But at the time I took her refusal to eat as a vote of no confidence. I do not think I was mistaken in perceiving a number of quizzical looks from her quarter.

I discarded my boots next. Although I walked a great deal in town and the boots were broken in perfectly well, they were not the thing for the road. Everyone advises the traveler to wear sensible shoes, and I have not found a better piece of advice.

We were in Comfort for most of the day. Several other hitchhikers appeared and got rides. I got a short ride late in the afternoon and made five dollars in the process. The driver offered to let me out at a rest stop or to drive me a few miles farther. As I did not then know the advantages of hitchhiking from a rest area, I asked to be driven the few miles farther.

We were let off at a crossover near the little town of Mountain Home. Here the median of the interstate expanded to several hundred yards and there were several shady trees. I left our gear under a tree and Lizbeth and I walked over the crossover to a store the last driver had said would be there.

It was a little country store with sparsely stocked, unfinished wood shelves. They were discontinuing cigarettes and had only a few stale packs of unfiltered Camels. I bought two packs and a Big Red, a caffeine-laced cream soda popular in Oklahoma and Texas, and I watered Lizbeth from the hose outside. Thursday afternoon had become very warm.

We returned to the tree where I had stashed our gear and I drank the Big Red and wrote a letter to Billy. Then I tried thumbing until dark, but it was useless.

I still do not know whether it is better to have a sign or not, if it is worth the effort of standing all the while, whether to look as presentable as possible or to try to appear down on my luck. I think perhaps none of that matters. Many, many people still pass by.

I was not so discouraged that night when I decided it was time to lie down. I was better off than when the day had started. I had smokes and some change in my pocket.

About dark we walked back on a little rise through which the road cut. When we were about sixteen feet above the road I decided to stop. I dropped the gear, left Lizbeth strapped to the gear, and raced another twenty or thirty yards.

When you live out of Dumpsters, dysentery is an occasional fact of life, although it is less frequent in cool weather. I had eaten nothing save the chicken à la king since we left Austin, but the day before that I had eaten some suspicious Dumpster pizza. In the middle of nowhere the result was inconvenient. In the city, as I had yet to discover, intestinal distress and the dearth of truly public rest rooms provide a number of unpretty options.

I had a magazine-premium battery-powered radio. From it I got enough of a weather report to hear that a low of twenty-eight degrees was expected somewhere, but the station faded before I learned its location. Suddenly Lizbeth broke loose from her moorings and ran across the rise. A white tail disappeared over a fence. Lizbeth had discovered deer.

FRIDAY MORNING WAS overcast with high clouds. The grass was very dewy and, in patches, frosty. Because I was bigger and stronger I eventually dislodged Lizbeth from the bedroll. As we were up at first light, I believe I had packed and we were down at the road before sunrise. Very many semitrailers passed us. I tipped my cap or waved at most of them and a few of them sounded their horns. So far as I know, no trucker has ever done me any good in my travels, but I had heard it was a good idea to be friendly toward the truckers, so I was. Lizbeth curled up on the gear and shivered. I hate it when she shivers.

Quite soon, although at the time it seemed not so soon, we got another ride. I did not notice him until he had passed us and stopped and honked his horn.

The old pickup was very battered, mostly lime green, with a Florida license plate taped in the rear window of the cab. It sat on the shoulder under the crossover some two or three hundred yards beyond us. As fast as I could move with all the gear was hardly more than a brisk walk, even with Lizbeth towing me as hard she was able. The truck did not pull away as sometimes happens in these situations. The cab was nearly full of gear and delicately balanced arrangements for brewing coffee with power from the cigarette lighter. The bed of the pickup was loaded with exactly what all I never discovered, but Lizbeth would have to ride there.

Lizbeth is a fool. Off her leash she cannot be trusted not to dart out into traffic. In the last couple of days she had ridden more than she had in her whole life before and she had never been in the back of a pickup alone. I tied her leash to the hub of a loose spare tire in the bed of the pickup.

It was far from clear that she could not hang herself by jumping overboard or be lost over the side by slipping her collar. There was not room for me to ride with her. I worried about her constantly for she rode standing on various objects and precariously balanced. The worst was when we would overtake a livestock truck. She clearly appreciated only the very slight relative motion of the vehicles and gave every appearance of being willing to dash herself against the slats of the livestock trucks, just as she might jump against a stationary fence.

The driver's story was that he had been a couple of years in Florida with a girlfriend, but the relationship had gone sour. So he was returning to Tucson, his hometown, and a previous girlfriend.

To Tucson seemed quite a ways and I was very much encouraged. I had pored over the map without absorbing many facts of geography. I thought, for example, that the continental divide was somewhere in California, rather near the San Gabriel Mountains. I was not entirely sure how far I would have got when I reached Tucson, but from the mile markers I could see this ride would put at least five hundred miles of Texas behind me.

We stopped fairly soon at a rest stop. I scraped a razor over my face, washed my neck and forearms, and since I had a ride already, changed into my most ragged jeans. The driver wanted to be sure that Lizbeth was walked. She seldom wants walking more than twice a day. But I welcomed the chance to lash her to the tire again, this time with much less slack. Nonetheless, she managed to get up and about and to keep my heart in my throat for the rest of the ride.

The last of the grass and the trees petered out a little past Junction, Texas, and then for many miles there was nothing except what is called cedar in Austin but elsewhere is known as juniper scrub. This is a long and desolate stretch, but what is more, the few wretched settlements that exist are several miles from the highway and no cafés, gas stations, or even tourist traps are visible from the road. I was set to work brewing coffee. The driver was well into his second day on the road, without stopping and had no intention of resting until he reached Tucson. Again I was offered a part of a roach from the ashtray, but once it was clear I had no interest in marijuana, I was given the job of rolling joints for the driver from a stash in a Bull Durham bag. We did not talk much. The driver was determined to coax something out of the radio. For the most part we got static and whenever he did pick up something he overpowered his speakers so the result to me was little different from static.

I was suitably impressed by the mountains as we got to them. I had seldom seen mountains and never such as these, young and rising from a treeless landscape.

It was another hot day and we were climbing. The temperature gauge in the old pickup read hot, but the driver insisted it was stuck. We pulled into Las Cruces to get gas and the radiator blew.

The cap is supposed to blow first, just as a safety valve on a boiler blows before the boiler reaches the bursting point. But this cap had not. Yet as the steam dissipated and things cooled off, it appeared the radiator had only split a seam. A welder was found who would draw a bead down the seam for seven dollars.

This exhausted our folding cash and I was set to the task of sorting through the driver's change pot. There was enough for a couple of packs of cigarettes and, perhaps, gasoline to get to Tucson. I had about three quarters besides of my own, which I did not mention. We would press on.

As we pulled out of the service station in Las Cruces, Lizbeth finally managed to hang herself, but inadequately. She was attempting to get from the back of the pickup to the cab window. I made a bed for her in the hub of the spare tire and then lashed her to it again with as little slack as I thought possible. Night was falling and I knew it would be cold. I hoped she would nest in the tire. Of course she did not. I was set back to square one in worrying about her. I became accustomed to the shadow of her head in the lights of the vehicles that overtook us, only to be alarmed again by the absence of the shadow when she finally fell asleep.

The sun set as we passed Vail, Arizona. We were climbing again. The driver explained that Tucson was in a box canyon and if we reached the top of this climb we could coast into town. This was far from an idle observation, for fuel was precariously low. Eventually the truck did make it to the top and it was all downhill from there.

The driver let us off about 9:00 P.M. at a truck stop south of town. I have since learned that this was a famous truck stop and elegantly appointed as these things go, but I had no chance of learning that firsthand. Immediately Lizbeth sat on a prickly pear and thus struck the keynote of our tenure in Tucson.

The shoulder of the frontage road was under construction for as far ahead as I could see. That would pose a problem in getting away from the truck stop.

I know now what I should have done. I should have found a dark spot and gone to sleep. Our situation did not appear to me to be good, but it was far from desperate and unlikely to deteriorate overnight. "Things will look brighter in the morning" was the sort of adage I always sneered at. Now I was to learn it was valuable advice and in Tucson it was a dear lesson. A long ride is such a piece of luck that one is tempted to try to press on before fortune shows its other face. I suppose that was why I hoped to get farther that night. But instead, Lizbeth and I were fallen upon by thieves.

A young Latin man distracted me with some discussion that I never understood. I was holding Lizbeth and we were not more than twenty feet from our gear. When I turned to the gear, it was gone, and when I turned again, so was the young man.

His confederates must have had a car, for there was no other way they could have made such a pile of gear disappear in so short a time. Naturally, I had laid my heavy coat on the bundle.

I find it hard to believe that anyone would have thought I had anything of much value. My clothes, besides being worn, would not fit many other people, and this should have been obvious to look at me. The little radio was of no appreciable value. Besides my papers, most of the bulk of what was taken was the remainder of Lizbeth's food and the bedding, which was warm enough, but could not have been sold. Other than a few dollars in postage, nothing could have been readily converted to cash. I was left with what I was wearing, a football practice jersey and my most ragged pair of jeans, and Lizbeth.

My mistake, besides not getting us out of harm's way after dark, was in not lashing Lizbeth to the gear the minute I set it down. While Lizbeth is harmless, most people would require some time to discover the fact and in the meanwhile she would make noise.

Tired and disheartened, I sat by a telephone pole, and in spite of the cold I must have dozed sitting up.

When I awoke I discovered a further disaster. Lizbeth had curled up at the base of the telephone pole, and cold as it was, she had heated the tar on the pole until it flowed all over her back. Clearly no one would want this mess in his vehicle. When the sun rose I saw it was even worse than it had first appeared.

My own stamps and envelopes had gone with our gear. But just before I left Austin, Billy gave me a whole book of stamps with a face value of $4.40, which I had put in my wallet. By chance the wallet was in my jeans and not in the pocket of the coat that had been stolen.

Billy had told me his phone credit card number and I used it to call a bookstore that was listed in the copied pages of a gay travelers' guide that Billy had given me with the stamps. I supposed the bookstore was a gay one, and in my experience these little stores, which are not to be confused with adult bookstores, take a proprietary interest in their authors. The clerk I spoke to, however, seemed less than gracious and only grudgingly agreed to give me cash for the stamps. My object was to buy some rubbing alcohol to clean the tar off Lizbeth's back.

The immediate problem was to get to the bookstore.

South Tucson consists of huts and shacks and sand dunes, with here and there the occasional obvious federal housing project. It is unremittingly barren and ugly. There are few improvements of any kind. Street signs are restricted to the housing projects where they identify various *stravs*. Using the dictionaries of several languages, I have been unable to discover what a *strav* is, and have concluded that it is a compromise between *street* and *avenue*.

South Tucson simply has no sidewalks. I thought at first this was merely in keeping with the general wretchedness of the place, but eventually it seemed to me that the public policy in Tucson is to impede pedestrians as much as possible. In particular, I could find no way to walk to the main part of town in the north except in the traffic lanes of narrow highway ramps.

I could not believe this at first, and Lizbeth and I spent several hours wandering on the south bank of the dry gash that divides Tucson as I looked for a walkway. More than anywhere we have been, adults like teenagers shouted threats as well as insults at us in Tucson, and did so whether I was trying to hitchhike or was merely walking. More than one man found it necessary to brandish a firearm at us although we were afoot and presented no conceivable threat to those cruising past us at upward of fifty miles per hour. This atmosphere did not make the walk across the high ramp in the traffic lane any less exciting.

The usual medium in Tucson for vulgar displays of wealth

appeared to be the conspicuous and wasteful consumption of water. As we walked north things got greener and more affluent. The ritziest neighborhoods were positively swamplike. Lizbeth could drink from the runoff of the sprinkler systems that ran throughout the heat of the day. Still, there were no continuous sidewalks.

Perhaps the bookstore was no more than seven miles north of the gorge, but it was late in the afternoon when Lizbeth and I got there. The bookstore was not of the sort I expected. It was not after all a little gay bookstore, but was a very large general-interest bookstore with a gay-interest section.

The clerk took the book of stamps and said he would have to check with the owner, although I mentioned having phoned earlier. I suppose they counted the stamps each and every one, for it was some time before he returned to give me $4.40. I noticed that a couple of magazines that contained my stories were on display behind the counter, over the clerk's head.

I took the money to a nearby drugstore to get some rubbing alcohol.

If I had then had a better grasp of the geography I might have saved us considerable trouble and heartbreak. The bookstore was not so very far to the east of the interstate. But as we had crossed the gorge, the interstate appeared to veer off sharply to the west. I thought the nearest point of the highway was in the south, and to the south we returned.

We were quite in darkness by the time we crossed the gorge again. Lizbeth could no longer walk.

We were far enough west now that convenience stores no longer had faucets and hoses on the outside. I went into a convenience store and bought a gallon of water. I returned to Lizbeth and carried her a few feet from the road, behind a sand dune.

I would never have thought a stout middle-aged man could outwalk a healthy young dog. I have since learned I cannot expect much more than five miles a day out of Lizbeth on a consistent basis, and then only when conditions are favorable. In Tucson conditions are not favorable. Without sidewalks or grass, she had walked on cinders, sand, and rocks. The trip to the bookstore had worn the pads off her paws.

TWO

Tucson to La Puente: The Desert Rat

It gets cold in the desert at night.

I scouted around for something to cover us and found a piece of packing material that appeared to be shredded plastic pressed into a sheet. Lizbeth yipped and moaned every moment I was out of her sight. I stumbled about as if very intoxicated. I found Lizbeth again only for her crying. I was too cold to sleep. I sat up with Lizbeth on my lap, under my jersey, and the sheet of plastic wrapped around us. I shuddered until dawn. Then I found a piece of cardboard to lie on and fell asleep.

We were there four days and I cannot account for that time. It is hard to say what was the worst of it. The nights warmed a little. When I went to find an unlocked and unattended water tap, Lizbeth would whine and howl; I was afraid she would be taken away when I got back. My lips crusted over. My face and exposed forearms burned.

We were spotted from time to time by mobile thugs who drove by over and over shouting insults.

One of the evenings, I forget which, something good finally happened. A young couple stopped on the road and set something out of their car. When they were back in it, they called to me and drove away. They left a paper plate of cold cuts, evidently left over from a buffet, for some of the slices were fanned out.

We had eaten nothing since the night of the chicken à la king. I meant to give most of the cold cuts to Lizbeth, but I had my eye on a piece of cheese for myself. As soon as the plate was within her range, Lizbeth scarfed down all the food in a swoop. I held her in my lap, said, "Good dog, good dog," and cried.

Day and night strange planes flew in and out of the Air Force base. I reflected on what our last ride had told me; Tucson—or so he said—was one of the few cities in America that was off-limits to Soviet citizens. I supposed for that reason the Soviets had a number of missiles aimed at Tucson. I took that as a reassuring thought. Arizona is a desolate wasteland, but it might be considerably improved by detonating a few H-bombs in and around Tucson.

I recalled an anthropology professor I had studied under once, who in proposing a list of cultural universals cited the duty to aid the wayfarer as a common aspect of desert cultures. He had never, I supposed, been to Tucson.

One morning I went behind a bush and Lizbeth came after me. I had not needed to tie her while she recovered. She tackled me from behind at the knees, almost causing a minor accident.

We rolled around in the sand, playing her favorite puppy-hood game, Piranha Fish, which consists of her chewing on my hands and wrists and wrestling me about while I shout, "Oh, the razor-sharp piranha teeth strip the flesh from my fingers! Oh, the pain!" and so on. Then we played Brain-Sucking Spider from Outer

Space, in which the creepy brain-sucking spider-hand lands on the dog's head and, of course, starves to death in short order.

Lizbeth was well.

In the meantime I had got most of the tar off her back. What tar remained was fairly inconspicuous because that part of her coat was black. Now I was the weak link.

I had fasted before for much longer periods, but always with vitamins and, at least, caffeine to keep my spirits up. The sunburn and the chill of the nights were beginning to tell on me. I became dizzy when I stood and exhausted by twenty minutes of walking.

I had found water in a distant park and when I went to fetch water I managed to rinse off my upper body in the men's room. I was surprised to discover over time how much bathing helps, even if one has to put on dirty clothes afterward. But I did not have a razor or even a comb.

I did not see how we would ever get out of Tucson.

I was deeply depressed.

My plan was to follow the frontage road through town, trying to hitchhike, but moving slowly through town in any event. Unfortunately, there was no frontage road in the direction we were going for quite long stretches.

The day of Lizbeth's recovery we walked again in the traffic lanes to cross into Tucson. Eventually we reached an on ramp in what appeared to be the central business district. We did not get a ride that day, but many jokers stopped twenty or thirty yards past us, blew their horns, and then sped off when we ran after them. I did not sleep that night, but sat at the corner with my head against a lamppost while Lizbeth slept on my lap.

The following morning we did get a short ride, the two of us in the back of a commercial pickup. But we were let off where the interstate ran below street level. We had no place to stand and no driver could stop for us safely. So we walked along the city streets, which of course had no sidewalks. I tried to steer us parallel to the highway, but often I could not see where it was.

Eventually we came to the Miracle Mile. Quite a number of Western towns seem to think there is something miraculous about a string of dilapidated tourist traps and fast-food outlets that have seen better days. Signs promised that the Miracle Mile would join the interstate, so we walked along until we came to the ramp.

The ramp from the Miracle Mile to the interstate looked too dangerous to attempt afoot. But I could see we had only to descend the artificial hill we were on and cross an exceptionally stark expanse of desert to reach what appeared to be the frontage road. Some of the sand we crossed to reach the road appeared to be the lot of a truck stop. I tried hitchhiking on the frontage road. But it was a two-way frontage road and those going our way had trouble enough getting into the lane to turn onto the highway. Stopping to pick us up was out of the question.

It began to rain.

This was the last thing I expected.

The real rain lasted long enough for me to cast about for some shelter on the treeless landscape, and then it turned to a drifting mist from which there could be no shelter. A cycle of rain and then mist recurred several times.

I spotted a Dumpster behind a restaurant that was next to the truck stop, but the Dumpster yielded nothing. Far out in the lot I had seen a wool horse blanket, evidently part of an abandoned bedroll. The wool would be warm in spite of the rain. I expected we would get no farther by nightfall, and if the blanket was not claimed then, I planned to make it mine. I sat on the abutment of a drainage culvert and Lizbeth stood, her forepaws on my knees, to lick the rain off my face.

Here then is the occurrence of my parable: We had been fallen upon by thieves, snubbed by the respectable elements of the community, I was dazed and weary, yet we were to be rescued by one of those most likely to disapprove of me, for just at this time appeared the Good Fundamentalist.

"Jesus told me to stop," he said.

I was in no position to argue with this bit of divine inspiration. Principles are principles, but it seemed to me that a cultural guerilla must make use of the resources at hand without regard to their origin.

He opened his trunk and gave me a bedspread of thin, quilted chintz, its fitted corners torn out. This proved surprisingly warm. And he gave me five bucks.

I was not especially surprised that he returned in about an hour with his wife. Jesus had told them to take me to Phoenix. They had brought a sack of groceries including dog food and a number of old flannel shirts, one of which would fit over my arms although I could not use the rest of them. They insisted I eat as we went. I made a sandwich of thin-sliced beef, but slipped most of the beef in the package to Lizbeth because I knew better than to break fast with a heavy meal. They did not press me too hard with their philosophy.

It was fully dark by the time we reached Phoenix. I had found a ten-dollar bill in the desert while Lizbeth was recovering. As anyone from hurricane country knows, genuine U.S. currency turns a sickly yellow when exposed after a flood, and that was the color of one side of the note I found. The other side was encrusted with sand.

I hoped to use the money in Phoenix to clean up and, perhaps, get some rest, but the discolored and damaged currency was sneered at when I presented it at the gay bathhouse.

At that time I-10 did not go through Phoenix but turned north and became the Flagstaff Highway. The through traffic on Interstate 10 was fed onto the city streets. This must have been very satisfactory for local commerce, which perhaps explains why the highway through Phoenix remained unfinished so long after the rest of the system was complete. I could not complain, for the situation seemed as promising for a hitchhiker as for the merchants.

Lizbeth and I took up a station on the city street that was the interstate as it passed through Phoenix. A number of prostitutes objected that this was their regular corner and our presence was bad for their business.

Highways, medians, and margins throughout Arizona are lavishly planted, thereby to convince the unwary traveler that the land is fit for human habitation. Along the Flagstaff Highway I found a spreading magnolia where there was some evidence of a previous camper. My only qualm was that the sprinkler system might be turned on in the night. But I laid out my new bedroll, reclined with Lizbeth at my feet, and the next thing I knew it was dawn.

WE RETURNED TO the corner and of course in daylight none of the working girls were in evidence. Promptly Jesus told a roofer in a pickup to give us a ride, a couple of oranges, and another five dollars. In return I had only to accept a fulsome little tract. The driver let us off at the Avondale ramp. Here were the signs of lengthy and fruitless habitation by other hitchhikers, and the graffiti on the lamppost were not reassuring:

"130,000 miles and still going strong—11–26–86—the Golden Thumb—6 years on the road."

"Trick Norton—12–17–87."

"1–29–88—Phoenix to L.A.—the Kalamazoo Kid—Fuck this ramp." This latter sentiment was repeated in many slight variations.

I wrote: "Lizbeth the dog and Lars . . . Austin TX to L.A. February 1988. Tucson sucks."

Thereafter whenever things on the road were not totally

wretched, I often thought of the Golden Thumb, six years on the road. A person could, it seemed to me, hitchhike forever, and had I been twenty years younger I would have been tempted to see just how long I could make such an adventure last.

Lizbeth and I walked down the cross street, found a truck stop where I replenished my mailing supplies, and stopped at a McDonald's. We returned to the ramp to split a Big Mac.

I did not expect to get out of Avondale soon, but in the afternoon a red-haired woman in a trashy car stopped and gave us a ride to the Burnt Well rest stop.

Burnt Well had shaded picnic tables and plenty of water. Indians laid out tacky turquoise and silver jewelry for sale in the shade of the pavilion that housed the restrooms. They had a fair number of customers, even for the obviously ersatz coral pieces.

Refreshed, Lizbeth and I walked far out on the reentry ramp where we could be seen both by cars on the highway and by those leaving the rest stop. A couple of women from the rest stop offered me a handful of change. They said they would give me a ride but for Lizbeth. I told them I would not part with her, and that was that.

Once again we were picked up by a vehicle I had not noticed until it stopped. I always tried to make as much eye contact with the drivers of approaching vehicles as possible, but I do not believe I stared down a single ride. Eventually I was picked up so often by cars I had not seen that I almost became superstitious on the subject. I did not see this ride because I had turned my head away from the blowing rain for a moment.

The driver's name was Dallas Matsen. His car was a beat-up Pontiac. Its drab paint had been mostly blasted away by the sand, and its windshield bore a spider's-web fracture. Rain leaked in at the top of the windshield and through my door, which was sprung. Many partial packs of cigarettes slid back and forth on the dashboard as Dallas drove.

Dallas was what I expected of Arizona and Southern California. He had long, stringy, dirty-blond hair, sun-bleached in streaks, blue eyes, and a very dark tan, and he was so slender that he gave the impression of being taller. He said he was going from Phoenix to Fontana and then on to L.A. He claimed to have a good idea where La Puente was and said he would drop me off there.

I thought our troubles were over.

Dallas's story seemed at first in no way alarming or far-fetched. He said he had fallen out with his girlfriend in Phoenix, which accounted for the crack in the windshield. Now he had a few days off and money in his pocket. He was going to Fontana to visit his son, who was with his ex-wife, and then on to L.A. to party.

I had lost my maps with the rest of my gear. I gathered Fontana was in Southern California, but whether it was ten miles or a hundred from La Puente I did not know. At least we had plenty of cigarettes. Dallas told me to help myself from the open packs. He opened a fresh pack about every third cigarette and had several unbroken cartons in the backseat. He must have known the road well, for soon he pulled off the highway and stopped at a convenience store that had not been visible from the highway. Dallas flashed a roll of bills. My job was to keep a foot on the accelerator. If the engine were to die, there was some doubt Dallas could restart it. Dallas went into the store and came out with a couple of bottles of cold duck and a couple of cartons more of cigarettes.

He popped the plastic corks of the bottles with his teeth and handed me one of the foaming bottles. In normal times I would have been dead drunk if I had finished off one bottle of cold duck, and would have been all the more so then, as I was scarcely accustomed to solid food again and was still somewhat dehydrated from our days in the sun while Lizbeth recovered. I took every opportunity to pour a little out of the bottle when I was unobserved, and I only sipped at the wine while trying to give the impression I was guzzling it. After only a few sips I was quite lightheaded.

Dallas told me he was thirty-four. Since he carried his cash in a roll, he left his wallet lying on the car seat, and I later verified his age and the name he had given me. He looked at least ten years younger. He had a certain je ne sais quoi that reminded me of Rufus. They were of the same physical type, and I soon learned that like Rufus, Dallas was a compulsive liar and a bad one.

We stopped again, this time for gasoline. I had to keep the engine running while Dallas filled the tank. This did not seem very safe, but then nothing about Matsen's car seemed very safe; his gas cap was merely a red shop rag. The roll of bills came out again and Dallas went in to pay for the gas. Again he came out with two bottles and two cartons of cigarettes. And so our journey went. After a while I noticed his bankroll was all ones. Dallas was obviously an alcoholic. If I had drunk as much as he did we would not have accumulated a surplus of cold duck, for he drank one of every pair of bottles he acquired. He continued to bring two bottles out of the store every time we stopped, though it must have been clear I would never catch up to his drinking. But it was the cigarettes I wondered about. The cartons in the backseat already amounted to a case or more. He was not buying them to smoke. Then I realized: He was not buying them at all.

I felt that by keeping my foot on the gas to ensure Dallas's getaway, I was compromising my policy of not stealing. Moreover, I was afraid of being arrested. Technically I became an accessory as soon as I realized what Dallas was doing. I did not think I would be convicted of any such thing, but I was afraid that if I was detained, even if I was eventually discharged, Lizbeth would be impounded and I would be unable to raise the pound fee to reclaim her. She was a handsome animal when she had her winter coat, but she was no longer a cute puppy. I feared that once she was impounded she would not be adopted and would be put to death. Sticking with Matsen was not wise and I knew it.

But we were moving toward Southern California and it seemed Lizbeth and I would reach our goal in just a few hours. I was too tired and too roadsick to insist that Dallas put us out in the desert. I believed Lizbeth and I had been near death in Tucson and to go afoot on the sand again voluntarily might tempt Fate.

A little after dark we were in the mountains and the car was climbing to the top of a rise. "I want to show this to you," Dallas said.

We cleared the rise and in every direction were the shimmering lights of the thickly populated valley below us: rose sodium lights, blue mercury vapor, neon and yellow incandescent; all before us glittering in the darkness. Tears rolled down my cheeks. It was beautiful and, so I hoped, somewhere down there Lizbeth and I might get off the road.

The novelty had worn off traveling so far as Lizbeth was concerned. She no longer sat up and sniffed the air, but whenever we found a ride she sought the warmest and most comfortable spot available and promptly fell asleep. When it was time to walk her she went about her business with uncharacteristic haste and then made a beeline for the vehicle, as if she had at some level grasped what a ride was and was afraid of losing one.

Dallas's car was a hazard. The engine died repeatedly, despite all precautions, giving up the ghost a couple of times on the open highway with no apparent provocation. Restarting the engine required liberal applications of some very volatile aerosol chemical that Dallas kept for that purpose, and as often as not the carburetor caught fire when he applied it.

I do not consider myself mechanically inclined, but I supposed Dallas knew what he was doing. Desert rat that he was, he seemed certain to have known something about cars to have kept his bucket of bolts running. I imagined he was born with grease under his fingernails. I mastered my fear and did as he said no matter how many times the results seemed alarming.

By and by we began to smell something like rubber burning. Dallas laid a heavy wrench on the accelerator and we got out to investigate. I do not like to fool with engines while they are running, especially when the radiator fan is uncowled, as Matsen's was. We found a wire of some kind that had joined its ancestors. Perhaps we had smelled the insulation burning off that wire. As the engine continued to run, we decided the wire had something to do with the heater or the radio, both of which had turned up hors de combat. Dallas seemed content with the situation. We shrugged our shoulders, got back in the car, and went on. I expected to find cultural differences in Southern California, and among the first I detected was Dallas's driving. There was, for example, the practice of passing on the right by jumping the curb and driving on the sidewalks. This was impossible in Texas, where the blocks were short and the sidewalks narrow. But in Southern California it works out well enough, provided the sidewalk is mounted and dismounted between lampposts, which are conveniently widely spaced. There is a stimulating effect on pedestrians.

Then there is the custom—custom, I say, because I observed that Dallas's driving habits were far from unique—of pulling up behind and gently nudging the bumper of anyone who has cut you off on the freeway. There are many others: backing up to a missed exit, impromptu crossing over at arbitrary points, U-turning on bridges, and yet others that I cannot describe because my eyes were clamped shut.

I came to understand that Dallas had not just left Phoenix when he picked me up. He had been living in his car for some time. His occupation was driving from Phoenix to L.A. and back, with side forays on the many long boulevards between San Bernardino and L.A., where there were enough convenience stores that he could shoplift for years, perhaps even for a lifetime without having to hit the same store twice, although he did seem to have his favorites.

At times I thought Dallas always knew where we were and where we were going. At other times I thought he had mastered only the general scheme of the boulevards and their strip centers, for they were so alike that a map of one would have served as a fair guide to any of the others.

We sometimes stopped at rest stops—or perhaps it was the same rest stop several times—where I observed that Dallas was only one of a number of young men who lived in this way and all the others traveled in pairs. I was never in earshot when Dallas talked to the others, but I gathered they talked shop—where the pickings were especially easy, how someone had got busted, that sort of thing.

Perhaps my imagination was running away with me, but I thought Dallas was grooming me as his sidekick. Some of his vehicular antics seemed calculated to try my nerve. Once he put me out when I gasped too audibly at one of his maneuvers. The wind was cold and hard. Dallas returned for me shortly and for a while after that he drove sanely and spoke sweetly. But after a bit he attempted even more spectacular feats, just to see, I think, whether I had learned my lesson.

I had not a nerve left in my body, for I am usually a poor rider, likely to pump the imaginary passenger-side brake even when I am in the hands of a model driver.

We were developing quite a surplus of cold duck. I had disposed of only two bottles while actually drinking about three wineglasses' worth. The cigarettes accumulated even more rapidly and were beginning to crowd Lizbeth in the backseat. At last Dallas left off calling on convenience stores. We headed into the wilds of Fontana, which it turned out had been close by for some time. The plan, Dallas told me, was for me to assist him in kidnapping his infant son.

I was certain, just about, that the plan was a lie, perhaps a part of my testing. Dallas embroidered on his story a bit, claiming to be wanted in L.A. for having hired there a couple of guys to break his ex-wife's legs.

We spent many hours driving back roads. Dallas was looking for something, perhaps a place he had been to only once or twice before. Again and again we returned to the highway. From the highway we followed a fixed sequence of roads so that we always reached a certain point in Fontana. From there Dallas was unsure of the way. We took various courses. Sometimes Dallas thought he almost recognized something. But finally he would realize the trail had gone cold and we would return to the highway and start over. Before long I knew the first part of the route as well as Dallas did. He remained tight-lipped.

At long last he pulled over at no place in particular and took the decisive action of turning off the ignition. The cigarettes went into the trunk. I walked Lizbeth. Then Lizbeth and I bedded down in the backseat, and Dallas in the front.

I cannot explain, exactly, why I had not parted with Dallas.

I was not sure where I was. But that was only an excuse. I knew I was in Southern California and I knew I could not be that far from La Puente.

As bad as things had been I cannot deny there is a romance of the road. The Golden Thumb and Dallas Matsen were part of something very appealing to me, and I suppose I will always wonder whether things would really have turned out so badly if I had given in to my desire for it.

Dallas seemed to have some use for me in mind and after my castaway days in Tucson I was grateful to be wanted by anybody for anything. I felt a little reckless because it seemed to me my life should have ended in the desert outside Tucson and whatever happened afterward I would be ahead of the game. And I was beginning to absorb a certain California something, something of the spirit of a rat race in paradise, something that whispered *"ma-ñana, mañana"* to my every nascent worry and fear. I was letting go. I was going with the flow. I was becoming Laid-Back.

IT WAS COLD duck for breakfast.

Lizbeth had never known quite what to make of sheep and cattle. But as it turned out we were parked near a corral that contained a swayback bay mare. Lizbeth reacted to this as if it were a large dog and I am sure that is what she thought it was.

We moved on rather quickly, the car cooperating for once. We returned to the same circuit we had traversed many times the night before. Then on one of the back roads, the car stopped. The starter would not crank. The battery was so flat it would not sound the horn.

The fan belt had joined its ancestors.

Dallas hailed down a pickup and went off to purchase a fan belt. His bankroll of ones was much diminished, although he had been paying for nothing but gas. Apparently Dallas sustained himself on cold duck. Lizbeth still had dog food, but I had exhausted my solid provisions.

I stood by the car and watched the locals drive by. Texas has rednecks, too, but Fontana seemed to have a particularly rugged and surly lot, and well-armed to boot. I developed a strong desire not to cross any of them.

The wind blew. Lizbeth sat out for a while, her ears streamlined back. But soon she preferred to sit in the car. The wind kept blasting unlike anything in my experience, far stronger than the winds from the Gulf of Mexico. Dallas said it was a Santa Ana, but it was not. It was the normal breeze in Fontana.

Across the road was a vista of a majestic, snow-topped mountain that rather looked like the Paramount Studios trademark. I jotted a postcard to Billy and flagged down a postal Jeep.

Fairly soon a pickup stopped in front of the car and Dallas hopped out with the new fan belt. I peeked under the hood with him. I believed I saw how the belt went on. Dallas began to remove the radiator. The way I saw it, that was unnecessary.

I still supposed Dallas was bound to have some mechanical knowledge to have kept his car running back and forth across the desert until most of the paint had been blasted away. He did have a large assortment of tools and most of them were greasy. So I stepped back and let Dallas proceed. Sure enough, he extracted the radiator rather neatly. That left more room to work, but so far as I could see it had not altered the geometry of the situation. Next Dallas removed a very large socket from his toolbox and went into the trunk of his car for a breaker bar. It took me a moment to absorb this.

The fool meant to pull the timing chain!

I knew from sad experience this is the last thing ever to do, even if the timing chain wants replacing.

Somehow I diverted Dallas for a moment while I slipped the fan belt on. "Look," I said, "won't it work this way?" Dallas studied the fan belt at great length, running his finger around the belt's path several times. This gave me a moment to slide under the car and to see what the situation was with the alternator.

The bolt that allows the alternator to be moved to adjust the tension in the fan belt had sheared off, or so it seemed at first. That had released the tension in the first fan belt and it had burned itself up from the friction of slipping. So I reasoned at the time, but I was not yet sure I was correct.

Dallas had sworn the old belt had been replaced recently. If so, a cure would require an explanation of the early failure of the belt, and the missing bolt seem to provide the explanation.

The bolt had threaded into a hole in the body of the alternator, and if it had sheared off we should now have had the problem of removing the remainder of the bolt from the alternator. This sort of thing keeps machinists out of breadlines.

But no. The threaded hole in the alternator was clean as could be; I could see through it. Evidently besides the hole itself being threaded, there had also been a nut on the far side. I asked who had replaced the fan belt the last time. Clearly Dallas had not done it himself.

"A friend," he said.

I suspected then that the bolt had not sheared off, but had never been replaced when the friend changed the belt. That in itself was odd, because the bolt should never have been removed, needing only to be loosened to adjust the tension in the belt. Yet I could not think of another explanation.

I sorted through Dallas's hardware. Of course I could not find a bolt to match the threads of the hole of the alternator. But I found one that was narrower and long enough. Dallas had discovered that a corrugated-metal building across the road was in fact a machine shop—I would never have inquired, for I would never have expected such luck. He took the bolt that fit through the alternator to the machine shop and returned with several nuts that fit it. Several square nuts. This was jury-rigging, but there was nothing else to be done.

"It will work now," I told Dallas, "but I can't say for how long."

I let Dallas replace the radiator. He seemed well-drilled in the procedure and I would have had to figure it out as I went along. Then Dallas waved his cables until someone stopped to give us a jump. We took to the interstate to build up a full charge in the battery. As we cruised the freeway we passed the West Covina exits several times, but I did not know that any one of them would have taken me to La Puente in short order.

We returned to Fontana with the battery fully charged. There was no more difficulty restarting the engine.

Dallas had no more to say about kidnapping children, his own or anyone else's. He was trying to score—crack or speed, I never learned which. He simply could not remember where his connection lived. It had been many years. I doubted that after such a time the connection would be where Dallas remembered even if he could remember.

At last Dallas thought he recognized something, either the house or the car. We stopped at a house we had passed many times before and Dallas went in. He was in the house a long time. It was not the place he was looking for, but he got an idea there of what to do instead. He began to try to set up a deal for the cigarettes. We rode around until it was dead dark. We went then to a number of sleazy places, including, I gather, a bordello. At one place he traded some cigarettes for a pint of whiskey, although there was cold duck aplenty on the floorboard behind the driver's seat. We went to various pay phones. At some of them Dallas placed calls and at others he waited for calls.

At last we went to the very dark parking lot of a very sleazy-looking beer joint somewhere in Fontana, not far from where we replaced the fan belt. People with guns and big flashlights came.

Flashlights shined at me and Lizbeth in the car. Dallas discussed something in animated whispers with a man and a woman in the parking lot. He got more and more excited. They leveled their guns at him.

Another man approached the car with a flashlight and a rifle or shotgun—I could not tell which because the light was in my eyes.

"Who are you?" he asked.

Lizbeth yipped. "Just a hitchhiker," I said.

"What's your connection with this guy?"

"He picked me up outside Phoenix."

"Where did he leave the cigarettes?"

"In the backseat," I said. The cigarettes had been returned to the backseat from the trunk as soon as I got up and about that morning.

The man shined his flashlight into the backseat. There was more than a case of cigarettes stacked up.

"These are the cigarettes?"

"That's them."

"And you rode from Phoenix in this car with this guy?"

"Yes. That's all I know about this."

The man chuckled. He backed away from the car until he was in whispering range of the others. He whispered. The woman shrieked a sort of laugh.

Dallas began talking quickly and earnestly. I could not quite make out what he was saying. The people with flashlights and guns backed away. Dallas kept after them, jabbering away. One of the men ordered Dallas to stay put. Dallas kept talking and did not entirely stay put. But the others backed away quickly, and when they were out of the parking lot and down the road in the shadows, the flashlights went out all at once.

Where the flashlights had gone out a big engine fired up and a big truck without lights came down the road. The truck passed the parking lot on the fly and disappeared down the dark back road. It came out bit by bit. Dallas was quite intoxicated. He had set up a deal to trade cigarettes for whatever it was he wanted. But the people got the idea that Dallas had a truckload of cigarettes. Dallas tried to convince them to deal for the cigarettes he did have, but they were not interested in such a small quantity. I suspected the people did not have anything to trade, but would have ripped us off and possibly killed us if there had been a truckload of cigarettes.

Dallas returned to the bordello and quickly disposed of a case of cigarettes for some small amount of cash. That left four or five cartons.

As we pulled onto the interstate we passed a hitchhiker standing on the ramp far past the NO PEDESTRIANS sign. I saw the highway patrol car pull onto the ramp, and at first I thought they were
going after the hitchhiker. I guess I had become used to Dallas's
driving, for I had not noticed his doing anything spectacular. He
was drunk.

The highway patrol pulled us over.

I thought if Dallas really was the wanted man he had said he
was, I would soon know it. I hoped this was nothing to do with
the shoplifting. For some reason Dallas had stuffed the remaining
cartons of cigarettes under the seat. The officers used their public
address system to order Dallas out of the car. Lizbeth barked. She
had never encountered police before, but she hated them—perhaps
the uniforms remind her of letter carriers. Eventually one of the
officers came around to check my ID.

"You boys been drinking some beer?" He shined his light into
Dallas's car, but he could not see the open bottle of cold duck Dallas had slipped under my leg.

"No, we haven't been drinking any beer," I said quite truth-
fully. I'd had a couple of swallows of cold duck for breakfast and
nothing alcoholic to drink since. I never saw a sip of beer cross
Dallas's lips.

We waited a long time. Dallas raved. At last a tow truck arrived. One of the officers said I could go. I did not have much gear,
but it was scattered about in the backseat. I bundled up things
haphazardly and got out of the car, holding Lizbeth's leash firmly
close to the collar. Dallas realized at last that he was not going to
be arrested, but his car was. He tried to unload everything out of
the car onto the road. He kept unloading even as the winch began lifting the car. The police ordered him to stop. Dallas seemed
to think he would never see anything in the car again.

We were on a narrow shoulder on a high ramp. I told Dallas I
had a fear of heights. As he shouted after me I led Lizbeth down

the ramp, across a bridge, and to a convenience store. I do have a fear of heights, but I suppress it by force of will when I must. I used it as an excuse. I wanted to get away to a phone. I used Billy's credit card number to call Rufus's benefactor Roy in La Puente.

Roy knew who I was, I was sure of that. But being a friend of Rufus's was not a sterling character recommendation. I had no idea how Roy would receive me or whether he would receive me at all.

I described where I was and Roy said he knew the place and would come after us right away. This gave me the impression that Roy was close by. He was not. He knew where I was only because he has a remarkable knowledge of most of Los Angeles county.

I had hoped otherwise, but Dallas arrived at the convenience store before Roy. One of the reasons I had wanted to leave was that I thought Dallas's attempt to get everything out of the car was hopeless and the officers were becoming impatient with the effort. But Dallas had got a great deal of it.

He considered my leaving as desertion under fire. Moreover he had missed a carton of cigarettes when he went through the car and he supposed I had taken them. I had repacked my few things in anticipation of Roy's arrival. I invited Dallas to look through them, for I knew I had not taken the cigarettes, not even inadvertently.

I told Dallas that I had contacted my friends in La Puente and I reminded him that after all La Puente was where I was going. Dallas seemed deeply hurt at this news. I was sorry for that. I had found Dallas attractive, and he had been almost affectionate at times. But he had never said explicitly that he had any other thought than to drop me in La Puente when he had finished his business in Fontana, and if he had thought of me as anything more than his shotgun rider, he had not given me a hint. If I had got a hint, I think I would have stuck with him, in spite of his dangerous way of life.

Dallas wanted to know if he could come to La Puente, too. That, I said, was out of the question.

I tried to explain that I was to be the guest of a friend of a friend, I was already imposing to an unthinkable degree, and I certainly could not propose any additional houseguests.

Dallas believed I could if I wanted to.

At last a horn sounded and Roy waved to me from his car. He had recognized me by Lizbeth.

Lizbeth leapt for the backseat of Roy's car and stood on it, licking Roy's face. I got in the car with our bundle of gear. I did not look back at Dallas.

THREE

Los Angeles: Pounding the Pavement

Roy was a pleasant, avuncular man who loved dogs. He had a good income and no expensive habits except Rufus. I cannot think of our visit as anything but a great imposition on Roy, but at least it was no hardship.

I spent several days on Roy's sofa, making reconnoiter of his refrigerator as Sherman made of Georgia.

Rufus had not yet been released from prison. He explained by telephone that he expected to be released at any time, but prisoners were not told much in advance of their precise release dates.

My friend Aaron Travis sent me some money as a loan against payment for some short stories I did before I left Austin, and I bought a pair of jeans and few shirts so that I could look for work. With only one complete change of clothes, I managed to get into Los Angeles only a couple of times a week, but it did not take me long to exhaust all the possibilities that had occurred to me.

I went to the office of the magazine that had advertised for editorial assistance. I was cordially received by the editor himself. He told me there was a glut of editorial workers in Los Angeles and he had not heard of an opening anywhere for years. I had not mentioned his own ad. Much later I learned that this magazine often advertised in its own pages and elsewhere for editorial help. Whatever the purpose of the advertisements, they never reflected a genuine vacancy.

I visited the offices of similar publications. The prospects were much the same. The publications had no openings and expected none. Several editors told me they had adopted a policy of reducing staff through attrition and would not fill any vacancy that might occur.

At the AIDS agencies things were different, but the prospects were no better. I was told they had many applicants, many of whom were better qualified than I. Yet they had money to fund many more positions and waiting lists of clients that might be served. The problem was facilities. City Councilmember Woo, at what was reckoned to be a great political risk, had just cut the ribbon on the first group home for people with AIDS to be opened in Los Angeles. Neighborhood groups opposed all such facilities. Several other projects had long been tied up in the process of obtaining the various approvals necessary. No one could say when another facility might begin operation.

I was surprised to learn this, for several Texas cities that I thought of as backward in comparison to Los Angeles had long had an assortment of hospices, group homes, and assisted-living apartments for people with AIDS.

I began to put in applications with other kinds of agencies. At the hospitals I discovered that California required licenses for many kinds of lower-level aides and attendants, and for that reason I was unqualified for positions like the mental-health worker

and nurse's aide jobs I had held for many years in Texas. The requirements for the licenses were not stringent, but they were beyond my means.

I had exhausted all the possibilities I could think of by the time
Rufus was released from prison. He returned to Roy's only to get
his car and several thousand dollars. Roy had agreed to finance a
vacation for Rufus. I believe Rufus was supposed to travel around
the country to consider what he might do with the rest of his life,
and then to return to Roy's or not, depending upon what Rufus
decided he wanted to do. The aspects of consideration, reflection,
and decision seemed only to exist in Roy's hopes for the trip.
Rufus had in mind a cross-country party and urged me to accom-
pany him on his junket. But he was afraid Lizbeth would damage
the upholstery in his car. He wanted me to have her destroyed.
That put the matter out of the question, though having recently
spent a few days riding around Southern California with Dallas
Matsen, I was not, in any event, eager to ride around the country
with Rufus.

Roy remained perfectly gracious and never gave me the least
sign that I was exhausting his hospitality. But once Rufus left, I
could not justify continuing to impose on Roy. I had scheduled
a couple of job interviews, and I resolved to leave Roy's if nothing
came of them, although I had no idea where I would go or what I
would do.

The third day after Rufus departed I received a call from
Aaron Travis. One of the magazines Travis worked with re-
viewed adult videos. For that reason Travis had received a call
from Jack Frost. Jack Frost was producing an adult video and,
although the taping of the picture was complete, Frost felt it
needed a voice-over script. He asked Travis to suggest a writer.
Travis suggested me.

I called Frost, who described the work he wanted as just a

couple of paragraphs to set the scene for each of his sequences. Foolishly, I gave him a bid that was a fraction of what Travis had suggested. Frost was very pleased and gave me directions to his apartment in Hollywood.

I had just replaced the phone in its cradle when the phone rang again.

It was Rufus. He was very intoxicated. He was calling from a motel room, but he did not know which city he was in. All of the money Roy had given him was gone and so was his car. He said he would call back when Roy would be home from work.

Since Rufus could call Roy at work if need be, I hurried off to Hollywood as fast as the Rapid Transit District buses would take me. I spent most of the next two weeks at Jack Frost's apartment, which was also his office. In describing it to me, Frost had very seriously understated the amount of work his script required. Nonetheless I completed the script in a couple of days. After that, Frost found various small office tasks for me to do. He said he would like me to do the script for his next picture, which, he said, would pay far better. We spent many hours discussing what he wanted for that picture.

The real reason Frost did not discharge me as soon as I had finished the voice-over script was he did not have the money to pay me. His picture was over budget and behind schedule. The distributors would not give him any more cash until he delivered the final cut of the video.

We dined at trendy restaurants that would accept Frost's credit cards, but we did not have enough cash to buy a loaf of bread and a jar of peanut butter. One morning at about 4:00 A.M. while we were at the postproduction studio, Frost decided he needed a particular sound-effects record. Much of the motion picture industry has moved out of Hollywood, but in Hollywood one can still find a record store that is open at 4:00 A.M. and that stocks bins of sound-effects records. Frost shook down me and his models for change to buy the record.

Only later in the morning did I realize I had given Frost the bus fare I needed to attend the job interviews I had scheduled. I was disconsolate, but there was nothing to be done for it.

I began to form a vague plan.

Jack's assistant Eugene had mentioned to me that many people camped in a fire zone only a few yards north of Jack's apartment. I did not know what a fire zone was, and I did not even bother to look at the one that was at hand. But I perceived that shelter was not a strict necessity of life in Los Angeles. Rain was rare and things dried out quickly when it did rain. Although the mornings could be very brisk, the cold would not be life-threatening. I thought I might obtain a mail drop, which I would need to collect what was owed me for work I had done and work I might do, buy a portable typewriter, and camp in the fire zone until I completed the script for Jack Frost's next picture.

In the meantime I continued to pore over the want ads, and I found something promising in them.

A private mental-health agency in West Hollywood had bought a new offset press. As the manufacturer of the press included training in the price of the machine, the agency was willing to hire someone without experience to operate it. The address was within walking distance of Jack Frost's apartment. I put in an application with the agency. I called my references in Austin and several of them sent letters to the agency. Evidently the letters were quite good, for the executive director described them as impressive when he interviewed me for the job. The aspect of my application that most appealed to him, I think, was that with my experience I could handle calls to the agency's crisis hotline. The hotline had to be answered at all hours, but late at night there were few calls. The press was supposed to be run late at night and if I ran it I could answer the occasional crisis call, saving the expense of having a crisis counselor on duty to stare at the phone.

The position especially suited me because it would entail a small apartment in the attic of the building that housed the crisis center and Lizbeth would be welcome there. I would have to run errands in the agency's van, so I would have to get a driver's license and to do so I would have to obtain eyeglasses. But, the director said, if I could tell him at our next meeting how I planned to get a driver's license, the job was as good as mine. Otherwise our next meeting would be a mere formality. I would be working with the art director—in West Hollywood a private mental-health agency can be expected to have an art director—and he would have to approve my appointment, but that could be taken for granted.

When I returned to Jack Frost's apartment I told Eugene about the interview.

"They think you are a lush," Eugene said.

I knew Jack Frost had that opinion of all writers and that Frost had been observing me carefully for the signs, but I did not know why Eugene would think the private mental-health agency would share Frost's prejudice.

Eugene explained that in Southern California a driver's license is considered such a necessity of life that the only believable explanation of an adult's not having one is that it has been taken away for drunk driving. Like Sherlock Holmes, Eugene often made remarks that seemed at first astonishing but seemed less so once explained. I was far from convinced that the executive director of the mental-health agency had calculated as Eugene thought he had, but I was less certain he had not.

At last Frost delivered his video to the distributors. They paid him and he paid me with a tip that would have been generous if it had been timely. Before I left Hollywood for Roy's I tried to secure a mail drop but discovered I could not do so without a

California ID. I found this very irksome, for one cannot get an ID without a mailing address. But as I still expected to get the job with the mental-health agency, I did not think the mail drop was essential. Back in La Puente, I found Lizbeth in the yard with Roy's dogs. She sprang vertically into the air from all fours in a way that seemed to me physically impossible. I had left her for so long only once before, and then she had been in her puppyhood home with familiar things all around her. In the weeks past she had reached an accommodation with Roy's dogs, but upon my return she became so jealous I was afraid she would start a dog fight before I got in the house.

Inside, I hardly recognized Roy's home. All the while I had been there, Roy's house had a comfortable degree of bachelorly disorder. Grateful to be off the road, I had washed the dishes and ironed Roy's shirts, picked up the newspapers and swept out a bit. But Rufus had made the place shine.

Roy had driven all night to some desert city to pick Rufus up from the motel. Rufus's car was not misplaced; it had been stolen, flipped, and burned. Over dinner I told Rufus and Roy that I planned to leave in a few days, after my interview with the mental-health agency. I supposed that Rufus's burst of domestic energy reflected some genuine effort at reform and I was eager to be out of his way. Such a change is difficult to effect in even the best of circumstances, and Rufus, who was supposed to be my friend, seemed not entirely reconciled to my presence.

After dinner Rufus asked Roy for money for beer. Roy made it obvious that he thought Rufus was drinking too much again. Nonetheless, Roy gave Rufus the money. I was very tired and I did not want to encourage Rufus's drinking, but he insisted I walk with him to the beer store on the boulevard.

When we got to the beer store, Rufus walked past it. We were not going to the beer store but, as it turned out, to a crack house.

Actually it was not a house. This was the suburbs and the

crack depot was an ordinary, or better than ordinary, apartment complex with a prominent location on the boulevard. The complex showed only a nine-foot red-brick wall to the street. There were two driveways with a sentry at each. The drives led to several rows of covered parking stalls and beyond these was another wall, this one with several door-shaped openings.

We passed the first sentry without a word, but we were challenged as soon as we reached the parking area. This was a drive-through operation and walk-up business was neither expected nor encouraged. Three cars in the parking area appeared to be occupied by customers waiting for their orders to be filled by runners.

I came to understand that Rufus had been here many times before, but no one on duty recognized him. Nonetheless, they seemed willing to deal with Rufus. Rufus looked like a drug addict. I, on the other hand, looked like a plainclothes cop. I was escorted through one of the door-shaped openings to a courtyard and was told to stay there. In fact I was told not to move.

After a long time my escort came back for me and I was returned to the parking area. My escort returned to working the cars, for the operation had fallen behind while accommodating Rufus. Rufus and I left.

The complex could not have contained less than thirty units in the four or five cubical buildings that surrounded the courtyards. The complex was not very old and was well maintained. The lawn and the plantings in the courtyard revealed an attention to detail that indicated regular professional care. Although the crack operation was as smooth and orderly as any such enterprise could be, I could not help wondering what life might be like for the other tenants of the complex and who the other tenants might be. As soon as we were off the well-lit main boulevard, Rufus pulled a small glass pipe out of the pocket of his jacket and showed me the five-dollar rock he had bought. He had told me we

were going for dope, by which I first thought he meant marijuana. I knew we had not visited any neighborhood pot dealer,
but until he pulled out the rock I was not sure what Rufus had
got.

Rufus's five-dollar rock was the size of a baby pea. I began to
think that crack was not as cheap as television news stories had
led me to believe. I knew five dollars' worth of powder cocaine
was hardly enough to be seen with the naked eye. But Rufus
largely disposed of his rock in the time it took for us to walk the
four or five blocks to Roy's. As the euphoric effects on Rufus
seemed especially short-lived, I estimated that one could easily
spend as much on crack as on powder cocaine, and therefore the
popularity of crack in the ghettoes was more a matter of availability than of price. Rufus admitted that he had spent most of his
vacation money on crack: the better part of two thousand dollars
in two days. He told me the gentlemen running the drive-through
depot were Crips. I had noticed that they all wore the signal blue
bandanna.

Rufus was not in fact drinking heavily again, but only let
Roy think so. Indeed, as the euphoria of the crack wore off, Rufus became morose to the point of tearfulness, just as he did
when he drank. I would have assumed he was drunk if I had not
known otherwise. But Rufus got to this point in a matter of
minutes with crack whereas it would have taken him several
hours of hard drinking to reach the same state with alcohol, and
there would have been plenty of empty bottles and cans around
if Rufus had been drinking. So I do not know whether Roy was
fooled.

I went for the interview at the private mental-health agency.
The art director had no questions at all for me, which seemed
either a very good sign or a very bad one. I explained that I had
made enough money to buy eyeglasses and had arranged to bor-
row a car in which to take the driving test. But if I bought the

eyeglasses I would be flat broke and so I dared not order them unless the agency was committed to hiring me.

The executive director told me that I could consider the job mine and that I should get the glasses.

The next day I again took the RTD into Los Angeles. When I reached the office where I was to have my eyes examined, I felt uneasy. I decided to call the agency once more. I looked about for a pay phone. By this time I had learned to go into a bar when I wanted to use a phone. Unlike the phones on the streets, phones in bars usually had all of their parts and were in working order. And in even the noisiest bar it was easier to hear a telephone conversation than it was on the street.

The receptionist at the agency remembered me. I told him I was in Hollywood to have my spectacles made and had only called to check in. He told me to hold on. Sure enough, the executive director had something to tell me. The art director had vetoed my appointment.

"Well, it's a lucky thing I discovered this before I expended the last of my resources," I said. I was disappointed not to get the job. But I was angry that the executive director, who knew I was about to spend the rest of my money according to his assurances and who must have known the art director's position very soon after the interview had been concluded, had not bothered to call me with this news. I strained to remain civil.

As the conversation closed, almost as an afterthought, he asked me where I was calling from. "A bar," I said. Surely he had heard the pinball machines in the background anyway.

I supposed Eugene had been right. They had thought I was a lush. And now they would congratulate each other on not hiring me. "Told you so," I imagined one would say to the other, "he called from a bar." But what would the executive director have said to me if I had spent the last of my money for the glasses and the driver's license and had shown up at the agency expecting to go to work?

I was reminded of a saying I had heard once: Little boys squash ants in fun, but the ants die in earnest. So the executive director had urged me to get the glasses, and once he knew the glasses would do me no good, he had not bothered to inform me, for the price of a pair of eyeglasses was nothing to him.

The only hope I had was to write the script for Jack Frost's next picture. Frost had described what he wanted in great detail and had acted as if it were a given that I would write it. But I knew it suited his purpose at the time to hold out the promise of more work. Naïf though I was, I knew it was speculation to work on the script, but I had no better prospect.

I took the RTD back to La Puente and bought a rollbag and another pair of jeans.

LIZBETH AND I walked to California Highway 39 two blocks at a time. It was a warm weekday in late March.

The size of my new red rollbag had encouraged me to over-pack. Although it would have saved me much pain on the road, I never learned to travel lightly enough.

I did not intend to return to Roy's. I had packed everything, and as I packed, everything had not seemed like much: a couple of pairs of jeans, a few shirts and underwear, writing pads and pens, a copy of Syd Field's *Screenplay* I had bought in West Hollywood, a couple of cans of Spam for myself, a large beach towel Rufus reluctantly let me have, and the ragged bedspread I had been given in Tucson.

In anticipation of buying a new wardrobe with his payment from the video distributors, Jack Frost weeded out his closet while I was at his apartment. I am very large, but Jack was even larger. He kept trying to give me his cast-off clothing, for it seemed especially to please him to patronize me in this way. Most of Jack's clothes were enormous on me and too dressy for someone of my station, but I would have accepted more if I had any hope of keeping it.

I kept a pair of running shoes that Jack could not have worn more than once or twice and a down jacket that he discarded because of a very small rip at one of the pockets. I would wear the shoes until they fell apart, and for a long time I had nothing so valuable as the jacket.

Most of the weight I carried as we left Roy's was dog food and water. I had learned my lesson and never again went in arid country with less than a gallon of water.

The rollbag was a new kind of mistake. All of its weight depended from its one shoulder strap. However well I padded the strap, it dug into my shoulder. I learned to shift the strap from shoulder to shoulder as I walked, a procedure complicated by Lizbeth's utter ignorance of the heel command. Although I never traveled with an adequate frame backpack, I am now convinced that is what I always wanted.

Where private yards backed up to the noise-abatement walls along the boulevard, branches of orange trees spread over the walls and the walk was spotted with dropped, decaying fruit. I was told this fruit was too hard and bitter to be edible, but I did not verify this. The fruit on the trees looked as wholesome as any I had tried in the Rio Grande valley.

According to my map, California 39 ran north into the national forest. When we reached the highway, the intersection was occupied by a shopping center, but a few hundred yards north I found a place to stand on a broad grassy shoulder. I stuck out my thumb.

We were there several hours. For once Lizbeth did exactly as

I wanted and lay on the rollbag in front of me so that she was clearly visible to any driver who might consider stopping.

A young woman, alone in a beat-up yellow Datsun, stopped for us. She said she worked in a veterinarian's office, so I attribute this ride to Lizbeth.

The driver wanted to proselytize on a text of not giving bones to dogs.

I had always avoided giving Lizbeth chicken. When in the press of necessity Lizbeth did have chicken, she never had any trouble with it, and she is not a dainty eater. I suspected the supposed dangers of chicken bones were more of the stuff of fable.

But no. My driver did not mean merely that a dog should not have chicken bones. She meant that dogs should not have any bones at all.

I pictured the many hours of pleasure that Lizbeth could derive from a beef rib. She would light into it with all the radiant enjoyment of doing what she was born to do. When the good had been had of it, she kept the bone and on occasion I found her going through her collection as an old woman goes through a family photo album. I nodded politely at our driver's remarks. But, I thought, no one had been around to tell cavemen not to throw bones to their cavedogs, and Lizbeth herself was good evidence that the cavedogs survived. The driver asked if Lizbeth was spayed.

Yes, she was. I can hardly imagine how much more exciting our adventures might have been had I tried to travel with a bitch in heat.

I asked the driver about heartworms. By Texas standards the mosquito season was near at hand. I had been worried because Lizbeth's heartworm prophylactic had been stolen with the rest of our gear in Tucson. I had asked Roy, but he had never heard anything about heartworms. Our driver said she had heard of a case or two of heartworms, but had never seen one. That gave me hope that heartworms were not endemic to the area.

That settled all the pending dog business.

I explained that I was planning to camp in the national forest while I wrote a script for an adult video. This my driver took in stride. To write adult videos in Southern California is rather analogous to being a bankruptcy lawyer in Austin or an undertaker elsewhere. It was an essential line of work, even if not everyone would desire it as an occupation.

She asked whether I had decided which foothill I would camp on. Only then did I realize that the massive rocks looming ahead of us were *foothills*. They were not the mountains. I was awestruck.

My driver warned that gangs of desperadoes of various kinds were holed up in the wilderness, quite beyond the reach of the law. The banditos would surely kill an intruder, and indeed the intruder would be lucky who was no worse than murdered.

The L.A. area was then fixated with the belief that satanic death cults from Mexico were rampant. From time to time juvenile delinquents in the suburbs would mutilate a house cat, or something of the sort, and would leave to be discovered with the remains such symbols and indications as seemed to them to be satanic. This sort of thing was easy pickings for the evening news.

Southern California is in reality queer, but as it is pictured by its own local evening-news programs, it is positively fantastic.

In Azusa, California 39 split into opposing one-way streets. Going out of her way, our driver took us to the north end of town where a convenience store was lodged in the triangle formed by the lanes rejoining.

I still had money in my pocket and I bought a very large fountain drink at the store. I had recharged our water bottles just before we got the ride and I did not want to break into them.

Finding no other source of water, I scooped the ice out of the drink and gave it to Lizbeth. By my map, all to the north of where we stood was national forest. Yet up the road to the right was an extensive development of townhouse condos, both occupied and under construction. I had learned that the foothills would appear nearer than they were in fact, but I still estimated that they were within walking distance.

I drank slowly and watched the customers at the convenience store. To this day I have the impression that people throughout Southern California are especially attractive. I expected as much in Hollywood, where several generations of the most attractive people in the country have gathered in hopes of careers in the movies. But it seemed to me there were disproportionate numbers of beautiful people throughout the region. Late in the afternoon Lizbeth and I made our move.

We walked on the right, past the condos. The land on the left, too, seemed to be in private hands, for there was a defunct tourist trap with propped-up flats painted to resemble, vaguely, an Old West village, and there was a lodge: Odd Fellows, as I recall.

The road turned sharply to the right. There was a tourist information station of the forest service. The station was closed, but from its posted map, and for the fact of the station itself, I formed the opinion that we had entered the national forest. Yet as we walked on I found evidence to the contrary. On the right the road hugged a cliff, so closely in places that we had to cross the road and walk on the left. On the left, at regular intervals, were PRIVATE PROPERTY, NO PARKING, and NO TRESPASSING signs. Below the road was water that I call a creek, for so it seemed to me at the time, but as best I can determine now it was the San Gabriel River, or what was left of it, below a great reservoir.

We walked on.

The light was fading. I was weary of carrying the rollbag, and I had got as much mileage as I could expect of Lizbeth in one day.

We were amid the foothills that I had estimated to be within walking distance, but I had not seen a possible campsite.

Then the road turned sharply to the right, but the cliff on the right turned more sharply. In the armpit of this curve was an abandoned tavern. That seemed promising enough, at least for the night, but beyond the tavern there seemed to be a fairly dense residential development.

On the left the road had a very wide gravel shoulder. Here were NO PARKING signs, but I had not seen a NO TRESPASSING sign for some time. A graded dirt road, wide enough for a vehicle on it to pass another, led downward and backward from the left shoulder. I was almost sure there were no dwellings between the road and the creek. I led Lizbeth down the graded road.

I found footpaths cutting off toward the creek, and we went down one of these until I found a wide spot. By then it was dark. I made our bed. The wide spot was relatively level, but not level enough. This was the first time we tried to sleep on an incline. We were not very good at it and we never got better at it. In the course of the night we slid, scattering our bedroll, gear, and things from my pockets.

The night turned chilly and again Lizbeth abandoned her more usual popliteal position and climbed up into the down jacket with me. Fortunately Jack Frost was precisely one dog stouter than me.

At first light I left the gear as it was and we went about exploring.

We had slept about halfway down a footpath that led to a convex-lens-shaped field of smooth rounded rocks, each about the size of a flattened tennis ball. Beneath the rocks, evidently, were more rocks of a similar kind with the result that trying to walk on the rocks was not very different from trying to walk on several layers of ball bearings. A little of this and Lizbeth insisted on being carried, or at least, on not moving voluntarily.

At the upstream point of the lens, the road we had walked the night before bridged the creek. I kept the bridge in mind in case of rain, though the area under the bridge was even steeper than the incline on which we had just spent a restless night.

Near the bridge, but not quite under it, was a large block of concrete, evidently poured on the site. I could never tell why it was there. It was no structural part of the bridge that I could determine. The top was square, about nine feet to the side, and roughly level. The top surface was ten feet above the ground on the downhill side, but the block could be mounted easily from the uphill side. Lizbeth and I sat on the block for a while.

That it was flat and above the ground seemed to recommend it as a campsite, or at least as a place to sleep. It was exposed to the sun. I thought I might work under the bridge in the daytime and that we could sleep on the block at night. I considered that an object thrown from the bridge might fall on the block. But I saw no broken glass or cans in the vicinity. I am not sure why I decided against our sleeping on the block, but I did so decide and thus I am here to tell the tale.

We found a very large rusty object that looked to me to be a sluice of some kind. I developed the romantic notion that it had something to do with panning for gold. Later I was told this notion was not so far-fetched.

Nearer the water the rounded rocks got smaller and supported several grassy patches, some shrubs, and two or three small trees. Here I found signs of picnickers and campers. The signs of the campers were not recent but, to judge by the many empty bean cans and the soot on the rocks of the fire circle, several of the campers had remained a long time. The small rocks gave way to gravel and, at the edge of the water, to coarse sand.

On the far side of the creek, a steep cliff rose from the water. A few boulders and a narrow ledge formed all there was of the far shore.

Whether we were on public land or not, I thought lying low Lizbeth and I might remain the week I figured would be required to finish Jack Frost's script. One willowy tree among some shrubs seemed to offer good cover from every direction. I tied Lizbeth to this tree and went after our gear.

The rounded rocks under the tree were very discomforting. I gathered several large pieces of cardboard from abandoned camps and found these made a good base for my pallet. No doubt that was why I found them where I did.

I opened a can of Spam and gave Lizbeth all of the jelly. Eventually she also got most of the meat. I was prepared to be adult about the texture of Spam, but I had forgotten—or I had not realized when I had eaten Spam as a child—how very salty it is. I wonder whether I am not merely more sensitive to the salt now that so many other products contain less of it.

I set to work on Frost's script.

Several groups of picnickers came along. Some went into the water and some just looked at it. One of these groups gave me the opportunity of observing the Valley girl—as I never visited a Southern California mall, this was as near her native habitat as I would get.

Two girls and a boy, all of high school age, I would guess, arrived in the afternoon, dressed for bathing. I found it hard to believe her accent was not a conscious parody when one of the girls, having stalked the shore skeptically and stuck a toe in the water, exclaimed, "Ricky, we have got to talk. This water is gurreen. Gur-reen water is not one of my favorite things!"

The water, of course, was quite clear, but the rocks and boulders were covered with algae.

No one spoke to us or bothered us in any way, and the variety of visitors seemed to confirm that this was some kind of public area.

A few of the men and boys went into the water nude or in

their underwear, but not so many that I was convinced the practice was accepted. I had nothing to wear into the water, so I
waited until sunset to bathe. By then the others had left the area
and I let Lizbeth off her leash, confident she would not cross the
field of rocks voluntarily. I hoped to coax her into the water.

Lizbeth is supposed to be half Labrador retriever and she has
swimmer's paws. As a puppy she would beg to get into the bath-
tub with me, and always seemed to enjoy splashing around when
I hefted her in. But as an adult she refuses to go into the water,
however still the water or gently sloping the shore. She watched
me in the water but would no more than get her forepaws wet.
She drank the water, with no apparent ill effect, and then wandered off out of my sight. I was concerned about her, but when I
came out of the water I found her curled up on our bedroll.

The creek had a few deeper holes but mostly was less than
waist deep. In several places anyone able to maintain footing on
the slick boulders could wade across.

Despite the NO PARKING signs, the wide gravel shoulder up on
the road across from the abandoned tavern turned out to be
something of a lovers' lane. After dark, cars came and parked and
left at various intervals. But none of the cars came down the
graded road to the field of rocks.

I did not sleep very well. I spent much of the night watching
the stars. Although there were occasional headlights up on the
road and a few distant security lights, this was by far the darkest
sky I had seen since I had arrived in Southern California. There
were two bright objects in Sagittarius where there is no fixed star
of comparable magnitude, but it had been months since I had
known the positions of the planets and I could not guess which
two these were.

The following day was a Friday. Many more picnickers came,
especially in the afternoon. I spent the day alternately working
on Frost's script and reading Field's book. Field, of course, had no

specific advice for the writer of an adult video. But I enjoyed the way he expressed himself and, as I had never given any thought to the structure of screenplays, it was all news to me. As an exercise I began to put Frost's script into screenplay form. Frost would not have liked that, but as he had never learned to read I could prevent his knowing how I had formed his script.

At sunset I went in the water again. By the time I got out, a party was forming up on the road among the parkers, but I had not slept well in two nights and I soon fell into a dreamy sleep.

I believe I dreamt a *whoosh*. For a few moments I was neither asleep nor awake, but I do recall thinking how peculiar it was to have dreamt *whoosh*. I was soundly asleep again when Lizbeth began licking my face. Without opening my eyes, I tried to quiet her, but she was very insistent.

Then I supposed she had the runs—all the salt in the Spam would have had that effect on me. I had extended her leash with the shoulder strap from the rollbag. But no matter how much I ever extended her leash, Lizbeth would not relieve herself unless she was being walked. When she had to go urgently at night she would lick me awake, and I supposed that was why she was licking me then.

I sighed, sat up, and opened my eyes. I saw Lizbeth had a very different reason: fire.

Upstream, near the bridge, was a huge fireball that seemed to be growing larger every instant.

"Good dog, Lizbeth. Good dog," I said. By the orange light reflected by the cliff on the opposite shore I could see Lizbeth's face. I thought she was at once both worried by the fire and relieved that I was awake at last.

I led her from our willowy cover, taking the beach towel with me, thinking we might have to escape downstream with the wet towel over our heads. Indeed, the fireball had expanded until it seemed a wall of flame. The fire seemed to be upon us, but then I realized—from the silhouettes of the intervening shrubs and saplings—that the fire was no nearer than a hundred yards. Even so the fire was hot on my face and it stirred up strange air currents in the canyon. By watching the intervening objects I became convinced that the fire was coming no nearer, and then that it seemed slowly to recede. Without additional fuel I saw no way it could jump the field of rounded rocks. My theory was that a gas line under the bridge had ruptured. This I supposed accounted for my dream of *whoosh*, for the *whoosh* I had dreamt was the *whoosh* of lighting a gas oven with a match, only very much louder. I noticed the cars were gone from the shoulder of the road above and I deduced that either the hour was very late or the lovers had fled. I tried to reassure Lizbeth. We returned to the bedroll.

Then the screaming vehicles came.

One of the emergency vehicles up on the road shined a powerful spotlight. By watching the cliff on the far side of the creek I could see the shadows of the people and things up on the road. Some of the equipment I could not recognize in shadow form.

Suddenly Plato's cave came to life for me as it never had before, proving—or so it seems to me—that one pertinent experience is worth more than a volume of commentary. I had read the cave passage dozens of times—the central analogy of idealism—and I had got no more than a tenuous grasp of the general drift of the argument. Now although I recognized the shadows of people as the shadows of people and the shadows of police cars as the shadows of police cars, I saw also the shadows of many things I could not identify and I would not recognize the things that cast the shadows if I saw the things themselves in daylight. I was wonderfully excited by this new light on an old text, but then too, the event was exciting in a grim way.

Several of the emergency vehicles had piped the radio traffic to their public address horns. Because of the echoes in the canyon and the various dispatchers speaking at the same time, I could only understand a little of it. The main question was whether there was one victim or two. The answer to that question I never discovered, but the gist of the situation was that a car had not made the turn onto the bridge and had plunged off the road.

The remains of one victim had been seen in the car, but evidently there were reports that the car had taken a pedestrian with it as it left the road.

Despite the excitement I dozed off and on and finally fell asleep again just before dawn. I slept late in the morning.

I heard the wrecker come down the graded path and cross the field of rounded rocks, sometimes spinning its wheels. It returned with a horrible scraping noise and I sat up to take a look. The wrecked vehicle was being dragged upside down across the rounded rocks. The roof was crushed. No one could have escaped.

LIFE GOES ON. Lizbeth and I needed to return to town to buy water—I still had some change. I also wanted to mail some letters and postcards. I stashed the gear except for the empty water bottles. I decided we would investigate the crash site as we went.

From the scorch marks and the broken glass I could see that the car had pancaked onto the flat concrete block I had considered sleeping on. This provided me with a vivid mental image, but I supposed we would never have known what hit us.

To judge by what I had seen of the fire I would have sworn anything remotely inflammable in the car would have been reduced to cinders. But as we followed the drag path I found a remarkable number of things intact and unmarked by the fire, shed from the wreck as it was towed away.

There were a couple of pairs of jeans that had been worn too long without underwear by a beer drinker, and several shirts that smelled strongly of alcoholic body odor. I found one unmarked Western boot, not custom-made but of the more expensive kind of ready-made. From the cut of the clothes I guessed the victim was a tall, slender young man.

He lived in his car.

Lizbeth and I had accepted a ride with a young man who lived in his car and drank too much. If we might have been sleeping on the flat rock, then we might have been pedestrians on that side of the road, or we might have been riding in the car.

I found a shaving kit: pomade and an Afro comb with coarse curly black hairs in its teeth. The driver had been black.

There were other things: the rear-view mirror, coat hangers, and an empty suitcase, evidently broken before the crash.

Then I found the railroad book. I thought at first it had been singed in the fire. I put the book in my pocket. When we had got the water and returned to camp, I read the book through.

It was a rule book for the staff of passenger trains. Much of it concerned keeping correct time, reading signals, and placing emergency signals in case a train is delayed on the tracks. A number of rules pertained to assisting passengers in various kinds of emergencies. In these, women were classed with the insane and feeble-minded.

It began to dawn on me that this book had not been issued to the victim of the wreck. Age, not the fire, had made the pages brittle and yellow.

I had an education in ethnic studies and for once it cast some light. There was a time when a literate young black man without a well-connected family or money of his own had but a very few chances to avoid a life of back-breaking labor and miserable poverty. One of those chances was to get on with the postal service. Another was to work for the railroad. There was a limit to how high he might rise in one of these positions, but he might live in relative comfort, educate his children well, and give them a base from which they might aspire to the professions.

This was not the victim's book. It was his father's or his

grandfather's. It had been that one and only ticket out of hard times. Treasured and handed down, here it was, the progenitor's book.

Here it was.

And here, perhaps with only Lizbeth as a witness, this line whatever its aspirations and accomplishments had come to its fiery end.

FOUR

San Gabriels
and Hollywood

Late in the afternoon, when the last of the picnickers and bathers had left, a large new pickup came down the graded road and stopped at the far edge of the field of rocks. The driver was in Western attire. I estimated that he was the foreman of one of the nearby estates; he negotiated the field of rocks in his boots better than a weekend cowboy could have, but his clothes in spite of many washings acknowledged no recent acquaintance with hard work.

He could not have seen us from where he parked, but he knew we were there. He came directly to our camp. When he was near enough to see us anyway, I got up to meet him.

"You weren't planning on camping here overnight?" he asked. The only possible response was, "No, of course not." This, he said, was private property. The owners looked the other way for the picnickers, but camping was another thing. I began packing our gear as soon as he left. I still needed a couple of days to work on

Jack Frost's script. I thought we would not have to remove much farther north to reach the national forest and I foresaw no problems. But there is no twilight in the canyons and it was quite dark by the time we reached the road.

First there was the matter of getting across the bridge with Lizbeth and the gear. The bridge was very narrow and for the twists in the road I could not see the traffic coming from either direction. Bridges were a problem. Lizbeth always wanted to pull us to the middle of the road, and it was often difficult to restrain her when we were overtaken by vehicles.

Beyond the bridge the road was on a very narrow ledge. The left side of the road was rockbound. There was no shoulder and the pavement often was no more than a foot or two from the boulders. On the right there was a drop-off that seemed considerable, but the grassy shoulder was sometimes two or three yards wide. We came to a marker sign I could not read in the darkness.

When I saw the sign in daylight it proved to be the Azusa city-limit marker. My map was quite inaccurate on this point.

I laid us down on a somewhat wider part of the right shoulder. I could see ruts that indicated this was sometimes used as a turn-around. But I could not find a safer place and as it was too dark to see the ground I was walking on, I thought walking on would be no safer.

AT DAWN I saw that the road overlooked a vast reservoir. There were many NO CAMPING signs; no doubt we were near the intake valves of some public water supply. I could see, at intervals as it wound around the cliff, portions of the road ahead. I was glad we had not walked on in the dark. The bridges ahead were more treacherous than the one we had crossed and in places the right shoulder did not exist.

Before long we were picked up by a blond-bearded man who,

without his old station wagon, I might have taken for a forty-niner. His hobby, he said, was exploring the canyons. There were many things up the canyons, he said, that no one would guess: abandoned mines, ghost towns that had been cut off by flash floods, ruined bridges, wrecked wagons.

I explained that I just wanted to camp and work on my script undisturbed for a couple of days. Potable water was a consideration.

The driver had a place in mind.

As we went he pointed out a naval reservation on the reservoir. This was for torpedo testing. He said the reservoir had been used in World War II also to perfect the technique of skip-bombing, which was used against the German dams. I recalled seeing a motion picture on that subject. Indeed this was an excellent place, even in nuclear times, for a military installation. It would be invisible except from directly overhead and invulnerable to anything short of a direct hit.

After we crossed the river the driver pointed out what he said was the entrance to a gold mine. It was a box of chain-link fencing that appeared to go right into the hillside. He said the mines opened and closed as the price of gold fluctuated. Gold mining was now a business and the ore remaining in the mines was marginal. Lucky people still turned up sizable nuggets from time to time, but so rarely that no one could make a business of it. This all was put plausibly enough, but as it seemed to me the major gold deposits in California had been found far to the north of where we were, I never was sure whether to believe the driver.

Lizbeth and I were not let out entirely off the beaten path. One side of the road was a large gravel parking area where empty beer bottles and cans had been gathered into five-foot piles. We were a little downstream of a recreational-vehicle park that was ersatz bucolic and as near, I suppose, to inoffensive as such things get. No one else was up and about, for it was still early on a

Sunday morning. I could not find a way down to the river, but when I found a level spot out of plain sight, we lay down and slept.

I awoke about noon. The parking area was nearly full of cars. I had only to follow the people to find the way to the river. Five or six trails led down to a dozen or more little clearings and each of these had a little concrete grill. All of the sites were occupied by the time we got to the river, and we sat on a flat rock out of the way while I worked on the script.

Quite early in the afternoon the groups began to depart. I seized one of the areas at the end of a trail—so no one would have to pass through by Lizbeth. I accumulated a pile of old coals and lit these by using a piece of cardboard to carry hot coals from the fires that had been left burning. This was the only time we had a fire any place we camped. The water in the river was beautiful, clear, and cold and sweet smelling. Lizbeth drank it as it was. I was tempted to do the same, but owing to the RV park upstream, I boiled the water. I have had hepatitis B and have no desire to experience hepatitis A.

We stayed by the river two nights and it was as pretty and peaceful a place as Lizbeth and I have been in our travels. The crowds did not come on the weekdays. I finished the script Monday. The river was very broad and shallow where we camped. I had seen people wade across it Sunday and I wanted to do the same. Lizbeth refused to cross with me, and wisely—for I missed my footing on several slippery rocks—she refused to let me carry her across. Instead she stood on the shore and barked at the water while I explored.

Tuesday morning I read the script through once more by first light, and then I packed. I expected a ride would be hard to find on a weekday. I recalled we had passed a fork in the road shortly before we were let out at the parking area. I decided to walk back to it to take advantage of whatever additional traffic might come from the other fork. When we reached the fork, however, there was a NO HITCHHIKING sign.

I had noticed the road was marked by eighth-of-a-mile markers. We walked another mile and a half without encountering another NO HITCHHIKING sign. As always I was concerned that any confrontation with the law, whether serious or not, might result in Lizbeth's being taken from me and put to death. But I felt we had given the sign a respectful berth. I looked for a wide spot on the shoulder. At last the shoulder expanded and there was another large graveled area. Here was a very small building entirely surrounded by a chain-link fence that was topped with concertina wire. This seemed to me to be a telephone switching station. The fence bore NO LOITERING signs. These did not impress me as being official. In any event, I was by then disgusted. I set the gear down as far as I could away from the building while remaining in a position to take advantage of this stopping place for any car that might want to give us a ride.

After a couple of hours we had been passed by no more than a dozen cars.

At last a man in a pickup stopped and signaled me to get in the back. Lizbeth was still lashed to the gear—it had become my habit to do this whenever we stopped. I boosted her and the gear together into the bed of the pickup. As I got a foot up on the bumper, the truck pulled away. I almost fell on my face. Lizbeth was carried away; her paws up on the tailgate, she looked back at me until the truck was out of sight.

I was dumbfounded. After a second or two I shouted "Hey!" several times. The driver could not hear me or would not stop, I did not know which. I was afraid Lizbeth would try to leap off the truck. That would certainly be the end of her. Helpless, I watched until the truck was out of sight. I did not know whether the driver had meant to do this, perhaps from pure meanness or to see what I might have in my gear. The example of Tucson suggested either motive or both. Of course I was unconcerned about the gear. The driver's timing argued for intent—in another fraction of a second I would have had a leg over the tailgate. And the worst of it was the very puzzled way Lizbeth had looked back at me.

I sat down on the gravel, nearly in the road, limp and numb.

After what seemed like a very long time, the truck came back. I was not sure it was the same truck as it approached. It had, after all, been a mistake. The driver had heard me chunk Lizbeth and the gear into the bed of the truck and had not looked back, assuming I was in the truck as well.

The driver opened the sliding window at the back of the cab and we shouted back and forth as we went, although with Lizbeth on my lap I was too overcome to be a fit conversationalist for many miles. The driver had been fishing and had caught nothing.

I wondered then about the water Lizbeth and I had been drinking, for I realized I had seen no fish and that the water was so clear I would have seen any fish there were. The driver said I was very lucky he had picked me up. I had my doubts on that score. The driver explained that the NO HITCHHIKING signs were on account of a prison facility in the area. What is more, in my denim workshirt and blue jeans I was attired exactly as the prisoners were, save that their jeans had one white hip pocket, a difference bound to be lost on passing motorists as I faced them with my thumb out.

The drivers would not have calculated the likelihood of an escaping prisoner having acquired a dog and red rollbag. I wonder yet whether our driver had taken his opportunity to examine Lizbeth and my gear. He certainly was gone long enough to have done so.

We were let out on I-210, which runs north of I-10 and roughly parallel to it. We were picked up by a Latin man in a battered van. He spoke no more English than I spoke Spanish—I use the term *Latin* where I am not certain of a more specific word; the numbers of Central Americans found throughout the Southwest are now so large that Spanish-speakers cannot be assumed to be Mexicans or Chicanos. This was a fairly long ride and the driver let us out in a many-leveled freeway interchange.

I did not want to hitchhike there, for it was certainly dangerous and most likely illegal. But the driver had understood my destination was Hollywood and had seemed to indicate I needed to change roads here. At any rate, the interchange was fenced in. I tied Lizbeth and the gear in a shady spot. Even unencumbered I did not find a way out for more than an hour.

When we emerged from the interchange we were on another of the wide suburban strips. In retrospect I have come to believe we were in Pasadena. I found what I was nearly sure was the ramp we wanted, but there was no room for us to stand on it. I had to stand on the strip and to try to indicate I wanted on the ramp. We were there for several hours and it was especially frustrating because those who wanted on the ramp had to slow to turn onto it, and this gave me the impression we had a ride several times when we did not.

A gray-haired lady stopped. I knew this could not be a ride, but I thought it might be a handout. Instead she said she was looking for a missing dog. Obviously the missing dog could not have been her own, for she continued to question me closely in spite of her being near enough to see Lizbeth clearly. Having thought once that day that I had lost Lizbeth, I was unnerved by this interview. The woman still seemed suspicious even as she drove away.

I do not see how I could have thought the owner of the missing dog might appear and try to claim Lizbeth, nor do I think I really thought precisely that. But I was beginning to expect the worst of every situation and I had a strong impulse to flee with Lizbeth.

I do not remember much about the ride that took us to Griffith Park, except that I was glad to get it. We were let out near the tennis courts at rush hour.

I found pay phones at the tennis courts and used Billy's credit card number to call Jack Frost's apartment several times. Eventually Eugene picked up the phone and told me Jack was out of town, but that he might return the next day. I got the impression that Eugene was not being entirely frank with me.

Hitchhiking appeared out of the question in rush hour. Lizbeth and I walked down Los Feliz. Here were some of the grandest mansions I had ever seen, but many of them were going to seed. I supposed no one who could afford one of these places would want it. The houses were too near the central city. They would require large staffs, and security would be difficult to provide at any price.

After dark we came to a sharp curve that turned us onto Western Avenue. I knew that many of the streets north of Hollywood Boulevard were cut off by hills. I did not much want to negotiate Hollywood Boulevard with Lizbeth and the gear, but I did not want to wander around in the hills after dark. I was concerned that Lizbeth might misbehave in the crowds, but once I saw what the neighborhood of Western Avenue and Hollywood Boulevard was like, I was glad to have her with me.

Where the Hollywood Freeway passes under Hollywood Boulevard I found a weedy spot on a corner and sat down with Lizbeth on the gear. I had walked my limit with the gear and thereafter we moved at intervals from one bench at a bus stop to another. Lizbeth, on the other hand, was still feeling frisky because for most of the distance we had covered she had walked on sidewalks or grass.

By and by a prostitute came along, tears streaking her makeup, and forced two dollars on me. She said her little dog had been lost or stolen and she wanted me to buy Lizbeth something to eat with the money.

Although a considerable part of the weight I had been bearing was dog food, I formulated in that moment a new corollary to my existing policy of not stealing and not panhandling: I would not refuse anything that was offered to me.

Lizbeth displayed a talent for hustling. In this instance she surpassed herself—a wan look, a few feeble twitches of the tail, a languid, tentative lick. I found it difficult to keep from laughing. Lizbeth had never been taught this. At home she had been demanding if her food or water was overlooked. She had been forbidden to beg while people ate, but attended meals with quiet alertness, as she was allowed to have the scraps and lick the plates.

Her new set of behaviors I called the Dying Dog Routine. It is a wonder passersby who have seen it have not lynched me for cruelty to animals. I suppose one of her progenitors began working up this routine dog-eons ago and natural selection has preserved the bits most likely to affect human sympathy.

Of course as soon as the prostitute walked away, Lizbeth was up and about and in high spirits.

We continued west on Hollywood Boulevard. At one of the benches where we stopped, a wino—gray stubble on his face, clothes slept in, bottle in a brown paper sack—gave me a dollar to buy food for the dog. Lizbeth was shameless.

La Brea Avenue was the last convenient stopping place before we had to climb the hill to reach the fire zone. We rested there for a long time. I wanted to make the hill all in one move because the way was lined with fashionable apartment buildings and our lingering there might have aroused suspicion. On Hollywood Boulevard, we did not look so out of place.

I found no place to tie Lizbeth and I took her with me across the boulevard to a liquor store. There I tied her to the gear and went in to buy cigarettes. I worried because all of the gear would really only slow Lizbeth down if she decided to light out after a skateboarder or a cat or something of that nature. In the liquor store I had to wait in line. Sure enough, a man who had not realized Lizbeth was affixed to my bags tried to grab one of them.

Lizbeth snarled. I left my place in line and went outside where I saw the man fleeing down the boulevard. Encumbered by the gear, Lizbeth had managed to pursue him for only twenty yards. After I put things in order I went back into the store for my cigarettes and this time no one messed with the gear or Lizbeth.

I had no qualm about spending the money on cigarettes. The wino and the prostitute had meant for Lizbeth to eat, and eat she would.

We returned to the north side of the boulevard and remained there for more than an hour. About a half-dozen young men were drinking in the shadows near the intersection of La Brea and Hollywood. They were all dressed in the Nazi-punk attire that seemed to be fashionable among some young people. One at a time they stood on the corner, where they would get picked up quickly. I was told later that local Johns prefer the hustlers on Santa Monica Boulevard and consider the trade on Hollywood Boulevard to be fit only for tourists. Perhaps that is so. None of the young men was gone for very long.

When any of them returned, he went to the liquor store and brought a bottle back to the group. Whenever the corner was unoccupied for more than a few minutes some little discussion would arise in the group—over whose turn it was, I suppose— and eventually, with an obscene gesture for his comrades, someone would leave the group and take up his station at the corner. Generally the bottle stayed in the group, but once, on his way to the corner, one of the young men offered me the last swallows in a bottle, which I declined. He killed the bottle himself and chucked it into an empty parking lot.

Eventually the group broke up, the punks wandering off one at a time. By the time none was left, the hour was very late. Lizbeth and I went up the hill.

I was quite breathless when we reached the fire zone. When we got to it the avenue ended and there were barricades. We stepped over a six-inch-wide trench. Then there was a road that had been paved once.

We went up the road about a hundred yards and then cut off. I began looking for a flat spot. The weeds were quite high and I had begun to trample down a bed for us when I saw something peculiar. Several stone steps led to a stone platform, perhaps ten feet wide and twenty feet long. All I could think was that this was the stage of an outdoor theater. That did not seem quite right, for the stonework was above the surrounding ground and not below it. I did not care what it was besides being a clean flat spot to lay our bedroll on. I could hear several rowdy parties, or perhaps just one and its echoes, but I fell rather quickly to sleep.

I AWOKE AT dawn, which was a good thing. I had got turned around in the weeds. I thought the stone platform was distant from the old road, but the contrary was the fact. Joggers and little old ladies walking their dogs came along shortly after first light. I cached the gear, and Lizbeth and I went exploring.

The stone platform on which we had slept was once one of the porches of a house that had burned, although the rest of the ruins were so grown over that this was not at first apparent. There were ruins of many other grand places. At one, its chimney still standing, was a stone hearth, quite as large as the one in *Citizen Kane*.

This is what a fire zone is: a burned-out area on a hillside where the danger of fire is reckoned to be so great that rebuilding is prohibited. The fire zone I was in was almost completely walled round, so far as I could tell. Sections of the wall varied in style and there were various kinds of more-or-less ornate gates with stout locks. I deduced then that the walling off of the fire zone was the sum of various private projects. Indeed, the trench we had stepped over the night before was for the foundation of yet another section of wall, perhaps the last section. Then the area would be a private park for those who had keys to the well-locked ornate gates.

At a decent hour I brought Lizbeth and the gear down to the entrance of the fire zone and tied her and the gear to a tree there. Jack's apartment was in the first building on the avenue and I could see Lizbeth and the gear as I stood at the call box of the apartment building.

Eugene answered my buzz. He said Jack was still in San Francisco visiting another producer. As both Jack and Eugene were completely illiterate, I had done Jack's filing while I was there, and from sorting through his documents, I knew the other producer whom Eugene named spoke for most of Jack Frost's backers. Eugene said they were celebrating the completion of Frost's picture, but I still thought Eugene was hiding something. Perhaps Frost was being called onto the carpet. Frost's parking place could be seen through the automatic roll-down gate of the building's garage. I verified that Frost's car was gone and returned to the fire zone.

Not far from the stone porch, but farther from the road, I found a terraced garden, quite overgrown and wild. One of the levels was waist-high from the next, and as this spot was concealed by vegetation, it seemed a convenient place to camp.

I discovered the punks I had observed the night before, or some of them. They occupied a little stone building below. This structure was about twelve feet on a side, and although there was no evidence of pool equipment or a pool, I called it a pool house in my mind.

The punks saw me and I saw them at various times. Once when I was away from my camp I heard Lizbeth snarl. I returned quickly to her, but I found nothing disturbed. Thereafter the punks did not come near my camp and would avoid a trail rather than confront Lizbeth. But the punks did not have a dog, so in their absence I inspected their digs.

Perhaps the building had been no more than an ambitious garden shed. I found no plumbing or remains of electrical connections. The roof evidently had survived the fire, but since then had half rotted away. Swastikas had been spray-painted on all the walls. Whether six of the punks lived here or only three, the lot of them evidently slept en masse.

One corner of the room was given over to an altar: pentagrams, small animal skulls, drippy candles, that sort of thing. In another corner was an enormous pile of plastic Big Mac and Egg McMuffin boxes. They drank whiskey; I found no beer or wine bottles. I was somewhat surprised not to find hypodermic needles and spoons. All the clothing was in one pile—mostly black jeans and morbid T-shirts. I supposed they all dressed from this common stock; those I had seen were of the same size—about six feet tall and 180 pounds.

I checked with Eugene again in the evening. He assured me Jack Frost would be back the next day.

The moon was nearly full that night and the punks partied loudly until just before dawn. I napped through most of the following day. When I went to Frost's apartment again, I could see his car was back in its spot. But when I buzzed Eugene, he said Frost was still out of town. I mentioned the car. Eugene claimed a friend of Frost's had driven it back.

Perhaps Frost never intended to see me again after he paid me for my first script. I think it more likely that he did plan on a second picture and did want me to write it, although I expect he made the prospects sound more promising than he knew them to be. I think his backers had some bad news for him when he reported to them. At any rate, it was quite awhile before he made another picture that I know about.

I had not eaten in several days and was running low on water. Whatever Frost intended, I had to move on.

———

FRIDAY MORNING WE remained in the fire zone until after ten o'clock. Lizbeth drank the last of our water. I packed up our things. As we passed Jack's apartment I buzzed again and got more of the same story from Eugene. For what it was worth I told him I would mail the script whenever I could get it typed up.

I estimated our chances of survival on the streets of L.A. as very slight. The punks did well enough, but they were young, strong, and attractive. I had discovered another young man who camped in the fire zone and who fared not nearly so well.

He was arrayed in tatters, his pants held up with a length of cord. In Austin he would have been well dressed at least, for he was a normal size and easily could have worn the good clothes the students cast away. His camp was a pallet of cardboard in a clump of tall grass that may have been a kind of bamboo I had never seen before. He had obviously been there a long time, and his camp was well concealed, but he had not found the means to improve his digs. From my observations of the mobs of homeless people—mostly young and white—I had seen in Santa Monica as I had gone about looking for work, and the black families I had seen living in the central plaza in Los Angeles, I was convinced that I would be better off returning to Austin.

Lizbeth and I walked south on La Brea Avenue to Santa Monica Boulevard. Jack Frost had mentioned a grocery store there. I assumed that like all other grocery stores in Southern California, this one would have a machine that vended water, and of course it did. I filled our bottles. I wanted to be on the road to Austin that day.

But as night fell, the farthest east we had got was the bridge where Santa Monica Boulevard passes over the Hollywood Freeway. We had got only one ride and that had lasted only a few blocks. Moreover I had no good idea of where we might find a ramp to I-10.

We backtracked a couple of blocks to the gas station at Santa Monica Boulevard and Western Avenue. I called Roy. I might have found help nearer, but I did not know it then.

At Roy's, Rufus, who had been less patient with my visit, said I might stay longer. Roy agreed, but this time he sounded just a tad less convincing. I was not eager to get on the road again, but I no longer had even the most implausible plan for finding a situation in Los Angeles. I was afraid I would become too comfortable at Roy's. While I had some plans and prospects I could justify accepting and even requesting Roy's help; he could afford it. But I could not justify becoming a drone and I did not want to tempt myself to try it.

When I called from the gas station, I had in mind only getting to the interstate. I saw no reason to change that plan, but I had no objection to one more good night's sleep and the chance of getting cleaned up before I hit the road again. Saturday morning I laundered my things and repacked. I accepted some more cans of Spam and, of course, provisions for Lizbeth. In the early afternoon Roy and Rufus drove us to the interstate.

Lizbeth and I were on the road again.

FIVE

To Austin

We had three or four rides in quick succession. One of these got me no farther down the road.

A young man in a nice little car picked us up around sunset. We were hardly on the highway when he asked me whether I ever had sex with men. He drove us to a large, new home in—I would guess—the Riverside area. He said his lover was at work and that they had an open relationship. I would suppose this was so, for they obviously slept together in one bedroom while the other bedroom was reserved for sexual guests, with a plastic mattress protector under the sheets and various sexual appliances in and on the bedside table. For all of these provisions, I could not find a condom. I would have used one, if I had found it.

Aside from a couple of unsatisfactory daytime assignations with a young man who lived across the street from Roy and Rufus—and the rather pitiful five-dollar trick I had turned on the highway as we traveled west—I was sexually starved. I could not even remember the last time I was in a real bed with someone. Considering those circumstances I thought I did rather well, but I gathered it went rather too quickly for my host.

Afterward I discovered a stack of magazines in the living room. My stories were in almost all the magazines. I hope my host did have an open relationship with his lover, because I could not resist signing the stories. Although his home was considerably east of the ramp at which he had picked us up, the young man insisted on returning me to that ramp. I suppose he wanted to prevent my returning to the house, for he had told me that he was going to work and that his lover would not return for several more hours.

I was much encouraged, although it was long after dark and Lizbeth and I were still in the midst of the Southern California version of civilization.

At the same ramp we were picked up by some college boys in a small nearly new pickup. They were on their way to Palm Springs for spring break. Lizbeth and I were accommodated in the bed of the pickup, where I was given the task of fishing in an ice chest for beer. The boys suggested I continue to Palm Springs with them, but I got out where the road to Palm Springs left I-10.

The hour was then very late, but I decided to try hitchhiking awhile longer, for I supposed some drivers would make a point of crossing the worst of the desert at night. Before long a very small sports car stopped. Packing Lizbeth and the gear into the space behind the seat proved challenging. I do not believe the driver was drunk, but he clearly was not all there, either. The speedometer only went to 100 or a 120, but when we hit the highway the needle moved as far as it could to the right and stayed there.

The driver's story was that he was engaged in an over-the-highway race. Sometimes he described this as a onc-on-one wager. At other times this was an underground competition with a large purse and dozens of competitors. Besides the evidence that this was a lie, in that he never told it twice the same, the driver wasted several minutes in stopping to pick us up and our mass would be a considerable factor if the race was the near thing our driver said it was.

I have said I am not a good rider. And I am not. But on the dark straightaways through the desert, even with the strong crosswinds and the blowing dust, the speed did not bother me. What did bother me was that our driver allowed himself to be boxed in when we approached semitrailers traveling abreast. He could not, of course, make any better time than the trucks until one of them gave way. Several times we ran for many miles with the hood of the sports car actually under the overhang of the rear of a semitrailer. No driving skill a human being may possess would have done any good if the truck ahead had braked for any reason. Very simply, it was highway Russian roulette.

I was terrified.

Dallas Matsen had scared me because his judgment of what he could make his vehicle do differed from my own estimate of his abilities. But it was a matter of judgment. With the driver of the sports car, it was only a matter of chance whether we lived or died.

Perhaps I flinched too visibly. Perhaps he meant from the very first to strand me. He put us out at the Joshua Tree crossover. Although this was by far the most isolated and desolate place Lizbeth and I had yet landed, I thought we were lucky to be alive. I noticed the driver took the crossover and returned to the west rather than continuing his imaginary race to Blythe.

From the earthwork at the southern end of the crossover I could see a very great distance in all directions. I saw no artificial lights at all. Clearly our travels had come to an end for the night. I thought we would have great difficulty in the morning. But I had profited from our experience in Tucson. I would worry about tomorrow tomorrow. I picked a spot and we went to sleep.

I WAS ALARMED by how quickly Lizbeth and I went through the six liters of water I was carrying.

As might be expected of an Easter forenoon, there was little traffic of any kind. I was concerned as I poured the last of our water into Lizbeth's dish. Her dish was a plastic bowl. I had punched a hole in its lip so that it could be tethered to the rest of our gear and would follow us if we had to run after a ride.

I could form no suitable plan. My survey of the night before had revealed no evidence of habitation in any direction. Were we to walk, I knew we should stick to the road, but walking in the day-time seemed more likely to make things worse. In any event, we got a ride before I could think much further, and considering that California had lost an hour in the night to daylight savings time, perhaps this ride came much sooner than anyone could expect.

It was a beat-up panel truck of just the sort I expected to stop for us. The driver was a slender man, balding although he was several years younger than I. He had with him his son who was knee-biting high and perhaps five years of age. The child alternated between torturing Lizbeth and being terrified of her. Lizbeth had no previous experience with children, but she was a paragon, yipping once or twice for rescue and moaning in exasperation, but never snapping or growling.

The story was that it was the father's turn at custody. I envisioned a scene of wild rejoicing at the mother's household.

Fortunately we sometimes had respite as the child was able for short periods of time to amuse himself by maiming chocolate bunnies and mutilating toy chicks from his Easter basket. I became convinced that these behaviors did not represent the child's deep emotional scarring at being the product of a broken home, nor were they the artifacts of abuse, but rather enacted the child's self-realization that he was a spoiled, undersocialized, little monster.

The driver offered me soft drinks from the ice chest and I refreshed myself with Sprite while Lizbeth got water from the melting ice. The driver never said how far he was going. The panel truck contained the tools of several trades. From his spare remarks, I gathered the driver was an itinerant contractor.

At the first stop I filled my water bottles. After several oblique inquiries I still had not discovered how long this ride might last. Lizbeth then refused to get in the back with the child, and although it became quite warm there, she rode the rest of the way curled up under my legs. That very much frustrated the child, who was reduced to trying to poke at her with sticks and soda straws whenever the father and I were distracted.

We stopped at a number of flea markets. The flea markets were usually some distance from the highway and I never recognized any sign indicating their presence. The driver just knew where they were. Several of them seemed to have sprung up from the desert sand. But others were better organized, with portable toilets and electrical rigging of a temporary and dangerous appearance.

Much of the merchandise was trash, the sort of things one throws away before having a garage sale. Weapons, mostly knives, and rocks were the staple stock of the more prosperous-looking vendors. Dickering was de rigueur. I was astonished at the prices the rock specimens brought and even more so at the theoretical prices on their tags. Being rather deliberately out of touch with New Age mysticism, I did not appreciate the new demand for natural crystals.

The desert flea markets were clearly institutions of an alien culture, one I wished I had investigated more closely. The trade in Nazi memorabilia was especially brisk. My driver told me that automatic weapons, mortars, and a considerable variety of ordnance were usually available at these gatherings upon discreet inquiry, and of course no records were kept. Moreover, the vendors and the customers were entirely white. Not many blacks reside in this part of the country, but the utter absence of brown-skinned aboriginal people struck me as remarkable. Indeed, there was not a great variety of European stocks, for almost everyone seemed to be Scots-Irish. These sinister indications aside, I had a deep sense of cultural difference, as if I were not quite absorbing what was going on around me.

The child, however, was not likewise inhibited. As we approached a flea market, while it remained to me a tiny blur on the horizon, he would begin shouting, "Buy me! Buy me!" Most vendors had two-bit boxes filled with mangy stuffed animals and tooth-marked rubber and plastic things. The child could not get enough of these. Books, the mainstay of Austin garage sales, were rare in the Arizona flea markets. Occasionally there was a small box of two-dozen volumes of mass-market paperbacks—dog-eared, much-read tomes by Danielle Steele and Louis L'Amour. No doubt Arizona readers cannot bear to part with more substantial fare.

We circumvented Phoenix on roads that were little more than dry ruts. These took us through open range, and only then did I realize what open range was. There were no fences. Livestock wandered about freely, quite oblivious to traffic.

As we got on the interstate again and put the last of Phoenix behind us, I began to have a horrible suspicion. My worst fears were realized, for when we reached Tucson, Lizbeth and I were put out somewhere not far from the Miracle Mile. Before so very long we were picked up by three Chicano boys, locals who were cruising around on a Sunday afternoon. We rode around for about an hour. At times we got quite far from the highway.

My rollbag was new and the camouflage backpack I had persuaded Rufus to give me was in good shape. All my clothes were new, and I was still relatively neat and clean. I wondered whether I appeared a bit too affluent. Slowly I was reassured that the boys meant no harm, but they did propose, quite without premeditation, I think, to strand me far from the highway.

In no bargaining position I simply insisted on being returned to the highway. This the boys did, not graciously, but as if they had not realized I was utterly at their mercy. For all of that, this proved to be a valuable ride. We reached the south of town and we would not have to walk on the highway ramp to cross the gorge.

Not much daylight was left, but I stationed myself near an on ramp at a busy intersection. Just at sunset a young woman in a little car pulled over. I could not believe she was stopping for us, and I continued to face the traffic. When she had pulled abreast of us, she rolled down her window. She said she was alone and could not offer us a ride, but she wanted us to have something. She handed a wad of currency out the window. I thanked her profusely and all the more sincerely because she made no explicit religious reference in her little speech.

When she was gone I pulled the money out of my pocket and counted it: fourteen dollars. I wondered if I had not judged Tucson too severely. I could not really complain of indifference, for indifference is everywhere. I had been robbed only once. Against that were the couple who left the cold cuts, the couple who rescued us to Phoenix, the boys who had done me some good, however haphazardly, and this woman who gave me fourteen dollars. Yet my opinion of Tucson remained largely negative because of the many hostile indications from passersby who, if they could not help me and would not wish me well, could have at least remained as people elsewhere: indifferent. The brandishing of firearms, the pointless threat, the gratuitous insult: in these things I am grateful never to have discovered Tucson's peer.

The interchange was well lit, but shortly after the sun set I gathered up our gear, and Lizbeth and I walked south until I found a concealed spot. There we slept.

IN THE MORNING I shaved using Lizbeth's water dish. We were very near the truck stop where we were first let out in Tucson as we traveled west—and where we had been robbed. I recharged our water bottles at the service station there that catered to passenger vehicles.

In the forenoon we had a couple of short rides of which I cannot complain. We were carried beyond the suburban traffic, exactly as I would have wanted of a ride out of any other town. That we were let out in desolate areas with no shade cannot be blamed on the drivers; there simply were no better places. I knocked the dust of Tucson off my shoes.

At last a Chicano couple in a large, new red truck stopped. They already had one rider in the bed of the truck and he was quite afraid of Lizbeth at first. He told me he had no idea how far this ride was going. He had been drunk when he was picked up. He was not even sure where he had been picked up, but this had been a very long ride and the truck had stopped for many hitchhikers who had since reached their destinations and been let off. He himself was going to El Paso and he thought it possible the driver had said they would take him so far.

Soon we came to an old man who had walked past Lizbeth and me earlier. The pickup stopped for him. He did not say a word to either of us although the other rider tried to converse with him in the sort of Spanish that omits all articles and renders every verb in the present infinitive.

We were all put out rather suddenly in what seemed to me the middle of nowhere. Our hosts had become increasingly amorous as we traveled. They were indeed going to El Paso, but they were going to take a motel room first.

After I hopped out of the truck, I stopped to adjust my gear and by the time I had done that, all evidence of the other hitchhikers was gone. The terrain was hilly. I climbed a little rise to look around. The interstate arced to the left. Secant to it was a road almost as broad that passed through a little town before it intersected the highway again. Although walking is often a waste of energy and sticking to the main road is the best policy, I decided to walk through town. We wanted water and the distance did not seem so great.

Just after the fork there was a cattle guard—whether to keep livestock in or out, I never discovered. Lizbeth had to be carried over.

We got nothing of Benson but water and good wishes—I even spent a little money there. But I found it to be a wonderful little town, quite undeserving of being surrounded by Arizona.

At first I saw nothing that seemed to me very special: a new shopping center with a large grocery store. In the shade near the entrance to the store was a soda-vending machine, and wonder of wonders, attached to it was a free drinking fountain. I had not seen such a thing since I left Texas. Very rarely a free fountain could be found in the West, but this was the only time I found a fountain near a machine that took money. I filled our bottles and Lizbeth's dish. I bought myself a Coke with the fifty cents I had planned to spend on water. I sat down with Lizbeth in the shade. We got no dirty looks and people stopped to admire Lizbeth and to pet her.

By then it was the heat of the day and we moved through town slowly. We found a picnic table in the shade of a tree and sat down for a while. A respectable-looking old gentleman with very loud suspenders came and sat at the table too. He admired Lizbeth and inquired of me tactfully with no apparent motive other than to pass the time. I regret not learning from him anything of Benson except that he thought it was a nice little town.

When Lizbeth and I reached what I think was the principal cross street, I saw a Dairy Queen, still of the style I remembered from childhood. Lizbeth and I crossed the road. I tied her outside and went in. I got a cone as well as a dish. Lizbeth and I sat outside and she lapped at her dish while I licked my cone.

Adult dogs, of course, cannot digest ice cream, but I had heard the stuff at Dairy Queen is not a dairy product. At any rate, Lizbeth suffered no ill effects except thirst. Wonder of wonders, there was a free fountain at the Dairy Queen, too.

Evidently Benson was a rather old town by Arizona standards. Many of the buildings and storefronts on the road might easily have been a hundred years old. I did not see a hint of phony restoration. It looked like the Old West and it looked real.

Several of the old storefronts were for let and clearly had living quarters above. And since I saw them I have recurred to the fantasy of having one of them for a studio. Where the main street came to an end was a sign indicating that the entrance to the interstate was through an underpass. This was not made to accommodate pedestrians. So I stood on a grassy spot in the shade of a tree and stuck out my thumb.

Quite a number of high school kids were cruising around, but none of them yelled at me. Adults smiled and nodded. A sheriff's car came by, but the driver ignored me.

Another old man came along. I discovered he had parked his car nearby and got out to speak with me. He asked if there was some emergency. I said none immediately. I told him I had been to Los Angeles to look for work, had found none, and was returning to Austin although I had no particular prospects there.

He said he would return at sundown and if I was still there he would find some accommodation for me. I wish I could recall his exact words, for he graciously made it sound as if putting me up would be no trouble at all, while conveying nonetheless the idea that I ought not to interrupt my journey any further if the opportunity of continuing presented itself.

I was not in Benson at sundown.

I was very sorry to leave the town. Perhaps if I had stayed longer Benson would have shown another face, but I doubt it. If Benson was not genuine, it was at least very convincing.

As the shadows began to grow long I was picked up by a Latin man in a pickup. He spoke no English. Before we were quite out of town he stopped to fuel the truck and bought me a Coke. He seemed not to grasp that no matter how loudly and rapidly he spoke Spanish to me I would not understand. I caught one word, I thought: *"Paradisio,"* which I took to mean *paradise*—but I could not apprehend the significance of that. He became almost frantic, verging on tears in his utterances. I smiled sweetly and nodded.

I fancied he took me for some kind of mendicant holy man. Perhaps he hoped I might be induced to pray for him that he might attain paradise. This seemed a little less ludicrous at the time, for he could not have tried more passionately to communicate with me if his soul had depended on it.

Finally we went off down the highway, Lizbeth and I in the back. In the last bit of twilight he put us out. This was a place at least as desolate as the Joshua Tree crossover. He turned off the highway and was gone. He had let us out under a big green interstate sign. I had been facing the rear and had not read the sign as we approached. I backed away from it to read it. It indicated the exit to Paradise. Paradise, Arizona.

This is what he had been trying to tell me. He was only going to Paradise. No doubt he had become agitated because he knew he would be leaving me in the middle of nowhere. He took me not for a mendicant holy man, but for a lunatic or a fool.

Again our situation did not look good, so I laid out our bedroll. The moon rose. The moon must have been past full, else Sunday would not have been Easter, but the illusion that makes the moon seem larger when it is near the horizon is especially pronounced in the desert. All we needed to be the perfect Western cliché was the silhouette of a coyote against the rising moon.

That silhouette I never saw, but presently a coyote began to howl. The coyote's howl reached something primeval in Lizbeth. She insisted on getting under the covers with me, although it was really too warm. She whimpered and shuddered. But the sand was soft and I was soon asleep.

LATE THE FOLLOWING afternoon we got another ride after our water was quite exhausted. We had spent the day in the full sun, for there was not even a crossover.

He came along in an El Camino, which is a poor compromise between a small pickup and a car. In the bed of the decayed El Camino was a very large motorcycle, lashed upright on the diagonal, as it would not have fit lengthwise. All manner of gear had to be moved to accommodate my two bags. This left no place for Lizbeth except in the cab, and the driver wanted reassuring that she was a licker, not a biter. By then Lizbeth had absorbed, however dimly, that rides were a very good thing and she would lunge tongue-first to express her gratitude to our drivers.

Our driver's name was Dale, and he was a Texas native. I do not believe I learned much of his history, but if I did it did not impress me so much as his destination. He was going to his family's home in Bastrop, a little town to the east of Austin. I had expected to have trouble getting to Austin once I left the interstate, but Dale would be going into Austin, and this seemed the best I could have hoped for. Dale was quite saturated with biker culture. I had met such guys before—black T-shirts, flying-skull rings, back issues of *Easy Rider* magazine kept like other people keep *National Geographic*. I always suspected that real bikers did not put quite so much time and money into maintaining a biker image. Indeed, of the guys who seemed to be trying too hard to be bikers, Dale was the first I had met who actually owned a bike, although he admitted he had not been able to make his run since he bought it.

Part of the reason for the trip was that he hoped his father and brothers in Bastrop could make the bike run.

I believe the only reason Dale picked us up was that I had put on a black T-shirt that morning.

The El Camino had a slow leak in the radiator and its battery would not hold a charge. We limped from service station to service station. Dale had a case of a fluid that was supposed to be a quick fix for radiator leaks. Can after can of the stuff went into the radiator. I never could see that it helped any. Nonetheless we had some hope of reaching Las Cruces by nightfall until a tire blew out.

At once I dreaded the task of digging through all of Dale's junk to reach the spare tire. But Dale did not have a spare. To make matters worse, the blowout had occurred near a state prison and there were many signs advising drivers not to pick up hitchhikers. The nature of our plight was evident, but whether for the signs or for some other reason, no one would stop.

Signs on the interstate in New Mexico say that the highway is patrolled by aircraft. And so it must be, if it is patrolled at all, for I never saw a New Mexico highway patrol car. After dark we did begin to see light aircraft, a little to the north and east of us. We supposed these were the patrol aircraft, for they seemed to follow a regular circuit. The one part of Dale's bike that worked was the enormous headlamp. We swung it around and aimed it at the planes, alternately flashing the lamp in series of three flashes and burning the lamp steadily. Nothing came of this. We tried flashing the lamp at the prison. We could see the prison's searchlight sweeping the desert and thought it possible they might notice our light. We flashed the light irregularly, on the theory that the guards might send someone to investigate whether we were attempting to signal a prisoner. And nothing came of this.

At last Dale decided there was nothing to do except to ride into town on the rim, which could not help but ruin the rim, if it did no more serious damage. After midnight we pulled into a truck stop in Las Cruces.

Dale had some hope that his family would wire him some money. He began trying to reach them by phone. By ten o'clock the next morning it became clear to me that the family, for whatever reason, was not going to put the money on the wire. But Dale kept at it. In the meantime he met a man who was abandoning his car at the truck stop. The man wore a black T-shirt with a Harley emblem, so I ought to have seen how things would go.

Lizbeth and I remained to guard the gear while Dale and his new friend scouted around for a rim. The guy with the Harley shirt returned and extracted my last six dollars, saying it was for the rim. A rim arrived by pickup without either Dale or his new friend, but as the rim did not have holes to match the pattern of bolts on the hub, I sent it back. Eventually, the correct rim, complete with a serviceable tire, arrived.

Dale explained to me that the other guy, by virtue of having a Harley emblem on his black T-shirt, was a *bro*, and so he would ride in the cab. But by careful repacking we might make room for Lizbeth and me in the back. We did find a rather tenuous purchase on a pile of things in the back and Dale took off. This was a moderately terrifying experience.

To begin with, the bed of an El Camino is very shallow. With several layers of things under me, I was quite exposed to the wind and I had no handhold on any structural part of the vehicle. But mostly it was just very uncomfortable. The radiator's condition had not improved over the night. At the second stop for water, where there happened to be a bar, Dale told me they had decided to rest the car for a couple of hours. He and his new friend were going into the bar, and perhaps, Dale thought, it would be all to the better if I were not there when they came out.

Within a quarter of an hour they passed me as I stood on the highway and the guy with the Harley emblem shot me the finger.

At dusk a very large white car with Mexican plates stopped for me. The driver and his companion were quite as fair as I, but they knew only a few words of English. I gathered they were students. They took me to El Paso.

We passed the El Camino, broken down at the side of the road.

In downtown El Paso, where the highway was high in the air, the driver pulled over and stopped in the emergency lane. He indicated a bell tower not so far from the highway. He said—signing as much as saying—that this was a mission and they would take care of me there.

I had no intention of going to the mission, but Lizbeth and I slid down the concrete embankment in the general direction the driver had indicated. It was the only way I could see to get off the highway.

At the bottom of the embankment we confronted a very tall chain-link fence that was topped with concertina wire. Beyond the fence were the backsides of frame tenements, all very dilapidated. I found breaches in the fence, one or two perhaps large enough to admit me. But I knew some parts of El Paso north of the river had been ceded to Mexico. I suspected it was Mexico on the other side of the fence. I was afraid that if we did find ourselves in Mexico I might have difficulty repatriating Lizbeth.

We walked eastward along the fence and eventually the fence turned away sharply to the right. We were on the streets of El Paso. As we went east the highway descended below street level. We walked above it, on the street that fed all the on ramps. But at last that street came to an end. At the last on ramp I tried hitchhiking until midnight, but I had to get some sleep. The night before I had dozed only a little, sitting up in the El Camino.

We seemed to be surrounded by railroad yards. Everything I had heard about railroad detectives dated to the 1930s, but I did not want to learn whether these old stories were still applicable.

We walked through the downtown streets until I found a drunk passed out on the steps of an old office building. Around the corner of that building I lay down without laying out the bedroll. I supposed that whoever might molest me would find the wino a more tempting target. Perhaps I slept four hours and not very soundly, but my head was a lot clearer when I got up.

I filled my water bottles from the fountain at a service station that was not yet open for the day. The men's room was unlocked and I tidied up a bit. We walked back to the ramp and were there until the afternoon. We got a ride to the truck stop east of town, and we were there for three nights.

When we arrived at this ramp, two other hitchhikers were ahead of us. Before we left there were perhaps a dozen others. Here were two very large truck stops on both the east- and westbound sides of the highway. I did not investigate the one on the westbound side, but the one on the eastbound side was large enough to have an adult bookstore and arcade on the lot. The lot itself was huge and seemed always to contain several score big rigs and many more smaller trucks and passenger cars.

At night Lizbeth and I slept in a drainage tunnel under the earthwork of the crossover. The sand there was soft and previous tenants had left many candle stubs. The drainage tunnels were extensive and indicated, I suppose, the possibility of flash flooding—a phenomenon easier to imagine in the lush, narrow canyons of California than in the arid flats of West Texas.

Eventually I spoke to several of the other hitchhikers. Several of them claimed that the food stamp office in El Paso was issuing emergency food stamps to all comers. This was said to happen from time to time when the state had failed to issue its allotment. Funds for the stamps not issued would have to be returned to the federal government, and of course the state would rather hand the stamps out on the street than send money back to Washington. I often heard slight variations on this story, but whenever I investigated for myself I was told I did not qualify for assistance.

One of the other hitchhikers was the old mute man who had ridden between Tucson and Benson with us. All the rest I met were alcoholics, except perhaps for a college-aged man, apparently a weight lifter, who arrived on the ramp in a tank top and nylon running shorts. He got a ride within ten minutes.

Mogen David 20/20, called Mad Dog, was the choice beverage of the alcoholics here. When they pooled their resources to buy it at the convenience store in the truck stop, they debated whether to buy the purple or the yellow variety. Taste was not the issue. Some of the winos thought one or the other was more alcoholic.

They were astonished to learn I did not care for Mad Dog. In the afternoons traffic backed up on the off ramp, for evidently there was a large residential area somewhere to the south of this exit. The winos would go up to the ramp and beg from the drivers of the cars stuck in the off ramp. Many of the drivers gave the winos bottled water or fruit drinks. Having no use for that sort of thing, the winos gave the nonalcoholic beverages to me with the result that I had to go to the truck stop for water only once.

Peculiar things happened Saturday morning. One by one the winos were picked up by truckers. I think one of the trucks stopped for me, but for some reason I decided not to try to climb in the cab with Lizbeth and my gear without some more positive indication from the driver, who had merely stopped near us and sounded his horn. When all the others had been picked up, I regretted not pursuing the possibility of a ride with the trucker who had stopped. This seemed to have been my last chance and I had failed to take it.

I thought a sign might help. I had a sign when I started out, but had lost it as we got out of the sports car at the Joshua Tree exit. I found a piece of cardboard and painted it with Wite-Out, which is the sort of thing a writer will have saved and stored in his bag even though he had no immediate use for it. Whether the sign helped or not, a Pinto soon stopped.

The driver asked if I could drive. I replied that I could, but was not licensed. After a pause he said for me to get in. He was fifty-ish, deathly pale, grown fat with age, and he was wearing only boxer shorts. I wondered at this at first, especially as the open fly of the shorts exposed his sex whenever he shifted in his seat, but eventually I concluded that the driver's attire reflected only his practical nature. It was a very hot day.

The car was a wreck. Loose wires hung down from behind the dashboard, and most of the knobs, handles, and interior paneling was missing.

He was a salesman. He explained that as opposed to flying it was more economical to buy junk cars, such as the one we were in, for three or four hundred dollars and to abandon them when he reached his destination. He had no tangible product. What he did was to organize packets of promotional material that would be inserted in shopping bags at college bookstores.

He said he had planned next to go to San Antonio, but he had an old girlfriend in Austin, so if I would drive I could drive into Austin. This was very agreeable because I knew I otherwise might spend several days trying to get from the interstate to Austin.

As we went we passed, one by one, many of the winos I recognized from the truck stop. Each of them was far from any exit. That all of them had been picked up in so short a time that morning and that so many of them turned up stranded seemed to me to be more than a matter of chance. I suspected, and I still suspect, the truckers acted in concert to remove the winos from the truck stop and to strand them. I started driving about sundown, as we were among the Davis Mountains. Lizbeth insisted on lying in the front on the floorboard, and the weight of her head on the accelerator as she dozed off made a perfect cruise control.

Lizbeth and I got out in Austin about 3:00 A.M. A cold drizzle was falling. In Southern California I had forgotten about rain and cold.

Lizbeth realized where we were. It was a block from her veterinarian's office, where she had been going since she was whelped. It was three blocks from the shack on Avenue B, where she had been brought to me, where she had grown up, and where she had had her little yard to play in.

She pulled me in the direction of Avenue B.

I guess she thought I was crazy. Here we were back in Austin. But we were not going home.

Real rain began to fall. I led her to the bridge over Shoal Creek at Twenty-ninth Street. We got under the bridge.

SIX

Temporary Arrangements

In truth it was several more weeks before Lizbeth and I were on the streets for much more than a few nights at a time. But that first night in Austin I despaired. It was the first time I began to understand the reality of homelessness.

On our way to California I had my hopes. I was convinced at least once that we, or one of us, would die before we got there. But either I would die or I would reach California, and what is more, the outcome would be clear within some few days. To progress was to get nearer California. Some days we progressed and some days we did not. Whether we would end in Los Angeles or in our graves, our direction gave meaning and measure to the days.

Such a structure is utterly lacking in a life on the streets.

Home is the natural destination of any homeless person. But nothing can be done in a day, in a week, in a year to get nearer that destination. No perceptible progress can be made. In the absence of progress, time is nearly meaningless. Some days are more comfortable than others. And that is all the difference. A homeless life has no storyline. It is a pointless circular rambling about the stage that can be brought to happy conclusion only by a deus ex machina.

Rent, deposits, transportation, suitable clothing, living expenses: the kind of money required to obtain a home cannot be saved from pennies picked up on the street. Moreover, no homeless person would be likely to be able to obtain employment immediately even if he were somehow delivered from the streets. His fate is no longer in his hands. He may survive, but no more than survive. If he is to hope, he must have hope of the purest kind, unconnected to any intelligent appraisal of the actual prospects.

In the national forest and in the fire zone, I had work to do on Frost's script and I believed I had some possibility of selling him the script. On the return trip to Austin, I had the goal of reaching Austin. But once we were back I had not only nowhere to go, but also nothing to do, and nothing within reason to hope for.

Sometimes, especially when the rains had come and gone through the night many times and I had packed our gear up and led Lizbeth to some slight shelter and the rain had stopped and we had returned to our bedroll only to be woke by renewed rains, sometimes I would think, my mind still fogged with sleep, "The hell with this. I am going home," as if I were some backyard camper, as if I had only to admit that my expedition was not so much fun as I thought it would be, as if I could give it up, pack my gear, and go inside to my own warm bed. I did not have many nightmares, but this was the crudest dream.

My first thought, on our first day back in Austin, was to call Billy. I did not expect him to take me in, but I felt I could face the streets better if I got cleaned up and had a good night's sleep. But

Billy's telephone number had been changed and I could not discover his new number because it, like the old one, was unlisted.

While I was in California I had talked to Billy by telephone several times. He had rather encouraged me to continue to use his telephone credit card so long as it was useful. Now I did not know if he had changed his mind when the bill arrived, but he had his number changed fairly often in any event.

Billy was paid monthly and as it was still early in April I knew he would have the money to go out drinking. Sunday afternoon I went to Sleazy Sue's, then the oldest gay bar in Austin and the one Billy most favored, and of course he arrived soon and insisted I come home with him.

Billy was always expansive and generous at the first of the month, but once he drank through his salary, his mood darkened sharply. Moreover, he knew this was his pattern as well as I did. He suggested that I visit him in the first week of every month. He knew he would be happy to see me then, and I could get some respite from the streets. Beyond that Billy had stored my manuscripts and a manual typewriter, which I could use to prepare anything I had written in longhand on the streets. Of course, once the month had aged to the point that Billy would have to start hocking things to keep drinking, he would resent my presence and throw me out in an alcoholic snit—we discussed this explicitly—so I ought to be ready to leave at the end of the first week.

Billy and I had been platonic friends for many years, but more than this, his interest in helping stemmed from his job. He worked for the state welfare department. He had a back-office sort of job and he had often doubted that the welfare department did any good. His doubts had increased when the state moved its payday from the last day of the month to the first. Ann Richards, who would become governor, was then the treasurer of the state and she had realized that by moving payday one day the state might collect an extra month's interest on the money it used to pay salaries. Unfortunately a large number of state employees, many of whom worked in the welfare office, realized that the month this conversion was made they would not receive any check. They would be paid the last day of the previous month and the first day of the following month, but in the calendar month they got no check they would technically be eligible for food stamps. En masse state employees, some of whom had salaries of more than two thousand dollars a month, applied for and got food stamps.

This made Billy think his job, which pertained to food stamps, was a hollow mockery of what it should be. In order to prove otherwise to himself, he had gone around with me as I applied for assistance before I left Austin. Billy knew I truly was in need, he considered me deserving, and he believed that if I received some public assistance I would soon regain a productive place in society. In short, Billy thought I was precisely the sort of person that public assistance should benefit, and by following my case he hoped to prove to himself that the system worked and that his own job was really of social value.

In many respects Billy was more disappointed with the outcome of my applications than I was, for I had a cynical view of the system and had not expected much.

To give but one example, there was the matter of food stamps. In Texas a person cannot qualify for food stamps unless he or she does not really need them. A person who truly needs food stamps cannot be eligible to receive them. To get food stamps a person must have all to him- or herself a functioning kitchen; if the kitchen is shared, then all who share the kitchen must, as a group, qualify for food stamps. To prove that you have the kitchen, you must have a rent receipt, which opens the question of where you got the money to pay the rent. If you cannot pay the rent then you must get a written statement from the landlord that he allows you to live rent free, which statement the landlord will not give you if he is properly advised, because it prejudices his case in the event he wants to collect back rent or to evict you for nonpayment.

If someone in the household has a job and so the rent is somehow paid, then the employed person must get a statement from his employer that the amounts shown on the stubs of the paycheck are in fact correct and that the employee is not paid more. With Texas employers, this will endanger the job of any employee who asks for such a statement. Moreover, there is the problem of proving that the household members who have no income have no income. A person who has a slight income can get documents to show that it is slight, but a person with no income has no employer to provide a statement that no wages are paid.

Anyone who happened to have a place with a kitchen and yet had not the money to buy food would most logically do one of two things: He would find a cheaper place without a kitchen—thereby becoming ineligible for food stamps—or he would take in a roommate to help pay the rent—again making the household ineligible for food stamps unless the roommate was willing to subject every aspect of his finances to scrutiny and to ask everyone with whom he does business to attest to his poverty. People who do get food stamps are people who can afford to have a kitchen to themselves, or in other words, people who do not really need public assistance to feed themselves. People who cannot pay rent, or who cannot pay enough rent to have a kitchen to themselves—in other words, the people who really need food stamps—are ineligible to receive them.

Those are just a few of the immediate implications of one of many requirements for food stamp eligibility. There are of course many other requirements and regulations so that virtually no honest applicant is qualified for food stamps. People do get them, but only when they lie and some social worker decides arbitrarily not to look too closely at the application.

Billy could not at first believe this. His sense of identity was strongly connected with his job and it seemed to him his job was a fraud. Of course he still had his nice income and I had none, but in the end it was I who was trying to console Billy.

I explained to him that he had the wrong idea. The purpose of welfare systems is not to help poor people. If the object were to help poor people, then that would be most surely done by giving money to poor people. But that is not the idea, as our tax code proves. If you give twenty dollars to someone on the street, there is not a way in the world you can deduct that donation from your taxes. To claim a deduction you must give the money to an organization that employs clerks and administrators and social workers and that, more than likely, puts nothing material into the hands of the poor, or if it does provide some material benefit, those benefits are not as much as a dime to the dollar of the original donation. When the agency makes an accounting of the good it has done the poor, it will count the money it spent on paying social workers to hold the hands of the poor the same as money, if any, spent on bread. The purpose of welfare systems is to provide jobs for social workers and bureaucrats. This is, I said, I supposed a sort of good in itself. I told Billy he should be grateful to have a job in the poverty industry, but to ask that such a job be meaningful is to ask too much.

Somehow he did not find these remarks consoling.

AT BILLY'S I showered and washed my clothes and had a good night's sleep on his sofa. The next day I pored over my manuscripts and cobbled together a couple of short stories from various scraps. I sent the stories out and none too soon, for Billy found an exceptionally convivial crowd when he went out that night and he drank through his money much faster than anticipated.

In the morning Billy was reasonably contrite about the tantrum he had thrown the night before. But the fact was he had spent almost all of his money. He would have to hock his TV and VCR and to write hot checks just to have enough money to drink for the rest of the month. Insisting that I was still invited back on the first of May, Billy drove us to the Hyde Park area and let us out.

The two most serious problems, it seemed to me, were to find a safe place to sleep and to find a safe place to stash my gear. In hopes of getting some help with the latter problem I called on Dan Archer.

Dan was a speed freak I had known back in the hippie times—about 1971. He had begun doing more and more speed then. At first this made him ambitious. He got a job and then he got another, and for a very brief time he was holding three jobs at once. Then he had his psychotic break.

The textbooks say that amphetamine psychosis is often clinically indistinguishable from schizophrenia. The most reliable method of differential diagnosis is to withdraw the patient from amphetamines for three months and then to see whether he is still crazy. But Dan never stopped taking amphetamines for as long as three months. No one can say whether Dan is naturally nuts or whether it is only a drug effect. In any event, Dan was declared totally disabled and placed on Supplemental Security Income. Because he held the three jobs when he first became ill, Dan will receive in excess of $650 a month from the government for the rest of his life.

After he got on SSI, Dan stayed around Austin for several years, working as a roadie and doing other jobs for which he could be paid under the table. Then he moved to a small Mexican town where, from the standpoint of cash income, his SSI checks made him by far the wealthiest man in town.

He was much resented by the landed locals who, though they owned everything and had the power of life and death over the peasants, could not lay their hands on nearly so much cash. They plotted against Dan even as they trotted out their daughters in hopes of making a fortunate marriage. He was immune to the plots because his cash put the bishop and all the functionaries of the state at his disposal.

Dan did marry, but he admits he deliberately chose a girl from the tiny middle class because she had no dowry and thus would forever be under his thumb. She reigned as virtual queen of her hometown for several years, but was dismayed to discover, when Dan decided they should move to Austin, that he was far from the richest man in Austin. Dan's family, on the other hand, was wealthy even by Texas standards, and to celebrate his return and his marriage, they presented him with a condo in Hyde Park. Each year when they buy a new car, they give Dan their year-old one.

Before I left the shack on Avenue B, Dan had come over about twice a week with his Bible and several quarts of beer. He could see my finances were deteriorating and he thought my life might be turned around if, between swallows of beer, he managed to convert me to his religion. My own theory was that if I were spotted a condo, a car, $650 a month, and first claim on a spouse's wages, I might manage my finances better even if I remained a pagan. I explained my theory to Dan. He said that my having such an opinion was sure proof that Satan had sent a demon to infest my soul.

But Dan had usually been good for a donation of a couple of packs of cigarettes and he very quickly learned to keep his Bible shut, as I would not put up with him otherwise. He could not be caught doing any productive work for fear of losing his SSI. He had sent his wife to work as soon as they reached Austin, and as such was the custom among her own people, she had not objected. Dan dabbled in church politics for a while but lost interest when he failed by a few votes of being elected elder. He was bored to death and was always grateful for any little conversation.

When I looked him up, Dan agreed I could store what I wanted to in the storage closet at his condo. It had an outside entrance and he never kept anything of value there. I could also do my laundry and shower at his place from time to time, if I came while his wife was at work.

She had developed a morbid fear of germs since her arrival in the United States. Whenever she knew that someone else had used their bathroom she went through an elaborate ritual of disinfection and Dan objected to the smell of the many cleansers she used. Curiously, only the bathroom bothered her in this way. Dishes that visitors had used received no special treatment.

THE PROBLEM OF a place to sleep proved more intractable. Dan suggested I sleep on a covered porch behind the sanctuary at his church. The church had established a policy to ask people found sleeping there to leave, but not to call the police. Unfortunately, like every other place I tried, the church porch was infested with fire ants.

April had become warm. With most of my gear stashed at Dan's I could go about with a small bookbag and a large towel. At night it was warm enough for us to sleep on the towel, but wherever Lizbeth and I lay down, we were attacked by fire ants. Most nights I did not sleep at all.

I encountered a former roommate who let me stay the night at his place once or twice, and a few other times let me shower and nap on his sofa in the afternoon. I do not know how I survived April, but remember only that I always wanted sleep.

On the first of May I returned to Billy's. I slept through the first two days there. The third afternoon I began to feel human again and started to sort through my manuscripts. Billy's cat Phantom sat on Billy's bar and glared at me as I worked. Phantom was a cat of tastes so precious that he would not deign to lick a tuna can, insisting instead on having only the kind of gourmet cat food that came in tiny cans. Lizbeth, of course, is a gourmand, and whether it was Lizbeth's low standards or something else that inspired Phantom's disdain, Phantom very much resented Lizbeth whenever we visited. This caused Billy some concern at first. But Lizbeth rather likes cats and only chases them if they run from her. Phantom, after he was neutered, never ran, but stomped about in a stately manner. Thus, Billy had become convinced that Lizbeth was no physical threat to Phantom, and Phantom would just have to lump it. Lump it Phantom did, but never graciously.

Billy's friend Tim arrived before Billy did that evening. Billy was working the swing shift and would get off work at eleven. But since he had just been paid and all of his favorite bars were between his place of employment and his apartment, I could not say when he would return. Tim was supposed to meet Billy to transact some very small marijuana business, but whether Tim was the buyer or seller I never learned. At any rate I was sure Billy had forgotten this appointment or that he would forget it after his third cocktail.

I had met Tim once before at Billy's, just before I left for California. Tim had come there to change out of his work clothes before going to visit someone at a hospital that was very near Billy's apartment.

I learned from Tim that he had been visiting his very much older companion who had died a few days after Tim had come to Billy's to change. The companion had not mentioned Tim in the will. The family soon evicted him from the estate and did not recognize his claim to several valuable works of art that he thought his companion had given him. Nonetheless, the family had wished to conceal that Tim's companion had died of AIDS, and so in hopes of securing Tim's silence they had established him in an efficiency apartment behind an older home in Hyde Park.

Billy arrived home in a terrible rage, for he had spent all his money on cocktails. He told me immediately that I would have to leave in the morning. In that event, Tim said, I should come and live with him.

AS USUAL BILLY was not so venomous in the morning. But I was packed and ready to go by the time he got up. He took me to the address Tim had given me. Tim was not home. Lizbeth and I sat on his stoop and made the acquaintance of his flea-ridden dog, Harley. When Tim arrived I could see that he was not really prepared to receive us, but had invited us only to spite Billy. I had suspected as much and would not have gone to Tim's place at all had it not been close to where I thought Lizbeth and I might fare best on the streets.

Nonetheless, Tim drew a deep breath and said we would try to make a go of it.

From the first I noticed many peculiarities in Tim's behavior. For example, Tim had a poor relationship with inanimate objects. I once witnessed Tim's throwing a spoon across the room and cursing at it steadily for five minutes only because he had picked it up with its bowl facedown. Things were much worse with more complicated devices such as can openers.

That Tim had beaten Harley regularly was obvious from Harley's behavior. Even when I was present, Tim would summon Harley in an angry voice. Harley would cower in a corner, but he would be beaten nonetheless for not coming when he was called.

I never left Lizbeth alone with Tim, but he was always very kind to her. Sometimes I thought he was kind to Lizbeth in order to humiliate and torture Harley.

Tim's moods fluctuated wildly and rapidly. He was always at one extreme or another. He could not be accommodating, but at times he was servile. He was never firm, but sometimes was dictatorial. He could not be irritated, but was often enraged. He had joyous times, but never merely pleasant ones.

Tim professed to have found from the first some mysterious attractive quality in me. But it was always, "Come hither," and then "Drop dead." He attempted to tease me by going around naked and displaying an erection. Perhaps my indifference drove him to persist in this behavior. Although he was an attractive young man, I was indifferent because of his off-and-on attitude. We masturbated together fairly often, but he sometimes changed his mind about this activity just as one or both of us reached a state of high arousal, and this more than any health concern put me off the idea of any more intimate sexual involvement with Tim. Once he discovered I was a writer, he was affectionate almost to the point of undressing us when we went to Sleazy Sue's and told anyone in earshot that I was a famous author and he was my lover. But at his apartment again, his passion evaporated.

I attributed all of this to the stress of his having recently lost his companion. I supposed he had felt some affection for him. Beyond that, when his companion died, Tim had lost a comfortable situation in society and whatever expectations he had. Moreover, although he continued to test negative for HIV, and in fact sold blood plasma regularly to supplement his income, he might have contracted the virus from his companion—who had kept the diagnosis secret until the very last—and the virus could still manifest itself in Tim any day. Given his circumstances I could not be sure that I would have behaved any better.

I was never sure whether Tim was truly psychotic. For example, he claimed to be a Jew. I did not discount this immediately because I knew some blond Jews, but when I discovered he did not know a seder from a bris, I questioned him more closely. Eventually I understood that he professed to be a Seventh-Day Adventist and their dogma held that they were the spiritual heirs of the Hebrew tradition.

He said he could read my mind. Sometimes when he made that claim he clearly meant no more than that he could infer what was behind some action or word of mine. Other times he seemed to think he really could read my mind. He seemed to be arguing with himself sometimes, although I only heard one side of it, as if I were listening to Tim place a telephone call. When I questioned him about this, he said he was not arguing with himself but with me, although of course I had said nothing throughout the argument.

Tim went to his job for only a week or two after I moved in. I do not know what he had done with the money he had been making at the job. He had not spent it on food. He worked in the banquet department of a large hotel and whenever he went to work he had brought back stacks of plastic-foam boxes containing dinners that had not been served. That was what he ate. His companion's family had paid several months' rent in advance for his apartment, but he had not paid rent after that and was a month in arrears when I moved in. He smoked cigarettes and rarely pot, and he drank a quart of beer in the evening. But that should have absorbed only a small fraction of his income. At any rate he claimed to be supporting me, while the contrary was the case. A few days after I moved in, one of the checks for work I had done before I left Austin caught up with me and I received a surprisingly swift positive response to one of the stories I had typed up when I first stayed at Billy's. As Tim had heard I was a writer, when the check arrived he seemed to think that it was the first of many that would arrive in rapid succession. Indeed, I tried to do a little work at Tim's until he lost his job. But when he was home, as he was always once he became unemployed, he demanded to be the center of attention and could not bear for me to ignore him for as long as it took me to type a single line. He never appreciated the connection between the arrival of the check and my work.

Aside from cigarette and beer money, which Tim provided himself by selling his dubious blood plasma, we had almost no cash the last few weeks I was with him. But Dan Archer gave me—or rather sold me with little expectation of ever collecting the price—an old, junky three-speed bicycle that he had got for his wife so that they might bicycle together. Dan had finally realized the bicycle was never going to be used.

But with the bicycle I could get around to a number of Dumpsters. Many college students were then leaving town for the summer and I could feed us from the Dumpsters without having to bring home table scraps or leftovers. I brought home more canned goods than Tim's shelves could hold, and I often passed by excess frozen foods because Tim's little refrigerator could hold no more.

Tim accused me of stealing what I came by and demanded to be cut in on the action. I told him it came from Dumpsters and he had only to open a can to have his share. Tim did not believe me. One day he undertook to shadow me, thinking I was unaware of him. When he saw I had been telling the truth he began to dive in Dumpsters himself.

Around the first of June I discovered that the rent was in arrears. It was beyond my capacity to pay it. I also discovered why Tim was not worried about it. He and his companion had often met in bars in the afternoon and Tim had been in the habit of riding his motorcycle home afterward. His route home took him past the courthouse and before long the officers there were on the lookout for him. Tim was erotically fixated on police officers and said he always enjoyed being arrested. Thus he had acquired three drunk-driving charges. All three charges were to come before the same judge on the same day. As Tim had a previous record of drunk driving, he was bound, even in Texas, to receive a jail sentence.

He rather hoped I would make the money to keep his apartment and his dog until he got out of jail. At any rate he had not given the future much thought.

Once he discovered how to feed himself from Dumpsters and that I would not make enough money to pay the arrears and the current rent, Tim became even more abusive than usual and his mood swings became more pronounced. At last I felt I had to move out for the sake of my own sanity. I was getting no work done and I was hardly resting better at Tim's apartment than I had been on the streets.

I packed my things and bagged up some of the canned goods I had collected. I loaded up the bicycle, which I used as something of a two-wheeled cart, and Lizbeth and I left.

ALL THE TIME I was on the streets I managed, with only one exception, to maintain my policy of not panhandling and not stealing. I know people who doubt that claim, but those people do not know the Dumpsters. While I had the bicycle I could range far—I had to pedal fairly fast to keep Lizbeth from towing me. While the end-of-school harvest lasted I could load up the bicycle with canned goods in less than an hour. I would find so much I would have to dismount the bike to make room on it for the goods, and then I would let Lizbeth tow—indeed, I could not walk fast enough to prevent her from towing.

The Dumpster harvest continued for a week or two more. I found more canned goods than I could use or store and I formed the habit of taking the food that was perfectly safe to the drop point for the AIDS food bank at Sleazy Sue's. I often wished I had a little dog cart, for Lizbeth seemed to very much enjoy towing the loaded bicycle as we carried things to Sue's. Perhaps it is not too much to suppose a dog knows when it is doing something useful. And perhaps it was not much different for me.

We were now truly on the streets, where we would be for what seemed to me a long time. But those first few days I dulled my feelings of hopelessness by striving to collect canned goods for the food bank—and whether it was or was not, I convinced myself it was something useful.

SEVEN

On Dumpster Diving

This chapter was composed while the author was homeless.
The present tense has been preserved.

Long before I began Dumpster diving I was impressed with Dumpsters, enough so that I wrote the Merriam-Webster research service to discover what I could about the word *Dumpster*. I learned from them that it is a proprietary word belonging to the Dempster Dumpster company. Since then I have dutifully capital ized the word, although it was lowercased in almost all the citations Merriam-Webster photocopied for me. Dempster's word is too apt. I have never heard these things called anything but Dumpsters. I do not know anyone who knows the generic name for these objects. From time to time I have heard a wino or hobo give some corrupted credit to the original and call them Dipsy Dumpsters.

I began Dumpster diving about a year before I became homeless.

I prefer the word *scavenging* and use the word *scrounging* when I mean to be obscure. I have heard people, evidently meaning to be polite, use the word *foraging,* but I prefer to reserve that word for gathering nuts and berries and such, which I do also according to the season and the opportunity. *Dumpster diving* seems to me to be a little too cute and, in my case, inaccurate because I lack the athletic ability to lower myself into the Dumpsters as the true divers do, much to their increased profit.

I like the frankness of the word *scavenging,* which I can hardly think of without picturing a big black snail on an aquarium wall. I live from the refuse of others. I am a scavenger. I think it a sound and honorable niche, although if I could I would naturally prefer to live the comfortable consumer life, perhaps—and only perhaps—as a slightly less wasteful consumer, owing to what I have learned as a scavenger.

While Lizbeth and I were still living in the shack on Avenue B as my savings ran out, I put almost all my sporadic income into rent. The necessities of daily life I began to extract from Dumpsters. Yes, we ate from them. Except for jeans, all my clothes came from Dumpsters. Boom boxes, candles, bedding, toilet paper, a virgin male love doll, medicine, books, a typewriter, dishes, furnishings, and change, sometimes amounting to many dollars—I acquired many things from the Dumpsters.

I have learned much as a scavenger. I mean to put some of what I have learned down here, beginning with the practical art of Dumpster diving and proceeding to the abstract.

WHAT IS SAFE to eat?

After all, the finding of objects is becoming something of an urban art. Even respectable employed people will sometimes find something tempting sticking out of a Dumpster or standing beside one. Quite a number of people, not all of them of the bohemian type, are willing to brag that they found this or that piece in

the trash. But eating from Dumpsters is what separates the dilet-
tanti from the professionals. Eating safely from the Dumpsters
involves three principles: using the senses and common sense
to evaluate the condition of the found materials, knowing the
Dumpsters of a given area and checking them regularly, and
seeking always to answer the question "Why was this discarded?"

Perhaps everyone who has a kitchen and a regular supply of
groceries has, at one time or another, made a sandwich and eaten
half of it before discovering mold on the bread or got a mouthful
of milk before realizing the milk had turned. Nothing of the sort
is likely to happen to a Dumpster diver because he is constantly
reminded that most food is discarded for a reason. Yet a lot of perfectly good food can be found in Dumpsters.

Canned goods, for example, turn up fairly often in the Dumpsters I frequent. All except the most phobic people would be willing to eat from a can, even if it came from a Dumpster. Canned
goods are among the safest of foods to be found in Dumpsters but
are not utterly foolproof.

Although very rare with modern canning methods, botulism
is a possibility. Most other forms of food poisoning seldom do
lasting harm to a healthy person, but botulism is almost certainly
fatal and often the first symptom is death. Except for carbonated
beverages, all canned goods should contain a slight vacuum and
suck air when first punctured. Bulging, rusty, and dented cans
and cans that spew when punctured should be avoided, especially
when the contents are not very acidic or syrupy.

Heat can break down the botulin, but this requires much
more cooking than most people do to canned goods. To the extent that botulism occurs at all, of course, it can occur in cans on
pantry shelves as well as in cans from Dumpsters. Need I say that
home-canned goods are simply too risky to be recommended.

From time to time one of my companions, aware of the source

of my provisions, will ask, "Do you think these crackers are really safe to eat?" For some reason it is most often the crackers they ask about.

This question has always made me angry. Of course I would not offer my companion anything I had doubts about. But more than that, I wonder why he cannot evaluate the condition of the crackers for himself. I have no special knowledge and I have been wrong before. Since he knows where the food comes from, it seems to me he ought to assume some of the responsibility for deciding what he will put in his mouth. For myself I have few qualms about dry foods such as crackers, cookies, cereal, chips, and pasta if they are free of visible contaminates and still dry and crisp. Most often such things are found in the original packaging, which is not so much a positive sign as it is the absence of a negative one.

Raw fruits and vegetables with intact skins seem perfectly safe to me, excluding of course the obviously rotten. Many are discarded for minor imperfections that can be pared away. Leafy vegetables, grapes, cauliflower, broccoli, and similar things may be contaminated by liquids and may be impractical to wash.

Candy, especially hard candy, is usually safe if it has not drawn ants. Chocolate is often discarded only because it has become discolored as the cocoa butter de-emulsified. Candying, after all, is one method of food preservation because pathogens do not like very sugary substances.

All of these foods might be found in any Dumpster and can be evaluated with some confidence largely on the basis of appearance. Beyond these are foods that cannot be correctly evaluated without additional information.

I began scavenging by pulling pizzas out of the Dumpster behind a pizza delivery shop. In general, prepared food requires caution, but in this case I knew when the shop closed and went to the Dumpster as soon as the last of the help left.

Such shops often get prank orders; both the orders and the products made to fill them are called *bogus*. Because help seldom stays long at these places, pizzas are often made with the wrong topping, refused on delivery for being cold, or baked incorrectly. The products to be discarded are boxed up because inventory is kept by counting boxes: A boxed pizza can be written off; an unboxed pizza does not exist.

I never placed a bogus order to increase the supply of pizzas and I believe no one else was scavenging in this Dumpster. But the people in the shop became suspicious and began to retain their garbage in the shop overnight. While it lasted I had a steady supply of fresh, sometimes warm pizza. Because I knew the Dumpster I knew the source of the pizza, and because I visited the Dumpster regularly I knew what was fresh and what was yesterday's.

The area I frequent is inhabited by many affluent college students. I am not here by chance; the Dumpsters in this area are very rich. Students throw out many good things, including food. In particular they tend to throw everything out when they move at the end of a semester, before and after breaks, and around midterm, when many of them despair of college. So I find it advantageous to keep an eye on the academic calendar.

Students throw food away around breaks because they do not know whether it has spoiled or will spoil before they return. A typical discard is a half jar of peanut butter. In fact, nonorganic peanut butter does not require refrigeration and is unlikely to spoil in any reasonable time. The student does not know that, and since it is Daddy's money, the student decides not to take a chance. Opened containers require caution and some attention to the question. "Why was this discarded?" But in the case of discards from student apartments, the answer may be that the item was thrown out through carelessness, ignorance, or wastefulness. This can sometimes be deduced when the item is found with many others, including some that are obviously perfectly good.

Some students, and others, approach defrosting a freezer by chucking out the whole lot. Not only do the circumstances of such a find tell the story, but also the mass of frozen goods stays cold for a long time and items may be found still frozen or freshly thawed.

Yogurt, cheese, and sour cream are items that are often thrown out while they are still good. Occasionally I find a cheese with a spot of mold, which of course I just pare off, and because it is obvious why such a cheese was discarded, I treat it with less suspicion than an apparently perfect cheese found in similar circumstances. Yogurt is often discarded, still sealed, only because the expiration date on the carton had passed. This is one of my favorite finds because yogurt will keep for several days, even in warm weather.

Students throw out canned goods and staples at the end of semesters and when they give up college at midterm. Drugs, pornography, spirits, and the like are often discarded when parents are expected—Dad's Day, for example. And spirits also turn up after big party weekends, presumably discarded by the newly reformed. Wine and spirits, of course, keep perfectly well even once opened, but the same cannot be said of beer.

My test for carbonated soft drinks is whether they still fizz vigorously. Many juices or other beverages are too acidic or too syrupy to cause much concern, provided they are not visibly contaminated. I have discovered nasty molds in vegetable juices, even when the product was found under its original seal; I recommend that such products be decanted slowly into a clear glass. Liquids always require some care. One hot day I found a large jug of Pat O'Brien's Hurricane mix. The jug had been opened but was still ice cold. I drank three large glasses before it became apparent to me that someone had added the rum to the mix, and not a little rum. I never tasted the rum, and by the time I began to feel the effects I had already ingested a very large quantity of the beverage. Some divers would have considered this a boon, but being suddenly intoxicated in a public place in the early afternoon is not my idea of a good time.

I have heard of people maliciously contaminating discarded food and even handouts, but mostly I have heard of this from people with vivid imaginations who have had no experience with the Dumpsters themselves. Just before the pizza shop stopped discarding its garbage at night, jalapeños began showing up on most of the thrown-out pizzas. If indeed this was meant to discourage me, it was a wasted effort because I am a native Texan.

For myself, I avoid game, poultry, pork, and egg-based foods, whether I find them raw or cooked. I seldom have the means to cook what I find, but when I do I avail myself of plentiful supplies of beef, which is often in very good condition. I suppose fish becomes disagreeable before it becomes dangerous. Lizbeth is happy to have any such thing that is past its prime and, in fact, does not recognize fish as food until it is quite strong.

Home leftovers, as opposed to surpluses from restaurants, are very often bad. Evidently, especially among students, there is a common type of personality that carefully wraps up even the smallest leftover and shoves it into the back of the refrigerator for six months or so before discarding it. Characteristic of this type are the reused jars and margarine tubs to which the remains are committed. I avoid ethnic foods I am unfamiliar with. If I do not know what it is supposed to look like when it is good, I cannot be certain I will be able to tell if it is bad.

No matter how careful I am I still get dysentery at least once a month, oftener in warm weather. I do not want to paint too romantic a picture. Dumpster diving has serious drawbacks as a way of life.

I LEARNED TO scavenge gradually, on my own. Since then I have initiated several companions into the trade. I have learned that there is a predictable series of stages a person goes through in learning to scavenge.

At first the new scavenger is filled with disgust and self-loathing. He is ashamed of being seen and may lurk around, trying to duck behind things, or he may try to dive at night. (In fact, most people instinctively look away from a scavenger. By skulking around, the novice calls attention to himself and arouses suspicion. Diving at night is ineffective and needlessly messy.)

Every grain of rice seems to be a maggot. Everything seems to stink. He can wipe the egg yolk off the found can, but he cannot erase from his mind the stigma of eating garbage.

That stage passes with experience. The scavenger finds a pair of running shoes that fit and look and smell brand-new. He finds a pocket calculator in perfect working order. He finds pristine ice cream, still frozen, more than he can eat or keep. He begins to understand: People throw away perfectly good stuff, a lot of perfectly good stuff.

At this stage, Dumpster shyness begins to dissipate. The diver, after all, has the last laugh. He is finding all manner of good things that are his for the taking. Those who disparage his profession are the fools, not he.

He may begin to hang on to some perfectly good things for which he has neither a use nor a market. Then he begins to take note of the things that are not perfectly good but are nearly so. He mates a Walkman with broken earphones and one that is missing a battery cover. He picks up things that he can repair.

At this stage he may become lost and never recover. Dumpsters are full of things of some potential value to someone and also of things that never have much intrinsic value but are interesting. All the Dumpster divers I have known come to the point of trying to acquire everything they touch. Why not take it, they reason, since it is all free? This is, of course, hopeless. Most divers come to realize that they must restrict themselves to items of relatively immediate utility. But in some cases the diver simply cannot control himself. I have met several of these pack-rat types. Their ideas of the values of various pieces of junk verge on the psychotic. Every bit of glass may be a diamond, they think, and all that glitters, gold.

I tend to gain weight when I am scavenging. Partly this is because I always find far more pizza and doughnuts than water-packed tuna, nonfat yogurt, and fresh vegetables. Also I have not developed much faith in the reliability of Dumpsters as a food source, although it has been proven to me many times. I tend to eat as if I have no idea where my next meal is coming from. But mostly I just hate to see food go to waste and so I eat much more than I should. Something like this drives the obsession to collect junk.

As for collecting objects, I usually restrict myself to collecting one kind of small object at a time, such as pocket calculators, sunglasses, or campaign buttons. To live on the street I must anticipate my needs to a certain extent: I must pick up and save warm bedding I find in August because it will not be found in Dumpsters in November. As I have no access to health care, I often hoard essential drugs, such as antibiotics and antihistamines. (This course can be recommended only to those with some grounding in pharmacology. Antibiotics, for example, even when indicated are worse than useless if taken in insufficient amounts.) But even if I had a home with extensive storage space, I could not save everything that might be valuable in some contingency.

I have proprietary feelings about my Dumpsters. As I have mentioned, it is no accident that I scavenge from ones where good finds are common. But my limited experience with Dumpsters in other areas suggests to me that even in poorer areas, Dumpsters, if attended with sufficient diligence, can be made to yield a livelihood. The rich students discard perfectly good kiwi-fruit; poorer people discard perfectly good apples. Slacks and Polo shirts are found in the one place; jeans and T-shirts in the other. The population of competitors rather than the affluence of the dumpers most affects the feasibility of survival by scavenging. The large number of competitors is what puts me off the idea of trying to scavenge in places like Los Angeles.

Curiously, I do not mind my direct competition, other scavengers, so much as I hate the can scroungers.

People scrounge cans because they have to have a little cash. I have tried scrounging cans with an able-bodied companion. Afoot a can scrounger simply cannot make more than a few dollars a day. One can extract the necessities of life from the Dumpsters directly with far less effort than would be required to accumulate the equivalent value in cans. (These observations may not hold in places with container redemption laws.)

Can scroungers, then, are people who must have small amounts of cash. These are drug addicts and winos, mostly the latter because the amounts of cash are so small. Spirits and drugs do, like all other commodities, turn up in Dumpsters and the scavenger will from time to time have a half bottle of a rather good wine with his dinner. But the wino cannot survive on these occasional finds; he must have his daily dose to stave off the DTs. All the cans he can carry will buy about three bottles of Wild Irish Rose.

I do not begrudge them the cans, but can scroungers tend to tear up the Dumpsters, mixing the contents and littering the area. They become so specialized that they can see only cans. They earn my contempt by passing up change, canned goods, and readily hockable items.

There are precious few courtesies among scavengers. But it is common practice to set aside surplus items: pairs of shoes, clothing, canned goods, and such. A true scavenger hates to see good stuff go to waste, and what he cannot use he leaves in good condition in plain sight.

Can scroungers lay waste to everything in their path and will stir one of a pair of good shoes to the bottom of a Dumpster, to be lost or ruined in the muck. Can scroungers will even go through individual garbage cans, something I have never seen a scavenger do.

Individual garbage cans are set out on the public easement only on garbage days. On other days going through them requires trespassing close to a dwelling. Going through individual garbage cans without scattering litter is almost impossible. Litter is likely to reduce the public's tolerance of scavenging. Individual cans are simply not as productive as Dumpsters; people in houses and duplexes do not move so often and for some reason do not tend to discard as much useful material. Moreover, the time required to go through one garbage can that serves one household is not much less than the time required to go through a Dumpster that contains the refuse of twenty apartments.

But my strongest reservation about going through individual garbage cans is that this seems to me a very personal kind of invasion to which I would object if I were a householder. Although many things in Dumpsters are obviously meant never to come to light, a Dumpster is somehow less personal.

I AVOID TRYING to draw conclusions about the people who dump in the Dumpsters I frequent. I think it would be unethical to do so, although I know many people will find the idea of scavenger ethics too funny for words.

Dumpsters contain bank statements, correspondence, and other documents, just as anyone might expect. But there are also less obvious sources of information. Pill bottles, for example. The labels bear the name of the patient, the name of the doctor, and the name of the drug. AIDS drugs and anti-psychotic medicines, to name but two groups, are specific and are seldom prescribed for any other disorders. The plastic compacts for birth-control pills usually have complete label information.

Despite all of this sensitive information, I have had only one apartment resident object to my going through the Dumpster. In that case it turned out the resident was a university athlete who was taking bets and who was afraid I would turn up his wager slips.

Occasionally a find tells a story. I once found a small paper bag containing some unused condoms, several partial tubes of flavored sexual lubricants, a partially used compact of birth-control pills, and the torn pieces of a picture of a young man. Clearly she was through with him and planning to give up sex altogether.

Dumpster things are often sad—abandoned teddy bears, shredded wedding books, despaired-of sales kits. I find many pets lying in state in Dumpsters. Although I hope to get off the streets so that Lizbeth can have a long and comfortable old age, I know this hope is not very realistic. So I suppose when her time comes she too will go into a Dumpster. I will have no better place for her. And after all, it is fitting, since for most of her life her livelihood has come from the Dumpster. When she finds something I think is safe that has been spilled from a Dumpster, I let her have it. She already knows the route around the best ones. I like to think that if she survives me she will have a chance of evading the dog catcher and of finding her sustenance on the route.

Silly vanities also come to rest in the Dumpsters. I am a rather accomplished needleworker. I get a lot of material from the Dumpsters. Evidently sorority girls, hoping to impress someone, perhaps themselves, with their mastery of a womanly art, buy a lot of embroider-by-number kits, work a few stitches horribly, and eventually discard the whole mess. I pull out their stitches, turn the canvas over, and work an original design. Do not think I refrain from chuckling as I make gifts from these kits.

I find diaries and journals. I have often thought of compiling a book of literary found objects. And perhaps I will one day. But what I find is hopelessly commonplace and bad without being, even unconsciously, camp. College students also discard their papers. I am horrified to discover the kind of paper that now merits an A in an undergraduate course. I am grateful, however, for the number of good books and magazines the students throw out.

In the area I know best I have never discovered vermin in the Dumpsters, but there are two kinds of kitty surprise. One is alley cats whom I meet as they leap, claws first, out of Dumpsters. This is especially thrilling when I have Lizbeth in tow. The other kind of kitty surprise is a plastic garbage bag filled with some ponderous, amorphous mass. This always proves to be used cat litter.

City bees harvest doughnut glaze and this makes the Dumpster at the doughnut shop more interesting. My faith in the instinctive wisdom of animals is always shaken whenever I see Lizbeth attempt to catch a bee in her mouth, which she does whenever bees are present. Evidently some birds find Dumpsters profitable, for birdie surprise is almost as common as kitty surprise of the first kind. In hunting season all kinds of small game turn up in Dumpsters, some of it, sadly, not entirely dead. Curiously, summer and winter, maggots are uncommon.

The worst of the living and near-living hazards of the Dumpsters are the fire ants. The food they claim is not much of a loss, but they are vicious and aggressive. It is very easy to brush against some surface of the Dumpster and pick up half a dozen or more fire ants, usually in some sensitive area such as the underarm. One advantage of bringing Lizbeth along as I make Dumpster rounds is that, for obvious reasons, she is very alert to ground-based fire ants. When Lizbeth recognizes a fire-ant infestation around our feet, she does the Dance of the Zillion Fire Ants. I have learned not to ignore this warning from Lizbeth, whether I perceive the tiny ants or not, but to remove ourselves at Lizbeth's first pas de bourée. All the more so because the ants are the worst in the summer months when I wear flip-flops if I have them. (Perhaps someone will misunderstand this. Lizbeth does the Dance of the Zillion Fire Ants when she recognizes more fire ants than she cares to eat, not when she is being bitten. Since I have learned to react promptly, she does not get bitten at all. It is the isolated patrol of fire ants that falls in Lizbeth's range that deserves pity. She finds them quite tasty.)

By far the best way to go through a Dumpster is to lower yourself into it. Most of the good stuff tends to settle at the bottom because it is usually weightier than the rubbish. My more athletic companions have often demonstrated to me that they can extract much good material from a Dumpster I have already been over.

To those psychologically or physically unprepared to enter a Dumpster, I recommend a stout stick, preferably with some barb or hook at one end. The hook can be used to grab plastic garbage bags. When I find canned goods or other objects loose at the bottom of a Dumpster, I lower a bag into it, roll the desired object into the bag, and then hoist the bag out—a procedure more easily described than executed. Much Dumpster diving is a matter of experience for which nothing will do except practice.

Dumpster diving is outdoor work, often surprisingly pleasant. It is not entirely predictable; things of interest turn up every day and some days there are finds of great value. I am always very pleased when I can turn up exactly the thing I most wanted to find. Yet in spite of the element of chance, scavenging more than most other pursuits tends to yield returns in some proportion to the effort and intelligence brought to bear. It is very sweet to turn up a few dollars in change from a Dumpster that has just been gone over by a wino.

The land is now covered with cities: The cities are full of Dumpsters. If a member of the canine race is ever able to know what it is doing, then Lizbeth knows that when we go around to the Dumpsters, we are hunting. I think of scavenging as a modern form of self-reliance. In any event, after having survived nearly ten years of government service, where everything is geared to the lowest common denominator, I find it refreshing to have work that rewards initiative and effort. Certainly I would be happy to have a sinecure again, but I am no longer heartbroken that I left one.

I find from the experience of scavenging two rather deep lessons. The first is to take what you can use and let the rest go by. I have come to think that there is no value in the abstract. A thing I cannot use or make useful, perhaps by trading, has no value however rare or fine it may be. I mean useful in a broad sense—some art I would find useful and some otherwise.

I was shocked to realize that some things are not worth acquiring, but now I think it is so. Some material things are white elephants that eat up the possessor's substance. The second lesson is the transience of material being. This has not quite converted me to a dualist, but it has made some headway in that direction. I do not suppose that ideas are immortal, but certainly mental things are longer lived than other material things.

Once I was the sort of person who invests objects with sentimental value. Now I no longer have those objects, but I have the sentiments yet.

Many times in our travels I have lost everything but the clothes I was wearing and Lizbeth. The things I find in Dumpsters, the love letters and rag dolls of so many lives, remind me of this lesson. Now I hardly pick up a thing without envisioning the time I will cast it aside. This I think is a healthy state of mind.

Almost everything I have now has already been cast out at least once, proving that what I own is valueless to someone.

Anyway, I find my desire to grab for the gaudy bauble has been largely sated. I think this is an attitude I share with the very wealthy—we both know there is plenty more where what we have came from. Between us are the rat-race millions who nightly scavenge the cable channels looking for they know not what.

I am sorry for them.

EIGHT

Summer in Austin: Dog Days on the Street

The night I left Tim's I led Lizbeth to Shoal Creek, where I had spotted a large concrete slab that ran along a bank for several hundred yards. There I thought we might avoid the fire ants.

Lizbeth and I and all of our things were clean. I could not see why a fire ant would cross many yards of barren concrete to molest us. Nonetheless, as I was drifting off to sleep, Lizbeth danced the Dance of the Zillion Fire Ants, ending with a leap that landed four paws on my belly.

I could not believe it. Fire ants are very small and I had to light several matches before I saw one. Then I saw many more than one. Sure enough, fire ants came in a line, across thirty yards of slab, right at us. Indeed, hundreds of them already had reached the freshly laundered towel I lay on.

I supposed I had settled us by chance on an ant trail. I got up, shook the towel, and moved about ten yards on the perpendicular to the line of ants.

This time Lizbeth ate the first scouts that approached us. But it was hopeless. The ants followed their old line, turned, and came directly at our new spot.

The next night I tried sleeping on a flat rock in the middle of another creek. We were surrounded by water. I never understood how the fire ants got at us, but get at us they did. I doubted my sanity. Surely nothing in nature could be as malicious as the fire ants seemed to me to be. The fabric of reality seemed to take on the ominous shadows of a cheap horror movie. Tiny creatures out to get me? Only psychotic patients think such things. Yet the ants were real enough or else Lizbeth had become my partner in a folie à deux.

By the third night I had found some household insecticide in a Dumpster. A fire-ant colony cannot be destroyed with ordinary insecticide. Even when the mound is located and sprayed directly, the queen will be removed to safety before the vapors penetrate her chamber. What is worse, the colonies now have several queens—the experts once supposed this was impossible—and the chances of eliminating all the queens in one stroke are vanishingly small. But, as I discovered, insecticides can be used to discourage the ants from adventures in a small area.

I took Lizbeth to Adams Park. Austin had a park curfew. But several parts of Adams Park are not visible from the surrounding streets. I knew no Austin cop would put down his coffee and doughnuts, get out of his car, and come wandering through the park unless there was some complaint.

I hoped there would be no complaint. Adams Park is fairly obscure. How to get into it, or even that there is anything to get into, is not readily apparent from the streets. The park had a water tap and failed of being the perfect place only in that it had no rest rooms. But until I found the insecticide, the fire ants made sleeping there impossible.

I secured Lizbeth upwind and sprayed a ten-by-ten foot area

until it was wet. The toxic vapors gave me a sick headache, but it did the trick. With only a little touch-up spraying after heavy rains, the area remained free of fire ants so long as I did not bring food into it. However much this procedure may offend wild-eyed ecologists, I do not know how Lizbeth and I might have survived otherwise.

Lizbeth and I slept in Adams Park when the weather was fair. As our spot was quite in the open, we could not stay in the park in the rain. Nights that it rained we sat up under the awnings of stores.

We had a spell of intermittent rains late at night. We would go to the park several times, only to be driven out by renewed rainfall. These storms often cleared at three or four in the morning, by which time I would be exhausted from all the packing and unpacking. Sometimes I overslept. Although in our bedroll we were quite invisible from the streets, by daylight we were obvious to anyone entering the park afoot. At first I was worried that my oversleeping in the park would result in a complaint that would lead to our eviction from the park or my arrest. The park curfew expired at 5:00 A.M. and I thought by first light we were within the law. But I was afraid if I were observed too often in the park in the morning, the police might look for me there at night.

I did not then know there was an ordinance against sleeping at any time in any public place. I did not know it because, of course, the ordinance is never enforced against picnickers or sunbathers, but only against those who have no better place to sleep. I often heard from attorney friends that the law in its majesty forbids the rich as well as the poor from sleeping under bridges. In truth I saw that the rich—or at least the middle class—slept in public places, unmolested by the law.

But for a long while, Lizbeth and I did not come to the attention of the law. We came to know, or at least to recognize, most of the morning visitors to the park. Lizbeth charmed several of the women who came in the morning to walk their own dogs. Strangers in the park were rare.

One morning I slept a little later than usual and was much alarmed to wake to see a green Parks and Recreation Department vehicle jump a curb and drive into the park on the grass. I thought we were discovered, and of course we were. But the truck merely pulled into an inconspicuous spot, where the driver fell asleep. The park, it turned out, was a favorite hideout for city workers of various departments. Whole crews came to the park for three- or four-hour picnics, and individuals often slept in their trucks through the whole workday. None of them would complain of me, for of course they did not want the park to come under scrutiny.

Eventually, as the Dumpster harvest was coming to an end, my bicycle was stolen. I had left it only so long as it took me to run into Sleazy Sue's with a bag of canned goods for the food bank. Because it was raining I had not gone directly to Sue's door, but left Lizbeth, the bicycle, and a small backpack under the awning of an abandoned taco stand that was attached to Sue's. I was out of sight of the things for less than a minute, but in that time the thief determined Lizbeth was harmless and made off with the bicycle and the backpack.

While I was collecting canned goods for the food bank, I reserved the perishable food I found for Lizbeth and me. All that was in the backpack was our dinner—some boneless chicken breasts for Lizbeth, some Velveeta and candy corn for me. Later I found the food scattered in the street and run over. The backpack would be easy to replace because backpacks are common in Dumpsters, but we missed our dinner. We came to miss the bicycle more, for it was taken just as good finds in the Dumpsters became scarce and we most needed to range widely. Hungry and not entirely sheltered from the blowing rain, Lizbeth and I sat under the awning until long after dark.

Soon after the bicycle was stolen, Dan Archer's wife finally succeeded in persuading him to return to Mexico so that she could visit her relatives. Dan wanted to lock his storage closet while they were away, which would be for an indefinite period, and I was told I ought to remove whatever I might want before they returned. I left my cold-weather gear and my books and papers. I took most of my clothes. I seldom had the money to do laundry and so I wanted as many changes as possible. Stung by the loss of my bicycle, I tried to carry everything for several days. That proved impractical. Reluctantly I began to stash most of my gear where I stashed the bedroll, in a clump of bushes in Adams Park.

Two or three times I returned to discover my gear dumped out and scattered. But except for a Walkman I had put together from Dumpster finds, nothing was taken. A group of white can scroungers and a group of black can scroungers came through the park regularly on their rounds. I believed the black can scroungers were the ones dumping out my gear. At least they had the sense to see whether I had anything worth having before they removed it. My stash spot was in an uninviting brushy area where no one would go except to look for things. I kept my gear in garbage bags, like the ones can scroungers used to carry cans. Stealing another's cans is an occupation of certain can scroungers, and I suppose the can scroungers first looked into my gear with the thought that the garbage bags might contain cans.

Fortunately I was in the park one day when the white can scroungers came through. I was writing a letter at the picnic table at the far end of the park and took little notice of the can scroungers. Presently Lizbeth began barking and straining at her leash. This was remarkable for we were not less than a hundred yards from the gear, yet Lizbeth perceived the thieves were at work. I looked up and saw the bushes shake. Then I saw the white can scroungers scurrying up the bluff beyond the bushes.

I only managed to catch up with them because they did not know I was after them.

I found them sitting under a tree, still going through my rollbag. As I approached them, the nature of my errand must have been apparent. The able-bodied ones scattered, leaving a single old lame wino who could not have escaped me in any event but who was especially immobilized because he would not let go of the group's can collection. The collection was the size of a water bed and I do not know where the can scroungers found a plastic bag so large.

All that had been in the rollbag seemed to have remained under the tree, but my new backpack was missing. I questioned the old man. He denied having been in the bushes, but I recognized his cap. He denied going through the rollbag, although I had seen him in the thick of it. Mostly he denied knowing where the backpack was. I had not seen any of the others run off with it. Once I determined I could get no useful information out of him, I ripped his can bag open and scattered the cans on the street.

Early in the day as it was, the old gimp was already quite intoxicated. He tried for a long time to gather the cans up in his arms, not seeming to notice that he dropped as many as he picked up. He continued to live his miserable life only because I thought of Lizbeth and that she would not fare well if I were arrested.

I repacked the rollbag. Of course nothing was missing from it because there was nothing of value to anyone else in it. I was desperate to find the backpack because it contained Lizbeth's heartworm prophylactic and we were living quite exposed to mosquitoes.

I had a flash of insight. The thieves were can scroungers, after all. I looked into the nearby Dumpsters and, sure enough, found the backpack in one of them. The contents had been scattered and it took me awhile to fish everything out. But I ended that day with as much as I had at dawn.

I still could not carry everything with me all the time. But I began to carry always a day pack containing the most essential things, such as Lizbeth's medication and a day's supply of her food, with the few small items of value, such as the Walkmans I found.

I tried to keep at least one functioning radio, and usually I had to keep a large collection of batteries, for I discovered I could get an hour or so of play out of otherwise dead batteries if I allowed them several days of rest between uses. I tried to hear the National Public Radio news in the mornings and in the evenings. When I could not find one, I sometimes spent five dollars on a digital watch. As I made my Dumpster rounds I always picked up the discarded newspapers and newsmagazines.

When each day was so much like any other, I had to make an effort to remember the day of the week and the date. I sometimes went for weeks without speaking to another person. I sometimes caught myself losing touch with reality. Material reality, the fact of a day, I never had trouble with. But social reality, the convention of a date, sometimes eluded me.

As I was sleeping under the stars, my lapsed interest in things celestial renewed itself. For a time, however, this served to further disorient me.

I had known for a long time that the local daily was far from accurate in reporting local politics. But then the events of local politics were occasionally less certain and less predictable, and certainly always were less harmonious, than the motions of the spheres. When I found the local paper I usually discarded the city-state section after I read the obituaries to assure myself that most of those dying were considerably older than myself. I turned my attention to the weather page, which had recently been made over in imitation of *USA Today* with a four-color map and various sorts of graphic excesses. I discovered about every other day that the paper's report of the times of moonrise and moonset and the phases of the moon were contradictory of my own observations.

I knew the paper was perfectly capable of concealing the true dimensions of some real estate development that was being proposed for an environmentally sensitive area. But I found it hard to believe they would misrepresent the moon, which anyone might see for himself. I began to wonder whether I really made my observations or merely dreamt them, or if something was wrong with my basic observational faculties.

Eventually I discovered that the paper was, apparently, lifting the times of moonrise and moonset from the *Old Farmers' Almanac* and that the times were quite correct for observers in Boston. But many days whoever prepared the weather page failed to enter the corrections necessary to make the predictions answer for Austin. How the paper went wrong so often in reporting the phases of the moon, I never discovered.

I gleaned information on the present positions of the planets from astrology columns. These too seemed at odds with my own observations. I did not then know that astrologers who pretend to consult an ephemeris at all most often use one that long ago ceased to be useful in accounting for the motions of the actual planets. Fortunately when I remembered to listen to the radio at nine in the evening I could receive *Stardate*, a little sixty-second program from the McDonald observatory, and it proved infallibly accurate.

TWO OR THREE times a week we went north to a park that had a public pool. Usually Lizbeth and I arrived at Shipe Playground between 7:00 and 8:00 A.M. depending upon the condition of the Dumpsters along the way. I liked to brush my teeth and shave in the restroom before the park became crowded. Whether the light bulb in the restroom had been stolen or not, there was not enough light for me to see my face in the little mirror I had taken from a discarded compact. Nonetheless I discovered I had to set the mirror on the hand-drying machine. Due to some psychological quirk, I could not tell the right side of my face from the left unless I imagined an image in the mirror. I do not know why, if I had to imagine the image, I could not have imagined the mirror as well.

Unlike Adams Park, Shipe Playground was not a bit obscure. The swimming pool was well attended. But I rarely saw other homeless people there. While swimming was not as satisfactory as a real shower with hot water and soap, if I stayed in the water long enough and toweled off vigorously afterward, I could get reasonably clean. Since the pool authorities accepted any cut-off jeans as a bathing costume, I do not know why the expedient of pool bathing did not occur to more homeless people.

I could not always stay in the pool as long as I wanted because Lizbeth continued to regard bathing as an inherently unsafe activity—or at any rate, she would bark at the water until I got out of it, and sometimes she became agitated enough to annoy other people. After my swim, Lizbeth and I would picnic in the park if I had found lunch on the way. If I had not found lunch yet, I would tie Lizbeth and the day pack in the park while I went to the Dumpsters at the surrounding apartments. I saw Clint at Shipe Playground many times.

Clint was the last roommate I had at the shack on Avenue B. As I remembered it he had promised to contribute a hundred dollars a month toward the rent when he moved in in August. I had never seen a penny of that money. As we fell further and further in arrears, I explained the situation to him many times, but he never gave any sign of appreciating the seriousness of the matter. I had left him a very bitter note when I took off for California.

In truth, Clint's share of the rent would probably have only postponed the outcome. He made only a little money as a kitchen worker in a vegetarian restaurant. He did some of the pointless running around to the various agencies as we tried to get some assistance. When he did no more, at least he provided for himself. In many respects he was much more mature and responsible than I had been at his age—he was nineteen when he moved in. We never did have hot water or electric power while he lived in the shack, and for little rent or none, as he well knew, he might have found a much better situation.

He seemed to be the leader of a little group of other young people who hung out at the park. I did not speak to him at first, for fear of embarrassing him in front of his friends, but any observant person would have seen that Lizbeth knew Clint very well.

One day when we stayed in the park late into the afternoon, Clint followed us when we left and stopped me to talk as soon as we were out of sight of the playground. I learned that after he had left me off by the side of the road, Billy had visited the shack and added a few of his own remarks to the note I left. Still, Clint evidently had not absorbed that the landlord meant to repossess the property. He had stayed in the shack another week or two until he returned to find that all of his belongings had been removed.

He told me he was living on a deck he built in the limestone hills west of town. He had some hopes for his latest get-rich-quick scheme and he said if things worked out he would get a house and I could stay there.

Clint was obviously starving. That he was a bodybuilder made it all the more obvious that he was consuming some of his own muscle mass. I gave him the canned goods I had collected as Lizbeth and I walked to the playground that morning. After that whenever I found a T-shirt or a pair of shorts that would fit Clint, I would take it to the playground when I went and would leave it on his bicycle. Although he told me he was not ashamed for the others to know he knew me, he never acknowledged my presence when the others were around.

The rumor went around the park that Lizbeth was a pit bull

and even the most macho of the other boys gave her a wide berth. Clint was regarded as incredibly brave because he did not dodge her.

Pit-bull hysteria was then in full bloom. I never saw Lizbeth's resemblance to a pit bull, but the issue was raised many times. I suppose many people were terrified of pit bulls who would not have known one if they saw it. The pit-bull phenomenon was at least the third avatar of the Killer Breed to occur in my lifetime. When I was a child the Killer Breed was the German shepherd. By the time I was in college it was the Doberman pinscher. I imagine it is a chestnut that journalists dust off on a slow day. Of course there are many dog attacks every day. Without too much trouble a single breed can be implicated in several attacks and a new Killer Breed is born.

Lizbeth's supposed likeness to a pit bull was not the only troublesome aspect of her appearance. In the summer in Austin she developed a scaly dermatitis on her back and hindquarters. This had been diagnosed as an allergy and there was considerable evidence to support that diagnosis. But she looked flea-bitten or otherwise infested in the summer.

In fact she did not get fleas while we were on the streets. I found this hard to believe, for it seemed we were subject to every other kind of insect attack. I formed the theory that Lizbeth did not support a flea colony because she did not have a fixed nest. At any rate, although Lizbeth did not have a problem with fleas, I received a number of gratuitous lectures from strangers on the subject of flea control.

Small children, however, were oblivious to any defect in Lizbeth and surprisingly few of them showed any fear of her. Having seen her reaction to the little monster we had ridden with, I felt certain Lizbeth would never intentionally harm a child. But I thought she might deck a child if she jumped up to greet it. Fortunately that never happened. I formed the opinion that the dog brain reserves some substance, equivalent to twenty milligrams of Valium, which is rushed into the dog bloodstream at the sight of a human child. Were that I so equipped.

Lizbeth was good with children, but she was far from fond of them. When she was mobbed by toddlers, as sometimes happened in the park, she would often look sidelong at me, as if she wanted reassurance that I would rescue her if need be. Curiously, boys seemed to be more likely to be afraid of Lizbeth. Although they would come to see her, they tended to hold back at a range of three or four feet. Girls walked right up to Lizbeth and would even try to ride her without so much as a by-your-leave. Girls always asked the questions. "Is he a boy or a girl?"

"She's a girl."

"How do you know?"

This was a stumper and it took me awhile to perfect the answer: "I read her birth certificate."

"Where do you live?"

"We don't have a home."

"Are you married?" As I have said, the girls asked the questions.

One evening when Lizbeth and I had stayed rather late at Shipe Playground, a little girl out with her father ran across the playground to pet Lizbeth. Things went well at first and the father stayed back. But as the girl petted Lizbeth and spoke to me, I saw that the father was drawing nearer slowly and he seemed more and more displeased with the situation. At last he dashed forward and snatched the child away. His movement was so sudden that I instantly commanded Lizbeth, "Stay, Beth!" for fear that she would react. That brought the father up short.

"Is the dog's name Beth?" he asked.

The child's name was Elizabeth and she was called Beth just as I often called Lizbeth Beth or Bessie. I offered to show the father Lizbeth's tags.

He had heard me saying "Be a good girl, Beth," "Stay calm, Beth," and "That's a good girl, Beth," all in the particular tone one uses to calm animals and children. He was alarmed to think I had known the child's name from the start and that I addressed her in such a familiar fashion. The child evidently also thought I was speaking to her, for otherwise she surely would have said, "Beth's my name, too." Fortunately the father had the intelligence to reevaluate the situation when he heard me command Lizbeth. The father and I looked each other in the eye. We were horrified.

I read in the father's face that he was ticking off the what-ifs, just as I was. What if he had thought the encounter should be investigated? What if the child had been subjected to a social worker who needed one more case to justify her budget? How many leading questions would it take before the child understood that it was supposed to implicate me or her father or both of us?

I suppose the crones of old Salem exchanged many such expressions of shared horror as they wondered which of their number would be the next to be condemned by the mouth of a child.

The father did not need to examine Lizbeth's tags and the situation was so plain to both of us that there was nothing more to say.

UNTIL I BEGAN to receive my mail at Sleazy Sue's, I used the gay bookstore in town as my mailing address. On Thursdays we went to check my mail. The bookstore was some distance to the west and south of our usual haunts, and we broke the journey by stopping at Pease Park to picnic on whatever had turned up in the Dumpsters along the way.

The rest room near the picnic tables was a traditional place that men met to have sex, usually on the spot. I found that a pair of very attractive young men had undertaken there to give guerilla workshops on safe sex, and they turned up almost every time I visited this rest room. They had plenty of condoms and leaflets describing the proper use of condoms, and they distributed these to the patrons of the rest room. Not only that, but the young men participated in the activities. They disrobed and modeled and gently redirected the others away from unsafe activities.

This struck me as a singularly effective form of education, for of course people who give formal safe-sex workshops usually find themselves preaching to the choir. Moreover, to see these young men with their first-rate physiques practicing safe sex dispelled the notion that safe sex was in some way second rate. No lecture or tract could ever be so effective. The young men seemed entirely selfless in this work, and gave as much attention and concern to the old and unattractive participants as to the young and handsome ones.

They succeeded in establishing manual sex as the preferred form in the rest room. Because my hygiene on the street was less than adequate, I was really rather happy that my partners in the rest room had been encouraged to satisfy me in that way.

Days that we did not go to Shipe Playground or to the gay bookstore, we went only a few blocks west of Adams Park. I made the rounds of the Dumpsters at the student condos as early as possible, for I hoped to find our sustenance before the day grew too warm. Usually we stopped for lunch, if I had found it, under the awning of the abandoned taco stand at Sleazy Sue's. The management at Sue's cast a benign eye on us and later I was allowed to receive my mail there. More important I could use the rest room at Sue's. Truly public rest rooms were few in Austin and far between.

I often thought, as I began to discover the numbers of other homeless people on the street, that a distribution of public rest rooms would be a useful investment in public health. I thought also that such rest rooms might, at little additional expense, contain a simple, cold-water shower, and I do not suppose that any-thing else could provide a better return per dollar in terms of morale.

Across the street from Sue's was a very small strip shopping center. The shop nearest Sue's was Ramblin' Red's. Head shops are illegal in Texas and it would be libelous to write that Red's was a head shop. Red's was a tobacco accessories and gift shop. When Red's had first opened some twenty years ago, it had been located in an old house that had a large front porch. I had not been into Red's since those days. I suppose I was not the only old customer who felt Red's was a little out of place in the steel and glass of the little strip center. Perhaps to mitigate this jarring effect, the proprietor had installed an old church pew outside the store and green canvas awnings.

Lizbeth and I began to spend much of our time on the pew. From it I could see when the letter carrier arrived at Sue's. Except for a couple of hours in the afternoon, the bench was in the shade, and the overhang of the roof and the awnings offered some pro-tection from rain. The proprietor at Ramblin' Red's suggested that I might water Lizbeth from the tap at the side of the build-ing, and he and the staff were always gracious about allowing me to use their rest room. The pew was near enough a streetlight that I could read or write there at night.

From the first there were many reasons the pew seemed a convenient place to spend time. After a while there was another reason. After we had spent so many hours at the pew, it began to seem a little bit like home.

NINE

Phlebitis:
At the Public Hospital

I pressed my thumb into my left ankle.

I easily produced a half-inch dent in the watery swelling, and the dent remained in my ankle after I lifted my thumb.

I had forgotten the system for classifying degrees of edema, but it seemed to me that the relatively sudden onset of this sign would require medical attention.

As I examined my ankle by the light of a convenience store sign, two men on a drinking spree passed on their way to buy more beer at the store. They insisted on buying a bag of dry dog food for Lizbeth. I could not refuse. My leg had been so painful that for more than a week I had been unable to walk more than a few hundred yards at a time. Lizbeth was hungry.

I must have looked pretty ragged. I had not been able to walk to Shipe Playground to bathe. And I had not shaved, conserving the water I could carry for us to drink.

Since I was not bleeding and was breathing regularly I thought it would be useless to go to the emergency room on a Saturday night. Besides, I had to make some arrangement for Lizbeth. As late in the month as it was I guessed Billy would have spent most of his state salary and probably would be at home and relatively sober. Billy had paid a pet deposit at his apartment because he had a cat, and since I now had a bag of food for Lizbeth, he would probably agree to keep her. I had his new telephone credit card number, so I called him.

Billy's plan that I visit him on the first of every month had been forgotten after May. Perhaps he felt guilty about that. He agreed to pick us up in the morning. He would take me to the emergency room and keep Lizbeth while I was in the hospital. I thought my condition was serious enough that I would be admitted to the hospital. I would not have thought of applying to the emergency room otherwise. Lizbeth and I returned across the street to the pew. I tried always to keep a supply of ibuprofen tablets and I had found some Vicodin, a synthetic codeine, in a Dumpster. Although I was in pain I decided not to take either drug. I did not want to cloud the clinical picture. Besides it had been some time since a safe amount of either drug had helped the pain much and I wanted to save the ibuprofen because it is the only thing I have found that is any good for my migraines.

If there had been ibuprofen when I was younger, when my migraines were more frequent and had disrupted my school and work, perhaps this story would be different.

At the pew I had light enough from a streetlight to write. I began to write out my medical history.

One of the winos came by and wanted me to drink with him, although I had told him many times that I do not drink on the streets. I showed the wino my leg and ankle. He gave me what turned out to be an accurate diagnosis, given the limitations of his language. At the time, however, I took it for drunken gibberish. The pain had exhausted my patience. I stood up, and Lizbeth and I returned slowly to our bedroll in Adams Park.

I ARRIVED AT the emergency room a little before eight on Sunday morning. A few joggers had reported with running injuries. From the years I had worked at the admissions desk of the state lunatic asylum I recognized a malingerer. He had discovered that he could get some attention by complaining of chest pain. I could see that the staff knew it was a sham, but they had to go through the motions of ruling out a physical cause of his pain.

Someone drew the drapes around my gurney and that was all I saw of my fellow patients for quite some time. My vital signs were taken and my blood was drawn. I told my complaint many times over and offered my written medical history to whoever looked important enough to have a use for it.

I heard one of the staff shout, "Dr. Leo." That is a hospital code for cardiac arrest. I was alarmed. Perhaps the malingerer had been telling the truth this time. There were several other calls of "Dr. Leo" during the next couple of hours. I was astonished that there were so many arrests on an otherwise quiet Sunday morning.

Finally a gentleman who looked a great deal like Pagliacci in a white coat came into my cubical. His name tag read: DR. LEO VELASQUEZ, RESIDENT. It was just a little ER inside joke to call him by his given name. I should have smelled a rat because the cries of "Dr. Leo" had not been followed by the usual crash-cart uproar. But what, I wondered, would they call out if they happened to have a cardiac arrest?

Dr. Velasquez finally accepted my written medical history and disappeared through the drapes again. When he returned he had developed a Chicano accent and spoke in what he must have thought was street language. In conspiratorial tones he inquired about my IV drug use.

I have never used IV drugs.

I explained that the hepatitis B I reported on my medical history had been contracted sexually. I assumed the questions about IV drug use were inspired by the history of hepatitis B. Dr. Velasquez clearly did not believe my denials. He warned me that he would send someone around to collect a specimen for a urine toxicology. That was fine with me. I had been lying on the gurney for many hours and was more than prepared, was in fact anxious to provide an ample specimen.

Eventually my gurney was wheeled out of the ER to the ultrasound lab. The ultrasound sensor was run over my affected leg several times. The ultrasound operator consulted the ultrasound physician. Then the operator ran the sensor over my leg again while the physician watched the monitor. Again they conferred out of my hearing. All was not as expected; so much was clear to me. But after a third pass of the sensor I was sent back to the ER.

I had lost my cubicle, and my gurney was left adrift in the ER so that it had to be moved whenever someone wanted in or out of the nurses' station.

Dr. Velasquez found me again. The Chicano accent was gone. He diagnosed me with thrombophlebitis—that is, a blood clot that is irritating to a vein. The danger is that it will break loose, and if it is large enough it will cause a pulmonary embolism, which in turn is a medical term for the end of the road.

Dr. Velasquez wanted to run an HIV screen on me. That I survived exposed to the elements and eating garbage seemed to me to be good evidence my immune system was functioning adequately. I asked Dr. Velasquez how my HIV status was related to the treatment of phlebitis.

He strung some words together, which did not in fact amount to an explanation. But I was no longer thinking clearly and I consented to the test. He sent a tech to draw my blood and promised that someone would be along to collect that urine specimen. He said he would admit me to the hospital.

Another couple of hours passed. No one came to collect a urine specimen. But eventually the drift of my gurney brought me in range of a men's room.

Finally someone came to wheel my gurney to the elevator. I got a chance to go through my ER chart. My vital signs were recorded for a couple of times they were not taken. I could not tell if someone else's vital signs had been recorded on my chart or if a busy tech had just made up some numbers. Dr. Velasquez had ordered a psychiatric consult. And all the bastard had ordered for pain was two Tylenol. I did not want an opiate, but I did want ibuprofen or Naprosyn. My gurney was wheeled out on one floor. But for some reason I could not be accommodated there and I was returned to the elevator and taken to another floor. I was given a private room.

A nurse gave me a shot of Lasix—a powerful diuretic. He hung a small plastic urinal on the bed and left a cup for the urine toxicology specimen. I made a nervous remark about whether they suspected Richard Nixon of IV drug use.

The Lasix came on like gangbusters. Fortunately, I hobbled to the bathroom with the toxicology cup; fortunately because I was passing enough water to have filled ten urinals the size of the one that had been hung on my bed.

The nurse returned after an hour or so. I had made a half-dozen trips to the bathroom by then. The nurse was very upset because he was supposed to monitor the amount of water I passed. Besides, I was supposed—he told me—to be on strict bedrest. That meant I was not supposed to use the bathroom for any reason.

I made another nervous remark about Richard Nixon. The

nurse said I seemed to be fixated on Richard Nixon and disappeared before I could reply.

Uh-oh. I was already down for a psych consult. I could easily imagine the kind of note the nurse was writing in my chart. He was too young to have remembered Richard Nixon's bout with phlebitis. I was not fixated on Richard Nixon; he was simply the only person I had ever heard of who had ever had phlebitis.

BUT I HAD more to worry about.

A person has to draw the line somewhere. Some people draw the line at brain death, some at ventilators. I draw the line at bedpans. I believe it is physically impossible for me to use a bedpan, and I have no intention of finding out if that is so. I planned at first simply to use the bathroom when I was unattended. I knew I was to have an intravenous infusion, but I did not think it would impair my mobility because I saw other patients moving about the halls, rolling their IV standards with them.

Unfortunately when my infusion was started I saw that it was controlled by an electric pump. The pump's cord would not reach the bathroom, and devices of this sort are commonly equipped with an alarm that sounds when the power supply is interrupted. I expected to find a way around this difficulty. In the meanwhile my plan was to eat as little as possible, thereby putting off the trip to the bathroom as long as possible.

Eventually Dr. Stalin came by. She struck me as the black-garter-belt, stiletto-heels, and riding-crop type—perhaps it was only that she resembled Cloris Leachman in Mel Brooks's *High Anxiety*. She explained the risk factors for phlebitis. One was sedentary life-style. That had not applied to me for a long time, since I customarily walked five miles a day scavenging for food. Another was trauma. I could not remember any recent injury. The third, and evidently last, risk factor was IV drug use. The text-books simply would not allow me to deny using IV drugs.

I complained that Tylenol was not touching my pain. Dr. Stalin nodded knowingly.

After she left a new nurse brought me some Vicodin. Another uh-oh. I could not remember how long it had been since I had taken any of the Vicodin I had found in a Dumpster. If it had been within the last few days my urine toxicology would come back positive for opiates and it would be a medically proven fact that I was a heroin addict. I don't know what heroin is like, but I hate Vicodin and codeine. In early attempts to control my migraines, doctors had given me rather large doses—two and more grains at a time—of codeine, to no avail. Codeine and Vicodin make me nauseated and keep me awake and never do any more for my pain than ibuprofen. I should have told Dr. Stalin that I wanted ibuprofen. She just assumed I was having opiate withdrawal and ordered Vicodin.

I took the Vicodin. I had had all of the hassles I could deal with that day.

A tech came to draw my blood. All the routine lab work that had been done in the ER was to be repeated on my admission to the hospital proper, and the specimen for the HIV screening that had been drawn in the ER had been lost. I noticed the tech was not gloved. I warned him that I had a history of hepatitis B—as he had the lab slip for the HIV screen I saw no point in belaboring the point because the precautions for hepatitis B and HIV are the same. He told me the policy of the hospital was now universal precautions; everyone was supposed to be treated as if he were known to be HIV positive. Still the tech approached me with the needle and his hands remained ungloved.

"The gloves are not made of steel," he said. "If I am careless enough to poke myself with the needle, it will go through rubber gloves as easily as it goes through my skin." I was drawn again at midnight and at four in the morning. That and the Vicodin assured me of no sleep at all. I did learn that the night nurse slept on duty. My infusion ran out in the night and the alarm on the pump went off. As the alarm continued to sound I pressed the call button on the console by my bed. The voice that responded was clearly that of a person roused from a deep sleep. This suggested to me that when this nurse was on duty I might unplug the pump and use the bathroom, for the alarm would bring no response. I had only to learn to reprogram the pump once I reconnected it. That could not be a great mental feat if nurses did it.

I picked at breakfast, avoiding the stuff with much fiber—which was practically all of it. That would be a nasty note in my chart. As things progressed and I ate little or nothing and did not call for the bedpan, they upped the ante. One of my last meals at the hospital consisted of stewed prunes, prune juice, a mound of lettuce, an apple, and whole wheat toast. Naturally I ate none of it.

I made another stupid and regrettable remark. When a nurse came to turn up the rate of my infusion, I said something about increasing the amount of rat poison they were pumping into my body.

I thought I was receiving Warfarin, an anti-coagulant often used in the treatment of thrombophlebitis. It is also the most common rat poison used in the United States. The rats eat it and bleed to death internally. Evidently they can detect and avoid many other poisons.

I regretted making this feeble joke as soon as it escaped my lips. In fact I was receiving Heparin, another anti-coagulant, but I seriously doubt the nurse would have appreciated my point in any event. I could imagine the chart note: "Patient expresses the belief we are trying to poison him."

THE SOCIAL WORKER called on me. He came right to the point: "How many fifths do you drink a day?"

I explained that if I drank a fifth of whiskey in a week I would be drunk the whole week.

Another uh-oh. Saturday afternoon I had gone into Sleazy Sue's. In the hottest part of the afternoon the pew where Lizbeth and I spent most of our days was in the sun. I often spent those hours in Sue's, for it had a powerful air-conditioning system. The owners of the bar were kind enough to allow me to remain there on one of the carpeted benches away from the bar, and they would even go so far as to offer to take some ice out to Lizbeth at her station under a shady tree. The bar did not have many customers at the times I went to sit in it. I had little difficulty in staying out of the way in the dim, cool bar.

A very rare thing had happened the afternoon before I went to the hospital. Someone sent me a frozen margarita. As the drink had already been prepared, I drank it. Had my urine toxicology come back positive for alcohol?

I did not think one cocktail would show up twenty-four hours later, but if it had, convincing the social worker I was not an alcoholic would be impossible. Social workers have a little saying: Alcoholism is a disease of denial. And so it may be. Unfortunately social workers take this saying to mean that anyone who denies being an alcoholic must be one. Of course anyone who admits to being an alcoholic is also an alcoholic.

It would have been greatly to my advantage if I could have admitted to being an alcoholic or a drug addict. The social workers have no way of assisting someone who is sane and sober. My interview with the social worker made it clear that only three explanations of homelessness could be considered: drug addiction, alcoholism, and psychiatric disorder. The more successful I was in ruling out one of these explanations, the more certain the others would become. Professional people like to believe this.

They like to believe that no misfortune could cause them to lose their own privileged places. They like to believe that homelessness is the fault of the homeless—that the homeless have special flaws not common to the human condition, or at least the homeless have flaws that professional people are immune to. They are glad to go through the motions of helping the homeless—and some, like the social worker, depend for their livelihood on there being homeless people to pretend to help—but on the ladder of being, homeless people are not quite up to the level of professional people.

The social worker had programs for alcoholics, programs for drug addicts, and programs for the insane. If I would admit to belonging to one of these categories—and if I would have my dog destroyed—then something might be done for me. Unless I were a drug addict, an alcoholic, or a lunatic, the best he could offer me—if I would have my dog destroyed and if I would destroy my conscience to the extent necessary to participate in a religious organization that often refused to agree to principles of nondiscrimination—was three nights' lodging at the Salvation Army.

The social worker prolonged the interview after it was clear he could not offer me any material benefit. He wanted me to apply for a program that would allow the costs of my hospitalization, including his services in advising me that he had no services to offer me, to be defrayed by the federal government.

This is of course all that social workers exist for: to keep the funds flowing to the institution, thus to preserve their own salaries. Otherwise they are just about as helpful as the average high school guidance counselor—to put the matter in terms that anyone who has attended a public school can readily understand.

I asked the social worker to explain what additional benefits I would receive if I filled out the forms he wanted me to fill out. Although he could not think of any way the forms might benefit me, he seemed genuinely surprised when I told him I would take the matter under advisement. The forms remained blank and the social worker remained in an agitated state until our interview was concluded.

I COULD SEE it was about time for me to have a look at my chart.

Someone who has never worked in a medical environment may think it is a rare thing for a positive pregnancy test to be reported in the chart of a seventy-four-year-old man, or for drugs—each relatively harmless in itself—to be prescribed in a lethal combination, or for several shifts of nursing notes to be so utterly fabricated that patients on leave from the facility are described as having slept well. But I have commonly seen such things. One of my duties at the state asylum was to review medical charts.

Face it. The employees of a public hospital are, despite being doctors and nurses, public employees. Public employees run the postal service, the military, and United States foreign policy. I know very well that some dedicated and competent individuals can—rarely—be found in public employment. And I sympathize with them. But I know, and I think they know too, their valiant struggle against Chaos is doomed from the outset. Perhaps you are willing to trust your life to a system run by public employees, or perhaps you are helpless to read your medical chart. As for me I began to demand to read my medical chart.

The patient's bill of rights at almost every hospital in America says that a patient has a right to read his or her chart. But in fact that right is very difficult to enforce. I was told that, in spite of the patients' bill of rights, the policy of the nursing staff was to prevent patients from reading their charts.

I asked if there were an ombudsman in the hospital. The person I spoke to had never heard the term, and my use of it may have been recorded in my chart as a neologism—a privately coined word, often taken as evidence of a psychiatric disorder. But eventually I discovered that the person charged with enforcing patients' rights was the director of nursing.

Oh? Wasn't it the policy of the director of nursing that prevented me from seeing my chart? Yes, it was. And the director of nursing was the person charged with enforcing my right to see my chart? Yes, that too.

If I were arrested I might expect sooner or later to have an attorney appointed to represent me, but in the hands of the medical system, I was on my own.

Dr. Stalin came into my room accompanied by a large number of nurses—including a couple of suspiciously burly types—and Dr. Velasquez. She flipped through my chart, reading such excerpts as she chose. She said as far as she was concerned I could read my chart whenever I wished. She still did not put the chart in my hands, but I took her at her word that I could examine the chart for myself later. Things calmed down. I asked that the Vicodin be changed to Naprosyn—another nonsteroid pain reliever and anti-inflammatory drug comparable in effect to ibuprofen. Eventually a nurse brought me some ibuprofen. Perhaps if I had asked for ibuprofen I would have got Naprosyn.

They were pumping Heparin into my body at an ever-increasing rate. Still my clotting time had not increased to the desired level, or so I was told.

By Tuesday night I was accustomed to the hospital routine. Dr. Stalin's apparent willingness to allow me to view my chart had reassured me that there was nothing in it of a diabolical nature. But it was time, so it seemed to me, to make a routine review of the chart. After all, I knew there were fictitious vital signs on my admitting chart. Every patient ought to make a routine review of his or her chart. Most patients, of course, will be in no position to make sense of the information in the chart. But anyone who will look carefully can spot a misfiled lab slip or report.

In many charting systems, lab slips are affixed to the chart so that they overlap. The results of the lab work are then available at a glance. But the name stamp on a slip is covered by the succeeding slips. Once the name stamp on a misfiled slip is covered by the next slip the chances of the error being discovered by the medical or clerical staff, applying their usual diligence, are vanishingly small. A patient who can do no more, can at least check to see that every piece of paper in the chart bears the correct name. This alone will enhance a patient's chances of survival. Patients who can do more for themselves should. One who can read medical orders should verify that the correct medications are supplied at the correct times, and so forth. So I called for my chart on Tuesday evening, suspecting nothing and desiring only to make a routine review.

The war began all over again.

Doctor Stalin was not in the hospital. Dr. Velasquez was. He claimed he would have to sit with me while I read the chart in case I encountered some medical terminology I did not understand. He claimed not to have the time to do that. I pointed out to him that the medical history I gave him had been written in medical terms and that we had always discussed things in medical terms. He knew I was perfectly familiar with medical language.

I pointed out that he had been in the room when Dr. Stalin had said I could look at the chart whenever I wanted. He claimed he had been called out of the room and had not heard her say that.

Of course he had not been called out of the room. I knew for a fact he was there. He was lying and I was certain of it. He had flimflammed me into agreeing to the HIV test; I had learned from Dr. Stalin that HIV status had nothing to do with the treatment of thrombophlebitis. And there was much else about my hospitalization that seemed to me vaguely dubious. But until Dr. Velasquez lied to me I had no real evidence that anything was amiss. The lie was a fact, and it renewed my suspicions that there was something in my chart that the staff did not want me to see.

A nurse had accompanied Dr. Velasquez into my room. She had been present for Dr. Stalin's remarks. The nurse corrected my recollection. Dr. Stalin had said, "As far as I am concerned you can look at your chart whenever you want." But, you see, it was not Dr. Stalin's concern. It wasn't up to her. The policy that prevented me from viewing my chart was a nursing policy. The director of nursing could not be bound by Dr. Stalin's remark.

I could think of no reasonable answer to this. Fortunately, Dr. Velasquez could not accept the nurse's argument—he could not admit the principle that a nursing policy could withstand a doctor's order to the contrary. As he insisted on this wedge, I calculated to drive it home.

I threatened to leave the hospital against medical advice. Dr. Velasquez asked if it would satisfy me to be allowed to view the chart for five minutes. I said it would. Dr. Velasquez said he would let me see the chart for five minutes after he had finished his rounds, which he expected to do within a quarter of an hour.

I was very pleased with this result. Evidently Dr. Velasquez had forgotten, if he ever knew, that I once had a job that entailed reviewing thirty charts in an hour. If there were a smoking gun in my chart, I could easily find it within five minutes.

Curiously, I never thought that anything the staff desired to conceal might be removed temporarily from my chart. In my job I had been thoroughly indoctrinated that nothing may ever be removed from a chart—even the most erroneous entry may be corrected only by a subsequent entry, and parts that must be corrected are struck out with a single thin line that leaves the error legible. Evidently the staff was as indoctrinated as I, for otherwise they might have brought my inquiries about my chart to an expedient conclusion.

Twenty minutes passed. When Dr. Velasquez returned to my

room he reported that he had talked to Dr. Stalin by telephone. The deal was off. I said I was leaving the hospital against medical advice. I asked that my infusion be discontinued. Dr. Velasquez said that it was up to me. He left my room. I called Billy to arrange a getaway car.

I stood. My leg hurt worse than ever. At least the Lasix had reduced the swelling in my ankle. I pulled on my pants and put on my shoes and got one arm into my shirt. I supposed that when Dr. Velasquez had said it was up to me, he meant it was up to me to remove my IV. I had to do so in order to get my shirt on. I hobbled down the hall and into the elevator.

The elevator doors closed. The elevator descended a few feet and lurched to a stop. Dr. Velasquez had gained control of the elevator system. The elevator returned to the landing and the doors opened.

Dr. Velasquez wanted me to sign the AMA (against medical advice) form. I told him I would sign nothing. He asked why I had discontinued the IV myself. I recalled to him that he had said it was up to me—but now I realized he had meant that as a response to my previous remark that I would leave the hospital and not to my request that the IV be discontinued.

When he at last released the elevator, he shouted at me that I could have a pulmonary embolism on the street. Although he had claimed to think I might be unable to interpret medical terminology, he knew I knew what a pulmonary embolism was.

Hospital security detained me in the lobby. They had no trouble doing so. I was barely able to walk. Besides, I knew they were not private guards, but city cops. My failure to obey their orders would be grounds for my arrest, and if I were arrested I might be returned to the hospital as a prisoner.

After a long time they let me go.

———

BILLY ARRIVED QUICKLY and whisked me away to his apartment. After a shower, not to mention the use of the toilet, I felt like a new man. Except for my leg. I had a good night's sleep on Billy's sofa. Lizbeth warmed my leg at least as well as it had been warmed by the hospital's heating pad. In the morning Billy returned Lizbeth and me to the park. Of course the things I had stashed there had been stolen.

That was Wednesday morning. I believed it very likely that I would die at any moment and considering the pain in my leg I almost hoped I would. I made a sign and slowly, painfully made my way back to the hospital. I concealed Lizbeth in a shady place in the park across the street from the hospital. I left her with her bag of food and a large bowl of water. It was the best I could do for her. I bade her a tearful farewell, for I believed I would die before I could return to her.

I picketed the hospital. The side of my sign that I kept toward the hospital building read, DEMAND TO READ YOUR CHART. The other side said something like, DR. STALIN DENIES PATIENTS' RIGHTS. I did not attract much attention. I did not expect to until I dropped dead.

After a couple of hours I could no longer put one foot in front of the other reliably. I made my way back to Lizbeth. Then in tears I called Billy.

With uncommon good grace Billy agreed to pick us up again. I got another good night's sleep at his place. Lizbeth, who had been on a hunger strike since we were first separated, began to eat again. Thursday morning things seemed very different. I did not, after all, want to die.

Billy saw the change in my attitude and revealed his plot to me. It was why he had so readily agreed to pick me up the day before.

He had called the hospital Wednesday and spoken to Dr. Stalin. She was, according to Billy's report, livid. She told him that I had a very serious medical condition. She was furious at Dr. Velasquez for allowing me to leave the hospital. She told Billy that she had arranged for a psychiatric SWAT team in the ER to be on the alert for me. If Billy could get some friends to wrestle me into the ER, the psychiatric SWAT team would then take custody of me and my life might yet be saved.

When I called him on Wednesday, he had seen it as very fortuitous, for he had not yet decided how he might lure me back to his apartment.

Tim was then in jail, but he was released to go to a job he had found at a nursing home. He was supposed to ride the city bus to work, but in fact he rode his motorcycle, which he kept hidden near the jail. The time he saved in transit—some two or three hours a day—he spent at Billy's apartment. Tim and Billy had discussed me and formed a plan. If Billy could get me to his apartment, he would wait until Tim was available. Then Billy would propose to go to Sleazy Sue's for a drink and would offer to take me too so I could check my mail. He knew it would be hopeless to try to wrestle me into the car, but if he got me into the car voluntarily he could go toward Sleazy Sue's by a route that brought us very near the hospital, and he hoped the ruse would stand up until I was brought to the door of the ER. Then he and Tim would wrestle me into the hands of the psychiatric SWAT team.

But this sort of deception does not come easily to Billy, and as soon as he perceived I was prepared to be reasonable he abandoned the plot.

Tim seemed relieved too. All evidence of his violent mood swings was gone. He seemed pleasant enough, and he had not looked forward to the prospect of trying to force me into the ER. I assumed he had got over his grief.

I let Billy drive me to the hospital.

It was fortunate that Billy and Tim had not attempted to realize their plan. When I arrived at the ER, there was no psychiatric

SWAT team. Had I been wrestled into the ER, the matter would not have been resolved neatly. Instead of a psychiatric SWAT team, I found a very reasonable and personable psychiatric resident. I told him he was supposed to be on the lookout for me, but he was baffled. Eventually he found a note about me, my name badly misspelled, amid a large number of notes on a bulletin board. "Jesus," he said, "I've told them over and over about this shit!"

He stepped behind a glass partition and had an animated telephone conversation with, as he told me later, Dr. Stalin. The conversation ended with his slamming the phone into its cradle.

He approached me in a calm and reassuring manner, very unlike the falsely reassuring and humoring manner I had come to expect in my ten years of working with psychiatrists.

I had never had a life-threatening thrombosis. I had clots in my veins, all right. But they were too small to pose a threat. This had been discovered when I went to the ultrasound lab, while I was still an ER patient and the decision to admit me to the hospital had not yet been made. That was the reason, as I had noticed at the time, that the ultrasound study had been repeated several times. They expected big clots but turned up only little ones.

I was not going to die. And I would have discovered this fact if I had read the ultrasound report in my chart. (Evidently the report had not yet been reduced to writing when I went over my ER chart.)

I had been admitted to the hospital because Dr. Velasquez wanted to work me up for a psychiatric commitment. In reading the ER chart, I had assumed the order for the psychiatric consult was routine for admissions from the street. But it was in fact the only reason for my admission. The tiny clots could have been treated on an outpatient basis.

Before I made any of my stupid remarks and unfunny jokes, before I refused to use the bedpan and refused to eat so that I could continue to refuse the bedpan, before I began to act suspicious of what might be in my chart, before all of it, I was pegged for a psychiatric case.

There had never been any medical reason I should not have used the bathroom. By insisting I not use the bathroom, the doctors had hoped to convince me that any attempt to leave the hospital would be fatal—they had hoped to restrain me by fear because they had no legal means of restraining me physically.

If, believing I had a life-threatening condition, I had now returned to the hospital treatment, then clearly I was not insane enough for involuntary commitment. If I had not returned, that would not necessarily have been evidence I was insane because there was plenty of evidence that I had perceived in some degree that I was being deceived.

The psychiatric resident had tried over and over to explain to the medical staff that they could not commit a person just because they disapproved of his way of life. Mine was not the first such case. Perhaps the medical staff could not learn their lesson. If I did have a mental illness, it appeared to be a largely iatrogenic one.

The psychiatric resident apologized and asked if I wanted further treatment for my leg.

I told him I realized my values were at variance with those of the society around me. Perhaps it would have been the normal thing for me to have my dog killed that I might obtain three nights' lodging. Perhaps a more normal person would steal or beg rather than dig through garbage for his sustenance. Perhaps I really was eccentric. But I did not think I was insane. And if I had no life-threatening condition, I desired to remain in the hospital not one second longer.

The psychiatric resident shook my hand and wished me well.

Billy had good news when he picked me up. His family had allowed him to cash a certificate of deposit his senile grandmother had put in his name. He would put me up until the tenth of September—for he figured he could not drink through the money before then.

He bought me a nice cane. I put my leg up and took aspirin. By the tenth of September I was well.

TEN

Alcohol, Drugs, and Insanity

There is no gainsaying that many homeless people are alcoholic or addicted to illicit drugs or insane. But I think the proportion of homeless people who belong to one or more of those categories is greatly overestimated.

This overestimation seems to stem from two otherwise opposing views. People who do not want to help the homeless seek to blame the homeless for being homeless. These people see alcoholism, drug addiction, and insanity as character flaws that somehow justify the condition of the homeless. This conservative line of thought is only one step removed from the conclusion that in addition to deserving homelessness, the homeless also deserve whatever mistreatment individuals or society may choose to mete out.

Those who wish to help the homeless, on the other hand, want to find a problem that can be fixed. Admittedly, alcoholism, drug addiction, and insanity are difficult problems, but something can be done about them. What is even better, for those who take the liberal view, is that what can be done for alcoholism, drug addiction, and insanity is likely to involve the creation of many jobs for social workers and administrators and other middle-class people. Although they find contradictory morals to it, both of these views subscribe more or less to a mythical history of the typical street wino. It is a myth that goes something like this: A man had a reasonably good job and reasonably happy home life. But he drank. At first it was only social drinking. But he drank more and more because he had either the disease of alcoholism or a character flaw that deprived him of the will to be sober, depending upon whether the myth is told in its liberal or its conservative version.

At any rate, he covered up his drinking for a while, but eventually everyone else realized he had a problem. Something dreadful happened at work, at home, or on the road, and the alcoholic had to admit, at last, that he might have a problem. Perhaps he tried one program or another, but without success because—as they say in the programs—he had not yet hit bottom. He lost his job, his family, and at last his home. And there he is, a wino clutching a brown sack, passed out in an alley.

Indeed, I met street winos who told this story of themselves. But in as many other cases I found the cause and the effect reversed: people who claimed to have drunk little or not at all until they became homeless.

Alcohol in some forms is cheap and readily available to people on the streets. The winos in El Paso favored Mogen David 20/20. In Austin, Wild Irish Rose was a favorite. The law in Texas requires a special license to sell wines with an alcohol content of more than fourteen percent, but every convenience store has one or two brands of wine that push as near this limit as possible. These products, of course, are not much sought after by oenophiles and are seldom served at intimate dinners. In Los Angeles, corner stores could sell liquor and I noticed the preference for wine was much less pronounced. For reasons I do not understand, malt liquor is favored in some black areas.

I do not propose to try to convince anyone that homeless people buy alcoholic beverages out of thirst, but many times when I could not find a water tap and had to buy something to drink, I noticed that whichever beer was on sale was cheaper than soft drinks or mineral water. I hope this will not be taken to imply that beer should be made more expensive, for my complaint is of the difficulty of finding nonalcoholic drink. When I could find it, distilled water was cheaper, but it would be found warm, on an out-of-the-way shelf, in unwieldy, unresealable plastic gallon bottles. Except that Lizbeth despises beer and I would not give a dog beer anyway, I am fairly sure I would have asked myself on several occasions: Why not get the beer?

Why not, indeed. Alcohol provides a sensation of warmth and well-being. In truth, alcohol can contribute to hypothermia in the winter and to dehydration in the summer, but many people, homeless and not, are unaware of this. Alcohol is a fair anesthetic and its sedative properties can produce sleep in restless circumstances. Alcohol induces the illusion of potency in the powerless—I can identify, but not quite understand, a nexus of alcoholism and issues of power, else why would so many politicians be alcoholic. In a life that seems utterly without meaning and purpose, the quest for the daily dose is something to do, is a reason to keep putting one foot in front of the other. Perhaps many people, perhaps all people, deceive themselves in some way or another to make it through the day, to the end of the quarter, to the closing of the fiscal year, to the season when the children leave for college. So a homeless person may become a wino by deceiving himself that paradise is at the bottom of the next jug.

If there were no alcohol, society would still have no use, no job, no home for the men, young and old, who sit on street corners with brown paper sacks. If the cities were filled with sober hopeless people, I doubt that the comfortable would find the results much to their liking.

So long as I had hopes of improving my position, I avoided other homeless people. I did not want to be acculturated to the street or resigned to my situation. Beyond this, I often avoided other homeless people because alcohol was the organizing principle of the street life I saw.

According to my observations, the homeless, aside from the whole families I saw in downtown Los Angeles, occur as loners, like me, or in pairs, or in groups of six to a dozen. Loners who were alcoholic tended to be in an advanced stage of alcoholism. When there was a pair, one of the pair was the star and the other was the sidekick, but I never detected any particular pattern of alcohol use among the pairs. There were also relatively stable groups of men who occupied more or less fixed areas. In some of the groups the men camped together. Eight seems to be near the optimal number of members in one of these groups— much larger groups, I surmise, would have been perceived as a threat to the peace. I never ran into such groups of men that alcohol was not present. Some of the men in these groups certainly were thoroughgoing alcoholics. But many others cared as much or more for the company. Whatever alcohol any one of them had was shared, and everyone was expected to drink. The men who seemed to care less for the alcohol tended to be younger, to have some gear, and to exhibit, usually, some sign of caring for their appearance. Also, sometimes they got drunk, whereas those whom I identified as alcoholics did most of the drinking but were hardly ever drunk.

The men in these groups shared with society at large the belief that every homeless man drank. As I refused to drink with them I could not gain any acceptance from these groups. Over the course of many weeks one man from one of these groups offered me drink whenever I met him. Time after time I refused; the last time he reacted as if I had insulted him. But then he reconsidered and asked, "Is it maybe that you do not drink?"

That was precisely the excuse I had always offered to him and the group. He had not thought it was anything but an excuse until just that moment. Then he explained: Since the assumption was that everyone drank, the only explanation of my refusing to accept a drink from him or from the common stock of the group was that I had some private store of alcohol I was unwilling to share. When individuals or groups refuse to drink with each other, it is a sure sign of deadly enmity between them.

I am certain that many members of these groups would be called social drinkers if they were not homeless. Indeed, they might be called social drinkers more accurately than better-off people, because the drinking group was the only society I found on the street. People in better circumstances can find many associations and activities that do not involve alcohol. On the streets one must drink, or at least pretend to drink, to have any company or entertainment at all.

Of course, some of the people on the street who begin drinking socially in the drinking groups will become alcoholics—just as some people who attend cocktail parties will. But a businessman returning from a three-martini lunch who sees a drinking group on the street is likely to think that every member of the group is alcoholic. That is not so, and furthermore, I think that many of the people on the street who are alcoholic are so as a consequence of being homeless. That is, in many cases, homelessness comes first and alcoholism second.

I lied, of course, when I told the groups and the man who tried to befriend me that I do not drink. I will take a drink when the circumstances seem to me appropriate. On the street I seldom found the circumstances appropriate. I found survival on the street challenging enough with a clear head; I never understood how the heavy drinkers got by.

If I had a secure camp and I found a half bottle of a good wine or two or three beers in a Dumpster, I would take them to camp to have with dinner or just before I turned in. I always had a better use for whatever small amount of cash I might get than to spend it on alcohol. Needless to say, when I did find two or three beers in a Dumpster it was really only two or three and not upward of a dozen, which is what some people mean by "a couple of beers."

I did find a considerable amount of liquor once—someone who was moving had discarded everything from a well-stocked bar, including a number of exotic liqueurs with unbroken seals. As it was late in a month, I called Billy and he gladly took the whole lot off my hands.

At one time I would have considered it hypocritical to refuse to drink with the groups on the street while I was willing to accept a rare cocktail in Sue's or to have a couple of beers in camp. But I have come to think that keeping up appearances is not altogether a matter of deceit. I was not, after all, an alcoholic. It was no deception to refuse to appear to be one. Mostly I did not want to give Mr. Three-Martini-Lunch an excuse to think himself better than I.

Many in the groups did not drink much more than I, at least not at one sitting—although most of them did drink every day, as I did not. That they did not care how they appeared to a society that was otherwise indifferent seems entirely understandable. One of the yuppie excuses for not giving money to panhandlers is that the money might be spent on liquor. Surely the money would not be put to a better purpose if it were donated to an agency and used to make a payment on a social worker's Volvo.

The truth is that the vices of the homeless do not much differ from the vices of the housed, but the homeless, unless they become saints, must pursue their vices in public.

Besides myself, I never knew a homeless person who would refuse marijuana. But I never saw more-addictive illicit drugs used by homeless people.

When I appeared in the university area, I was often approached by well-dressed students who wanted to buy "A" or "cid." I assumed these were two new drugs, which like XTC had appeared after I stopped experimenting with them. When I denied knowing what the students were talking about, they sometimes accused me of being disingenuous. Well they might, for eventually I realized or I was told that "A" plus "cid" is "acid," and I could be expected to know what LSD was. That the students were so bold in soliciting me for it led me to think that homeless people in the area supplied this drug.

When I met the drinking group in this area, I learned they did sell LSD, but my observations led me to believe that they sold LSD to raise money for wine and seldom or never used it themselves.

I gathered that those who used hard drugs usually were not homeless, but by trading in drugs themselves they usually had some accommodation, even if it were no more than a trashy shooting gallery. Of course, one can drink or even toke where shooting up would not be tolerated, so it is possible some people I met on the street concealed this activity from me, but I think I would have recognized the signs if that had happened often. Next to alcohol, illicit drugs were nothing among the homeless people I encountered.

As to myself, I am addicted to nicotine. The state asylum has adopted a smoke-free policy since I was compelled to resign. If I had been able to keep my job there, I am sure I would have lost it by now anyway for my dependence on tobacco. Nothing seems to go well unless I have caffeine. Like many other people in Austin,

I suffer from seasonal allergies and for them I take pseudoephedrine or phenylpropanolamine. The combination of caffeine, pseudoephedrine, and phenylpropanolamine is sometimes sold on the street for speed, but other antihistamines send me right to sleep.

I sometimes saved drugs I found in Dumpsters, but most of these were antibiotics or things of that sort that might be of value to someone who had no access to medical care, but that have no recreational potential. I think it unconscionable that poor people in the United States cannot buy such drugs over the counter, as they do in most other countries. I understand that society may not wish to provide poor people with medical care, but to make it illegal for the poor to care for themselves can only be attributed to society's spite or doctors' greed.

I saved two kinds of opiates. As my leg began to bother me I saved Vicodin in hopes of relieving the pain enough that I could continue to make my Dumpster rounds, or to take for my migraines if I ran out of ibuprofen. I have mentioned that dysentery was frequently a problem, so I saved Lomotil or paregoric when I was lucky enough to find it—over-the-counter medications for this problem are utterly ineffective. Not many sleeping pills, minor tranquilizers, or diet pills appeared in the Dumpsters, but I passed by those that did. I did not care for such things for myself, and although I knew some of them had a street value—just as I knew some of the other things I found could be hocked—I never thought of trying to sell them, by which I do not mean I thought better of it, but that the idea never occurred to me.

I had been an attendant at the state asylum in Austin for seven years, five of which I worked in the admissions office, and before that I had worked in a walk-in crisis center. I could recognize most of the chronic lunatics in the Austin area and I met many of them on the streets. A few of them recognized me, but for want of the proper context they rarely knew where they had met me before.

Moreover after some ten years' experience in the mental-health field, I could detect the symptoms of mental illness in many homeless people of whose histories I had no direct knowledge. The state asylum in Austin is a large institution that draws patients from a vast area. Often when patients are released they do not return whence they came. Austin is a liberal town and as good a place as any to be insane.

Most patients now are released from the state institution very quickly, but not because a rapid recovery has been effected.

In the 1970s a new strategy for dealing with the mentally ill was developed. It was thought that patients could be treated more efficiently, and more humanely, in their own communities. This seemed feasible because the most serious and the most common forms of mental illness responded well to drugs that were developed in the 1950s and the 1960s. The plan was to reduce the large central institutions and to establish many small clinics in the communities.

Whether this plan would have worked or not we will never know, for only half of it was implemented. The powers and resources of the central institutions were drastically reduced. But the community clinics were established in only a few places, and where they were established they were inadequate. Many communities did not want mental-health facilities right next door, although their being right next door, in touch with the neighborhoods, was a key aspect of the plan for the clinics. Breaking up the large institutions meant that economies of scale would have to be sacrificed, and neither the legislature nor the communities were willing to fund the clinics at a level that would have offered some chance for success.

To make matters worse, there were problems with the wonder drugs. They were so good in treating the disorders for which they were appropriate that they were often tried where they were inappropriate—in much the same way that penicillin was once

prescribed for viral disorders against which it could not possibly
be effective. If a little of the drug did not produce the desired result, physicians often increased the dosage. Inappropriate use of
the drugs often ended badly. But even when the drugs were prescribed appropriately, they produced some undesirable side effects. Patients won the right to refuse to take the drugs. Patients
who did not raise the issue of their rights often simply discontinued taking them.

Anyone who has had to take a medication for a chronic disorder will recognize the resentment one feels at having to do this
thing that other people need not do. Mental patients feel this resentment as much as anyone, and they as much as anyone can
deny they have the disorder and refuse to take the medication or
can conveniently forget to take it. In addition, I have always suspected that it feels good to be a little bit crazy. At least one person
has told me he tries to reduce his medication so that he can get
the good feeling of being a little bit crazy. Unfortunately, just a
little bit crazy is just crazy enough for him to believe he can do
without the medication altogether, which he cannot.

I do not believe that patients who discontinue their medications often do so for fear of the side effects. But the side effects,
though relatively minor, are real and are sometimes irreversible. A
reasonable person might conclude that the risk of the side effects
outweighed the benefits of the drug—or so thought the courts in
deciding that mental patients ought to be able to refuse the drugs.

But the idea of the community clinics was that patients would
take the drugs and would report to the clinics on an outpatient
basis for minor adjustments of dosage and such. The clinics were
supposed to have, at most, a few inpatients who would be stabi-
lized quickly and returned to their homes, families, and neighborhoods.

When the plan went smash, the central institutions no longer
had the capacity to handle large numbers of patients. As a result,

subacute mental patients must be discharged to the streets until they are again sufficiently ill to be readmitted to the central institutions. Unfortunately there is no solution so simple as refunding the central institutions. Many of the evils of the central institutions persist; abusive and neglectful habits are still inculcated in the staffs of such institutions. But the power to compel treatment, whereby the central institutions occasionally and haphazardly did some good, is gone. Moreover, while acute psychosis is a vivid and unmistakable phenomenon that presents a need for hospitalization, even involuntary hospitalization, that few observers would deny, the more common symptoms of mental illness are matters of degree and definition that in the question of involuntary hospitalization try the limits of human wisdom and justice.

Matilda Temple was a crazy woman who occupied very much the same territory that Lizbeth and I frequented. She was from a well-to-do family in a large Texas city. She came to Austin not as a mental patient, but as a student. Many schizophrenic disorders first manifest themselves in late adolescence or early adulthood. And so it was with Matilda. Her illness was a great shock for the family, but at first they were very supportive. They put her in the best private institutions, and whenever she was released the family would set her up anew with a nice apartment and a vehicle. But Matilda would not take her medication. After so many cycles of treatment and relapse, the family washed their hands of her.

As an admissions attendant I saw Matilda many times. Most often she was brought to admissions by law-enforcement officers— then she would be floridly psychotic and violent. Rarely she appeared voluntarily, when the weather was especially cold or her food stamps had run out—then she was less violent but just as psychotic.

In my latter years at the hospital I worked on a women's ward and had the opportunity of seeing Matilda when she was medicated. When medicated, she seemed as sane as anyone. She was an intelligent and strong-willed woman, with enough of a mean streak that it was clear to me that she was not drugged into a zombie-like state, but was for the nonce in her right mind. And she would say as much herself.

Of course, when I saw her on the streets again she was nuts. She talked nonsense constantly—anyone who has ridden a New York subway or the Hollywood bus in Los Angeles is likely to have heard this sort of talk, which mental-health workers call *word salad*. Fortunately, Matilda only rarely remembered that I had been her attendant, but it hardly mattered when she did, because she could not hold a thought for more than a few seconds. She usually carried a red sleeping bag with her and went from store to store begging for cigarettes.

Matilda slept on stoops and porches and sometimes on the pew at Ramblin' Red's—she got very upset with me when Lizbeth and I stayed too late on the pew. At night she screamed and shouted at imaginary people and monsters, and her threats to them were so graphic that she often alarmed people who did not know her.

Matilda received, at general delivery, an SSI check on the first of each month. Her allotment was not so generous as Dan Archer's, but with it she might have got a small apartment, and in the apartment she might have received food stamps. But she disposed of her check quickly. Sometimes she literally threw money away. Other times she gave it away. She would get four large carry-out pizzas or a gross of doughnuts, eat a little, and leave the rest on the ground to be claimed by the fire ants. She was a crazy woman and she did crazy things with money. In any event, the money would be gone by the third.

I describe Matilda's case in some detail because I know the most about it and because it is typical of the mental patients I encountered on the streets. (In particular, her sex is typical. In discussing alcohol I deliberately referred to men. I never saw a single woman in one of these groups. Very rarely a woman attended as the companion of a man in the group, and then she most often sat away from the circle. On the other hand, I seldom recognized insane men on the streets. A man as threatening and verbally abusive as Matilda would have been taken to jail. And I would guess some men kept themselves medicated with alcohol and camouflaged themselves among the drinking groups. Matilda sometimes drank a beer, but in general, the crazy women I saw did not drink. I cannot explain the difference.)

What should society do with Matilda?

By the time I saw her on the streets, she was no longer violent, although she could be threatening and verbally abusive. She had been through the state asylum so many times that they would not accept her as a voluntary patient. Yet, unless she was immediately dangerous to herself or others, she could not be committed involuntarily. When she was committed involuntarily she could be compelled to take her medication so long as she was violent, but precisely because the medications worked so well in her case she would cease to be violent almost as soon as she received her first dose. But then, because she would not take her medicine once she was allowed to refuse it, and her bed was needed for someone else, she would be discharged to the streets. She was obviously very unhappy on the streets, whereas when I had seen her medicated she had claimed to be quite content.

What may in justice be done for a person without his or her consent is a question treated in Platonic dialogues, yet for all the centuries passed since Socrates sought wisdom, it is a question I cannot answer.

Dr. Velasquez and Dr. Stalin did not mean to do me harm, but quite the contrary—or so I think when I am in a generous mood. Dr. Velasquez did not know whether I was mentally ill or not, and I do not think he believed he knew. What he did believe, that I know not to be so, was that the state asylum was a good place, that they would sort out my disorder if I had one, and that I would be better off for going there. He may also have known that by committing me to the state asylum, he could assure that the state would pay the costs of the treatment of my phlebitis. At any rate, I do not think he was wise enough to decide for me, and so I do not think I am wise enough to decide for Matilda.

I have heard psychiatrists say that anyone who is homeless is ipso facto a chronic schizophrenic unless there is some more evident diagnosis. By one school of thought it is a form of mental illness to be so much at variance with the commonly accepted values of one's society, and it was to this school the Soviets applied when they committed their political dissidents to mental institutions. By the criteria of homelessness and deviance, I was no doubt mentally ill.

But given my values I thought I was about as rational and consistent as anyone could claim to be. I was moody. But in my material situation I think it no wonder that I was sometimes depressed. The wonder was that much of the time I managed to buoy up my spirits.

On the streets, one day very quickly blurs into the rest, and without the checkpoints of ordinary conversation I sometimes found my mind had wandered far from the path of sound judgment. I counted myself as sane as I could be in my circumstances, but I am in no position to argue if this account leads anyone to another conclusion.

ELEVEN

On Institutional Parasitism

Strictly for my own amusement I began to compose a novel I called *Hoebecker's Diary.*

One of the winos had come by the pew one evening with a well-dressed drinking companion who told me he lived by going from hospital to hospital, masquerading as a doctor. I knew from my years of working at the state lunatic asylum that such a career was entirely feasible, and this occupation—I called it "institutional parasitism"—was to be one of the themes of my work of fiction.

My antecedents were Ellison's *Invisible Man* and Richard Wright's very similar short story "The Man Who Lived Underground." I suppose *The Phantom of the Opera* would be one too, but I didn't think of it at the time. At any rate, I thought a person might discover a niche in a large institution and survive there for a long time without coming to the notice of those who had legitimate places there.

I had seen malingerers at the asylum who very blatantly put the resources of the institution to their own purposes, and so did many of my coworkers—this was government work, after all. Hoebecker would sleep in unused wards. He would eat by ordering meals for inmates that did not exist and by pilfering food from the inmates' kitchen. He would do his laundry in the facilities provided for the inmates, and he would get new clothes when he needed them from stocks provided for inmates.

None of Hoebecker's misappropriations was anything out of the ordinary. Each was something I had seen attendants at the state asylum do; ordering extra meal trays to save the expense of lunch was especially common. Hoebecker would differ only in degree. He would obtain everything he needed from the asylum. Before the end he would not even bother to cash his paychecks. He would be a parasite.

Hoebecker, like the attendants he was modeled on and the malingerers, would begin with an official and legitimate role at the institution. Yet as I wrote I became more interested in the idea of an utter impostor—someone with no official connection to the institution—who might from the excess resources of the institution provide himself with all the necessities of life and even a few of the luxuries.

As the novel developed in my mind I wished I could have another interview with the impostor who had first planted the seed of the idea. Alas, he never returned.

I often sat up late at the pew, lost in the novel, and in the weeks I was absorbed with it I met Don.

I met Don through Alex, who had been my penultimate roommate in the little shack on Avenue B. Alex bore a grudge against me from that time, and he had walked by the pew with Don several times before he deigned to introduce us. In spite of the company he kept, I somehow formed the impression that Don was Burmese and a professor at the university, albeit an eccentric one.

Don was a squat, middle-aged, brown-skinned man. He seemed not entirely at home in English, but I could not detect a foreign accent—or perhaps he had a slight one I could not identify. He was very quiet when other people were present, seeming to devote all his concentration to observing the others. Between the two of us he was usually very talkative with occasional long lapses that I took for periods of profound thought.

I supposed Don was an academic of the field of social work and that Alex, whose situation was better than mine because he had attached himself to the social welfare system by virtue of being on probation for several offenses, was the subject of some practical experiment. Other times I suspected Don was a social anthropologist and I was his key native informant. Mistaken as my impressions proved to be, Don contributed to them by speaking of "cases" and "case histories." Alex certainly was Don's main case.

When Don had me to himself he would tell me in the manner of a shaggy-dog story all the minutiae of Alex's latest escapade. *Escapade* is too good a word. Don's stories simply recounted events as if approaching but never reaching a point: Alex borrowed five dollars from someone but did not repay the lender when he was able to do so; Alex said one evening he was going to look for a job the next day and he circled a number of help-wanted ads in the newspaper, but the following day he slept until noon and threw out the newspaper; someone came to the apartment and offered Alex a job, but he got drunk and overslept; Alex made some stuff of egg yolk and sage that he sold as hashish.

Don seemed to expect me to comment on stories of this kind, but I could never think of anything except to ask, "What did you expect?"

Most of Don's stories had less point than these. Perhaps he thought that having once allowed Alex to room with me I had some enduring interest in him and I would be pleased to hear of any news, however mundane, pertaining to him. Once he began, Don seldom spent less than an hour telling me of Alex. But after some weeks, Don did begin to talk to me a little of his other subject.

Don's other subject was his poetry.

I belabored my incapacity as a critic with the blessed result that I was only twice confronted with the wretched stuff. Perhaps Don's poetry was no worse than average; I am no judge. At any rate, had Don wanted criticism he could have got it from his little poetry group, a superficially civilized kind of literary snake pit. Since Don still spoke warmly of the group without expecting any member, I gathered none of them had taken him seriously enough to critique his poetry.

Don wanted his poetry to be published and he had heard I knew something of the writing business. In particular he wanted to know how much he should expect to pay to have his work published. I am always surprised at the number of people who believe that writers ought to pay publishers.

I explained publishing to Don as clearly as I could. He seemed never to understand what I was telling him. In many meetings with him I re-covered the same ground; I stressed that a promising work in a popular form might expect a vicissitudinous career, but the odds against poetry were very long indeed.

Don brought me a small ad he had torn from a magazine. The ad announced a poetry contest. The first three winners were to receive small cash prizes and the honorable-mention winners were to have their poems published in a beautifully bound book. Don proposed to enter the contest.

I pointed out the line in the ad that said winners might be required to purchase a copy of the book in order to have their poems published in it. Don saw this as no objection. He certainly would want to buy the book if his poem was printed in it.

I told him he would win an honorable mention. Unless it

contained language likely to shock the other subscribers, any poem entered in the contest would win an honorable mention. I said the society that placed the ad, contrary to what its name suggested, was not a philanthropic enterprise, but was a printing business that would print anything for money. Don sent for the brochure nonetheless.

The volumes depicted in the brochure did look impressive. They had leatherlike covers and gilt-edged pages. So far as I could tell from the brochure, the signatures were saddle-sewn. The endpapers were marbled. I marveled at this at first, but as Don got deeper into the scheme I understood it better. The books were not cheap; they were nearly forty dollars apiece. And they were fully subscribed before they went to press. Little wonder the printer could make both handsome books and handsome profits. The beauty of the books was the genius of it.

Anyone might think of this scam and might make some money at it by producing shoddy books as cheaply as possible. Many customers would be dissatisfied; some would ask for their money back or even complain to the postal authorities. Then, too, there would be the problem of turning up new suckers to keep the scheme afloat.

But if the books were beautiful, the printer could expect a brisk return custom. I thrill to see my words in print and all the more when the publication is well produced. I know the feeling and I can guess how much some people desire it. I know the desire to be published is but a spark and the desire to be published again is a flame.

The printer of the poetry books knew what I know. When the printer delivers a beautiful volume—fulfilling his only concrete promise to the poet—the poet will not want his money back. No investigation will turn up evidence of mail fraud. Far from being disappointed, the poet will surely want to enter the next contest. One such volume on a shelf cries out for companions.

What is more, suckers like Don tend to swim in schools. When one shows off his prize book, his envious rivals—including some who should know better—will not be able to rest until they have matched the achievement.

In attempting to dissuade Don from entering the contest, I took another tack. I asked him if he ever saw one of these books in a bookstore. He admitted he had not. But, he said, the contents of these volumes were too sublime for the grubby channels of commerce.

Aha, I said, then, you see, no one except the authors ever buys these books. No. He thought the great libraries subscribed.

I asked him if he had tried to find one of these books in the University of Texas library. That was a mistake on my part. The university's collections are nearly as indiscriminate as they are extensive.

Fortunately Don had not found any of this line of books in the library, but he found some that he thought similar. The printer took a name that might very well be like that of some nineteenth-century literary society and perhaps Don had found that society's annals.

In spite of my advice, Don sent off three poems, the limit, to the contest. In due course he received notice that two of the poems had won honorable mention. To see them both printed he had to purchase two copies of the anthology. That one of the poems was rejected answered any embryonic doubt I might have cultivated in his mind. It proved the publisher would not publish just anything.

Don sent a money order for the price of two books before he consulted me again.

Had I still believed Don to be a university professor I would have been less concerned. If he could afford his vanity, who was I to object to it? The books arrived. They were beautiful. Almost anyone who saw the books would have thought Don was a very accomplished poet.

But I had begun to suspect that Don was not a professor.

He rebuffed all my inquiries about his situation. Nonetheless, I gathered that the amount he sent the publisher was in his estimation a very substantial sum. Worse, he was counting on royalties.

Perhaps the printer inserted a clause in the publishing contract that suggested to him this possibility. Publishing contracts tend to devote many paragraphs to divvying up the proceeds of rights that are merely hypothetical. However he came by the idea, Don thought it very likely that this book—too sublime for the grubby channels of commerce—would be in such demand beyond its subscribers that his hundredth part of the royalties would provide him a considerable income. Don thought the price of the books was an investment.

When I understood this, my first impulse was to stone him to death on the spot. But with the thought that Don was unlikely at his age to reproduce, I restrained myself. The printer had a live one and he knew it.

He offered Don the chance of buying a certificate to celebrate his honorable mention in the poetry contest. Don sprang for that. Although it cost almost as much as one of the books, the certificate when it arrived proved not to be of the same quality as the books. It was the most ordinary sort of thing, like the certificates given out in grade school according to categories carefully manipulated to ensure that each child gets at least one.

I could see that Don was disappointed in the certificate. But he did not exercise his option of returning it for a refund. I believe he was afraid of alienating his publisher. Seeing he had hardly tried Don's credulity, the printer flooded him with solicitations.

Don had sent his best work to the contest. After it had been rejected, he began to perceive serious flaws in the poem the publisher had returned. Despite my protests, he was determined to enlist my aid in resurrecting the work. I developed headaches and

suddenly remembered previous engagements. Still I was subjected to the thing in its vile entirety twice. Don was threatening
to read me more revisions of the poem when relief arrived from
an unexpected quarter.

Don received a note from the printer. The poem had not been
rejected for lack of merit, so the note said, but only because its
theme seemed not to fit that volume. The printer was compiling
a special new anthology, not related to any contest, but composed
of very special poems by an elite selection of the very best poets
who had entered previous contests. Naturally enough, the printer
thought of Don and recalled his beautiful poem, which had not
seemed quite right for the contest volume.

The new anthology, while quite as elegant as the contest volumes, was to have a distinctive appearance so that anyone could
see that it was an honor above and beyond that of the contest series. But the truly remarkable thing was that if Don acted promptly
his poem might appear in the new anthology and his investment
would be no greater than that required for an ordinary contest
volume.

Don spoke no more of the flaws he had supposed he perceived
in the rejected poem. Evidently after he showed his contest volume to his little poetry group, several of the other members entered the printer's subsequent contests. Naturally the other members
won honorable mentions, but their books had yet to go to press.
Publication in the special anthology would keep Don a step ahead
of them.

According to Don, there were also in the group a few cynics,
like me, who raised the same objections to this form of publication in less gentle terms than I had employed. They were, Don
assured me, just jealous because they could get published, if at all,
only in cheap-looking little chapbooks. In any event, the new anthology would answer them because it could not be mistaken for
the contest volumes they had criticized.

Don admitted he would have to sacrifice to afford the new book, but he was determined to do so. By that time I sympathized with the printer. I had come to think the printer would treat Don's money with more respect than Don showed it. I could no more condemn the printer than I could condemn the lioness for her method of getting lunch.

In the meanwhile I had learned more about Don, all of it from his own lips, but in sum I think it was more than he meant for me to know.

He never was a professor and had never been involved in any recognized academic work. From time to time he held various menial jobs, some of them at the university. Whether he discovered accidentally that he had the image of an absentminded professor or whether it was an image he had deliberately created, I do not know. But I was not alone in having had a mistaken first impression of him. The university police, librarians, lab assistants, students, genuine professors—all took Don for an academic.

He made the most of it. He had the run of the university. He avoided the most secure areas, where everyone is challenged routinely, but he had no use for such places anyway.

Don had keys. The university has an elaborate hierarchy of passkeys with master keys, grand-master keys, and keys of many intermediate and lesser degrees. The loss of a grandmaster key is a catastrophe, for if it cannot be brought to account, many thousands of locks must be changed. Don's keys were reckoned to be of too low an order to justify the expense of changing the affected locks. Still, the wholes of several buildings and parts of many others were at his command. Perhaps if he had taken great advantage of the situation, the locks would have been changed. But he did not and they were not.

He lived at the university for a long time.

He could do his laundry in any of the dormitories. He could pilfer the coffee funds for change in any of a number of offices.

Most of the departments had refrigerators and these would always contain forgotten lunches and the remains of various party trays brought for one little office party or another. No one would miss any of these things. Almost all of the conference rooms and coffee rooms were within range of Don's keys when they were locked at all. He never had to take too much from any one place.

He showered at the gym. This was remarkable because the university had greatly increased security there in the years since I had been a student. Then the gym had been more or less a public facility. Hippies and Austin businessmen alike had used the gym as if it were an extension of a public park. But security had been tightened to the point that recently graduated varsity athletes were sometimes detected, apprehended, and arrested for using the gym without the proper credentials. Don was never challenged.

Graduate students contend sharply for carrels, but many want them only as a matter of status. Don's keys commanded all of the carrels. When he found one that was unused he kept his few things there.

At night he could sleep on a sofa in any office that was convenient. If he wanted to sleep in the daytime, he slept on a sofa in the student union. Students often napped in the union and homeless people had done the same until their numbers gave rise to complaints. Security officers had since been on the alert to roust the homeless from the union, but apparently Don could create his professorial impression even as he slept. In any event, he was not bothered when he slept there.

Offices contain equipment and supplies. Either Don supposed that stealing the equipment for resale would raise suspicions or the idea of doing so never occurred to him; I would guess the latter. As for taking the equipment for his own use, why should he do so? Where would he take it? Once he became a poet, he used the typewriters and copiers and the various related supplies. But there was no point in removing anything; one office was as much home to him as any other. Most of this I guessed bit by bit. Don would say he had been working late the night before and had slept in a certain office, allowing me to infer that had he been less tired he would have gone home. He would say he had become overcome with fatigue and had taken a nap in the union. He would say he had typed a poem on a typewriter he had found in this office or that, implying he had been in such a frenzy of inspiration that he feared his poem would evaporate by the time he reached his own machine. And so on through the rest of it: he happened to find it convenient to do his laundry at a particular dormitory; he happened to tap a coffee fund for a few quarters, as if it were the one in his office and he had contributed to it; he happened to shower at the gym, as if it were only a matter of convenience.

After many interviews I began to understand. Sometimes he slept in one office; sometimes he slept in another. But always he slept in some office. Sometimes he typed at one unattended typewriter; sometimes at another. He had no typewriter of his own. He happened to shower at the gym because it happened to be the only place he ever did shower.

Don had become in fact an institutional parasite of the kind I was then trying to create in fiction, but I came to realize this only in retrospect. At the time, he seemed an interruption, often an annoying one. And of course for a long time much of what I have just related concerning his relation to the university was only my surmise.

Don finally confirmed my surmises, filled in a few of the details, and told me much I had not guessed in a single conversation. He had come to believe he belonged to an arcane community of scholars. The members of this esoteric brotherhood comprised the true University, as opposed to the apparent university, which was composed of various sophists, charlatans, bureaucrats, and hacks. Unfortunately these latter were vested with temporal authority at the university and the true scholars were reduced to skulking about as Don did. This unsatisfactory arrangement existed at all the great universities: at Harvard and Yale, of course, but also at Oxford, Heidelberg, the Sorbonne, and so on. The situation would be reversed sooner or later, but until then the brotherhood of true scholars contented itself with nourishing the flickering flame of true learning.

Apparently Don was the only member of his fraternity who was assigned to the University of Texas; his was a lonely outpost indeed.

At last Don ran afoul of an actual professor who was even crazier than he. The actual professor, although tenured, was so terrified of the spies he supposed his academic rivals would employ that he resorted to taking attendance in a lecture class of five hundred souls. He took attendance so carefully that he detected Don's unauthorized presence—Don often attended classes and other university activities in spite of his enmity for the sophists in charge. The actual professor summoned the university police to apprehend Don. When the police arrived, Don surely would have emerged unscathed if he had assumed an apologetic attitude. Attending classes without the permission of the instructor is an infraction of the university's rules, but permission is commonly taken for granted. The rule is almost never enforced in large lecture classes unless there is a serious disruption. If they had even heard of the rule the professor was invoking, the police would have thought him peculiar for raising the issue and their sympathies would have been with Don had he agreed to leave quietly.

But Don finally had encountered all of the sophists and charlatans that he could withstand. Loudly, so that the surrounding students could learn the truth, he began to explain about the brotherhood, the true University and the false, the natural rights of true scholars and the abuses they suffer from the hacks and sophists, and a great deal more. Once he began to vent these views, Don could hardly shut up, and thus that evening I learned what I have just recounted.

After this incident the university police were on the lookout for Don, but they seldom managed to interfere with him. They had not discovered his passkey and had not understood, evidently, the extent of his use of university facilities. Nonetheless Don began to lose interest in the university and spent less and less time there.

For a while he slept in a car that was parked in the university area. The car was inoperable, but Don did have title to it. The city police made him stop sleeping in the car and he was irate that they could thus limit his enjoyment of his property. After that the car was stripped and left on blocks. Don believed the police were less than diligent in investigating this crime. He suspected the sophists and charlatans at the university had corrupted the civil authorities to the end of discouraging him as much as possible. The city removed what was left of the car and this confirmed his suspicions.

The car was taken away just as Don managed to find the money to send to the printer for the special new anthology. As the poem for that volume had proved perfect after all, he no longer wanted my services as a critic. I saw less and less of him.

I saw him about the neighborhood at dawn and late at night. When he did stop to talk to me, he talked mostly, as he had before, of things Alex had done. I gathered he often slept at Alex's.

Eventually I learned that after Don had been put out of his car, he had begun camping in various shacks and outbuildings on the alleys in the university area. Many old houses in this area have been rehabilitated and are rented to students. But as often as not a storage shed or garage on the property is allowed to ruin. The students seldom attempt to make any use of these unsightly and unsound structures. So Don had been undisturbed for a long time and had begun to think he had a right to his lodgings.

When he was at last discovered he raised such a fuss that property owners and the police were put on notice and he was turned out of several shacks in succession. By this time, although I had known Don to take a drink in the past, he was now very obviously and thoroughly drunk whenever I saw him, and after a while I saw him no more.

TWELVE

Eviction

Many omens preceded our eviction from Adams Park. These were, like many an oracle, more intelligible in retrospect. Several nights someone, or perhaps there were two of them, threw firecrackers at our bedroll. These episodes were accompanied by much rustling in the bushes. Several times I thought, by observing the rustle of leaves and the snapping of twigs, that I had located the culprit, only to hear a war whoop from the opposite side of the park. These events had many of the qualities of a nightmare, except that in the morning I would find the unexploded duds and the bits of wadding from the charges that had exploded. I supposed they were college boys from one of the nearby apartments. After successive nights of attacks, I made dummy lumps to represent Lizbeth and me in our bedroll and we sat up in the bushes most of the night. I learned nothing from this ruse, but the night raids stopped altogether soon afterward.

An alcoholic couple hauled a mattress into the park. I had seen it standing beside a Dumpster but had not thought of any way of concealing it in the park. The couple, however, did not bother to conceal the mattress. They camped on it in plain sight, night and day. The woman went to the convenience store for alcohol each morning as soon as she could lawfully buy it. On Sunday when they could not buy alcohol before noon they suffered audibly. They supported their habit by selling food stamps, which, since they were homeless, they must have obtained fraudulently.

Homeless people were fleeing the Northern cities in advance of winter, and by this time perhaps a half-dozen men were sleeping in scattered parts of the park. Aside from the wino couple, most of the rest of us left the park in the daylight hours, or if we did not leave we made some effort at maintaining appearances.

The most ominous change was that the private school on the bluff that overlooked the park began its fall semester.

In some respects Austin seems a liberal town. It is not altogether so. It was one of the last cities in Texas to integrate its schools. When integration came at last, a large number of private schools were established. These were not the crude lily-white academies of the Deep South. Many of the schools were quite good, and the strategy of the schools was to admit one or two token minority students, from selected families, to each class. Since the public schools had remained essentially segregated for so long, by the time the private schools were thought necessary, land was scarce. Few of the private schools could afford a sizable campus with athletic fields. A private school simply adopted the nearest public park as its own.

And so it was in Adams Park.

Every hour of the school day, instructors descended from the bluff with their classes in tow. They commandeered whichever court or field they pleased. They called roll, they organized the games, and they made notations on their clipboards. It was not just supervised play, but the private school used the park as a part of its regular course of instruction.

Several afternoons I returned to the park to discover the place occupied by classes from the school. I did not give the situation much thought at first, but it did seem to me that by giving the schools the use of the parks, the city was winking at the white-flight schools. With some regard for the likely range of a softball, I laid a single blanket on the ground, as picnickers did, and worked on my novel.

As it happened the police caught me abed. I had got little sleep in the night, but had closed my eyes about dawn and stayed in my bedroll later than usual. That was not really so very late. The police came at seven or seven-thirty, and I had just woke up.

I came to believe that the police had planned this raid in advance and that they meant to get me in particular. Yet if this is true, the police had faulty intelligence because on any other day I would have been gone by the time they arrived.

They were mounted police.

In Austin the mounted police are composed exclusively of volunteers from the police ranks who own their own horses and board them at their own expense. This arrangement tends to overrepresent, in the mounted force, officers who have seen a few too many cowboy movies.

I was sitting on the bedroll when they came near. The first officer demanded to know who was with me. In fact, a young man I had met at the pew had spent the night with me. I doubted that was the reason for any complaint there might have been against me. True enough, I had brought young men to the park in recent weeks and one night there had been three of us, but I thought our love-making had been reasonably discreet in comparison to that of the wino couple and of the young people from nearby apartments who sometimes came to the park at night. But the young man who had been with me left in the dark before dawn. I replied that no one was with me.

The officer indicated a largish lump in the bedroll. I pulled back the cover to reveal Lizbeth, who strange to say had remained asleep thus far. She did not remain asleep for long, and taking the horse for a big dog, she hopped up and barked and strained at her leash. Although it was evident she was tied securely to a tree, the officer drew his weapon.

Curfew had expired at 5:00 A.M. and the officers had not found me asleep. I thought I was in the clear.

While the officer who had drawn his weapon detained me, his companion rode up the bluff, directly to my stash of gear in the bushes. He must have been informed of its location, for it was not obvious and he spent no time looking for it.

I was ordered to leave the park and never to return. That, I knew, was quite beyond the officer's legitimate authority. If he could have connected me with the stash in the bushes, he might have charged me with dumping or something of the sort. Instead he lectured me on sleeping in a public place and could come up with nothing better when I pointed out to him he had no evidence that I was sleeping. I hoped he might give me a clue as to the source of the complaint against me, for I had observed that the police had seemed to have singled me out.

I learned nothing. The officers left the park without bothering anyone else, although they had to ride past the wino couple, who on their mattress were about a bottle-and-a-half into breakfast.

Perhaps the officers meant only to make an example of me. Against that is that the police seemed to know where the rest of my gear was stashed and that the wino couple stayed at least a few more weeks in the park without being bothered. I do not know who might have been observing me closely enough to notice the sex of my bedfellows, and I cannot think of any other reason that the police would want to bother me while leaving the others unmolested, but I think that they did come to the park to annoy me in particular.

My stash in the bushes had been scattered and trod on by the horse. Most of my stuff was common geegaws from Dumpsters. But Lizbeth's large bag of dog food—since my leg trouble I had always tried to keep a reserve for her—was a total loss.

If the police knew where to look for me in Adams Park, the game was up. I had no intention of trying to remain there. Indeed, I had not intended to stay so long as I had, for my first plan had been to move fairly often. At first I kept my eyes open for new campsites. But I had not moved because I did not want to poison another area if I could avoid it.

I gathered up as much of our gear as could be salvaged, and Lizbeth and I moved to a place I called the Triangle. One side of the Triangle was a very high, very steep bluff, another was a creeklet that prevented mowing machines from getting at the Triangle—and which, I thought, a horse could not jump for want of a sufficient landing area—and the third side was a large boulevard with fast traffic that made a pedestrian approach from that direction unlikely. Here between the limbs of a horizontal oak we camped through the fall and into the winter.

AS FALL PROGRESSED, the migrant homeless—the snowbirds—returned to Austin from their summer habitats. So long as I stuck to my orbit, from my new camp to the pew at Ramblin' Red's and around to the Dumpsters near the pew, I saw little of them, perhaps because Lizbeth and I occupied the pew so regularly and so completely or perhaps because the panhandling was better elsewhere.

The cause of the homeless was fashionable; it was a presidential election year. Some group of purportedly homeless people had adopted a goose and named it, of course, Homer. From time to time they threatened to eat Homer in order to dramatize their plight. I do not know whether Homer was eaten, but only that after he attended the Democratic national convention in Atlanta he dropped out of sight. Some activists built a flotilla of ramshackle houseboats which were painted in gaudy slogans and launched on Town Lake, which is what the Texas Colorado River is called in downtown Austin. Some homeless people supposedly lived in the houseboats, despite the questionable seaworthiness of the craft and their lack of sanitary facilities.

This last proved to be a divisive point. The Liberals—who wished to dramatize homelessness—rather overlapped the Environmentalists—who objected to people's defecating in the river. The houseboats violated a number of ordinances, but the civic authorities hesitated to create a cause célèbre. The university, however, could be relied upon to be less discreet.

The university had exercised its eminent domain to condemn several blocks of shacks in a black neighborhood east of campus. The shacks were shoddy and the university was certain to raze them, but for the nonce they were boarded up. Some activists, possibly including a few genuinely homeless people, removed the boards and moved into several of the shacks.

Whether to save trees or houses, people lying in front of bulldozers is a traditional theme of Austin political demonstrations, and—as it seemed easier than attempting to police the area—the university soon obliged by sending in the bulldozers.

Thus the activists had the illustration they wanted of their cause: Here was the university destroying affordable housing just as homelessness was becoming more apparent on Austin's streets and just as the issue of homelessness was beginning to penetrate Austin's middle-level-bureaucrat mentality. Of course the people the university had displaced were all black and the new squatters, to judge from the photographs in the newspaper, were white. Moreover I never saw anyone in the photos whom I recognized from the street. The people I recognized were the usual gang of semiprofessional spokespersons who seem always to be in the forefront of whatever issue is hot.

I had been in Austin for a long time. I knew what an Austin political movement was. This knowledge put me off having anything to do with the homeless movement. But I was curious about other homeless people.

Before I became homeless, I had a vague interest in astronomy. Once I was sleeping under the stars, I could not learn enough about them. Similarly, I thought it a shame to be well situated to learn of other homeless people and to neglect to try to do so. Besides being intellectually curious, I thought I might acquire some practical skills from them. I believed I got by as well as any homeless person might, but I was not smug.

I had discovered I could learn nothing of value from social workers. Social workers, after all, never try to use the systems they establish and operate. I thought that perhaps I would have better luck in learning the skills of homelessness from the homeless. I could not believe I was the only sober and reasonably sane homeless person; there had to be others whose society I might enjoy.

I read in the daily newspaper that some of the homeless could be found at the Renaissance Market near the university. When I was in college many hippies hung out in that area, but being a hippie of no particular address in 1970 was very different from being homeless in 1988. Before, during, and after the hippies, a band of panhandling winos frequented the market. If they were who the paper meant, I did not think I was especially interested in meeting them.

I had not been to the market in a long time, and years had passed since I observed it any longer than I required to pass through. On the remote chance that the newspaper had reported something really new, I resolved to go there.

One day I found the pew at Ramblin' Reds occupied by snow-birds who seemed to have settled in. I thought it was as good a time as any to take Lizbeth to the Renaissance Market to see what I could learn of the homeless people there.

The Christmas season was still sufficiently remote that only a few of the spaces were occupied by vendors. Lizbeth and I sat on a bench that had been erected around one of the planters. I remembered the tree in the planter as a sapling. But it had grown up so that Lizbeth and I were quite in the shade.

Austin was having a bit of a Sixties revival. I was amused to see the tie-dyed T-shirts being offered by one of the vendors; the dyes were very much brighter than anything I remembered see-ing in the Sixties. I supposed the colors were fast, too. Either because they had always dressed that way, or to capitalize on the return of the fashion, many of the vendors were dressed as hip-pies. I did not look so out of place, I thought, for I was anticipating cold weather by letting my hair and beard grow.

The Renaissance Market had begun in the late Sixties when hippies had sold love beads, tie-dyed T-shirts, sandcast candles, and similar things on the sidewalks near the university. The side-walks had become crowded and the established merchants had objected.

The issue posed perplexing dilemmas on all sides. Leftists tended to side with the vendors but wanted an ideological basis for preferring one sort of capitalist to another. Conservatives gen-erally sided with the merchants, but that flew in the face of their entrepreneurial myths. What settled the issue was that the mar-ket quickly became a tourist attraction, and in Austin politics there is no sacred cow save tourism.

A more-or-less useless cross street was converted to a market square. At first it was called the People's Market and it had many of the qualities of the so-called liberated zones of the time. The years went by.

The rules of the market changed to eliminate jobbers—that is, middlemen who did not produce the goods they offered. To reflect this change in the market's rules, the name was changed to the People's Renaissance Market. Those vendors who were successful began to have proprietary feelings about the market. Licensing requirements were stiffened, fees were raised, and a commission was established to examine the artisans and the products they intended to offer. The number of licenses was limited. The illusion that anyone could make things and expect the chance to sell them at the market was dispelled. The word *People's* was dropped from the name.

I had not grasped what the changes in the policies of the market might mean in practice, but I was soon to find out. Almost as soon as Lizbeth and I sat down, the vendors' enforcer, whom I call Mr. Two Dogs, noticed us and asked me to leave. The market is, legally, a public park. I declined Mr. Two Dogs' request. Mr. Two Dogs said that if I did not leave he would summon the police. I thought that very unlikely but replied only that I had nothing to fear from the police. When Mr. Two Dogs returned to his dogs, they greeted him by cowering and flinching.

Thereafter when I was in the market I made a point of observing Mr. Two Dogs closely. He was not a vendor himself—not an official vendor. He sold drugs, but he was very discreet and selective in his clientele. Evidently the vendors granted him this exclusive concession in exchange for his services in expelling undesirables, a class that seemed to include me. At any rate, Mr. Two Dogs enjoyed the vendors' confidence and he would be asked to sit at a table if its proprietor had to be away to get lunch or use the rest room.

Students solicited me for drugs but had better luck with a drinking group that was seated in a more remote part of the market. Allowing for the usual turnover in personnel, these were the panhandlers and winos who had been in this area for years. They evidently were the homeless people the newspaper had discovered.

At first I thought the winos were far enough away to be beyond Mr. Two Dogs' jurisdiction. A park patrol car cruised up the alley that bisects the market. The park patrol have brown uniforms, but their cars look like ordinary police cars except that the car numbers are prefixed with a *P*. The park patrol seemed to take no notice of the winos. And it was the same when the blue-uniformed foot patrol that polices the university area came through.

Presently, however, a patrol car on the Drag, as Guadalupe Street is called in this area, stopped at the market. The officers got out of their car and had a small conference with Mr. Two Dogs and one of the vendors. Mr. Two Dogs pointed first at me and then at the group of winos. The officers came toward me. I was not especially alarmed. I had done nothing wrong and if the officers spoke to me they would perceive I was sober. Lizbeth barked fiercely as the officers approached. They walked past us. The winos were not so fortunate.

The officers shook down the winos but did not find the contraband. Nonetheless they arrested three of the winos and manhandled their prisoners as much as circumstances might permit. The officers left without molesting me.

I remained where I had been sitting long enough to show Mr. Two Dogs that I was not intimidated. Then I joined the winos to learn what had occurred.

The three were arrested for public intoxication. If not entirely without foundation, the charge was reckoned by all present to be a bum rap. Public intoxication is a charge usually reserved for persons found unconscious or for the passengers in a car when the driver is arrested for drunk driving, in order to prevent the passengers' trying to drive the vehicle.

None of the three arrested appeared especially intoxicated,

certainly no more than any of their fellows. I was told the arrests occurred daily. The choice of whom to arrest, so far as any of my informants could tell, was arbitrary.

The park patrol and the foot patrol never gave the winos any trouble unless someone really was out of line. Little or no effort was made to enforce the drug laws. But sometimes someone would be careless enough that the drugs would be detected on his person. With a drug so easily concealed as LSD, the winos admitted, to be caught was criminal stupidity and they reckoned it only just that the party be arrested in that case.

(That this sort of stupidity came to light so often was owing, I would guess, to the duller members of the group being cat's-paws of the sharper ones. The dumb one always held the drugs and had little or no stake in the proceeds. When I questioned one of the dumb ones out of earshot of the others, I learned he thought of holding the drugs as doing a small favor for an admired friend.)

The group reckoned it fair, too, if the cops were to employ undercover agents. This had never happened to anyone in this group and they figured the police had better things to do with their undercover men.

But the public intoxication charges were bullshit. Everyone I talked to explicitly denied caring much whether he went to jail or not—it was a given in their lives that they would spend some time there. That part of their way of life was not especially pleasant, but it might be said, almost, that going to jail for a few weeks had its advantages.

Unfortunately public intoxication entailed only four hours in jail. The prisoner would not get his laundry done and probably would not get a shower or a meal. He would not get a medical or dental examination. He would not get as much as one night's sleep. He would be released downtown, far from his friends. It was all hassle and no payoff.

Had the officers on the beat been especially tough and made

the public intoxication charges a matter of policy, the winos would not have liked it but would have had to accept it as a matter of fact. The galling thing was that the cops who made the arrests were off their beat. That was the reason they took three prisoners, or so said my informants. Three would fit in the back of a patrol car. More would have required the officers to summon a paddy wagon, and that would have raised the questions of what the officers were doing so far from their appointed area and of why they had not consulted the officers assigned to the market area.

The answer to those questions, according to the winos, was that one of the officers who made the arrests was the brother-in-law of one of the vendors. The vendors wanted the winos out of the market.

The officers assigned to the market area—the park patrol and the foot patrol—had been disinclined to put themselves at the vendors' disposal. Perhaps the officers thought the vendors little better than the winos, or they had enough legitimate complaints to deal with, or perhaps it was their policy to leave well enough alone. However it was, the winos had no complaint of the officers on the beat.

The winos said the public intoxication arrests were examples of private law enforcement.

I had won the winos' confidence by telling them of my eviction from Adams Park. They sympathized. They said the mounted police were the worst. They told me they had never heard of a mounted patrol so far north, and that was in agreement with my belief that the mounted police had been off their beat.

The winos suggested that I had experienced another example of private law enforcement: Somebody at the school on the bluff had used private connections to encourage the mounted police to sweep through Adams Park—perhaps one of the officers had a child in the school, or perhaps the owner of a restaurant that abutted the park, though his establishment was out of sight of my place in the park, had been consulted and had used his influence, for he had once been a policeman and was very popular among his former colleagues.

I always suspected something of the sort. That the winos reached the same conclusion independently encouraged my suspicions. The police dispose of poor people however they will, on a whim, as a favor, and the officers know they will never answer for anything they do so long as their victims are not fortunate enough to afford a lawyer.

It is a crime to be poor, so the winos said. So it is, for it is a crime to sleep in a public place and a crime to trespass to sleep in a private place. But more than that, to be poor is to be subject utterly to the agents of the law. This as much as anything, I think, is what a middle-class person fails to appreciate about being poor. A middle-class man may want to avoid being stopped for speeding in his BMW, but if he is stopped he sees a face of the law very different from the face shown to the poor. The traffic officer who stops a man in a BMW knows the man's sister might be a lawyer, the man himself might be a lawyer, at any rate the man has the resources to make trouble if he is dealt with unfairly. Middle-class people have rights and they like to think that everyone does. The rich, of course, know that rights are bought and sold, and the poor know it too. Those between them live in an illusion.

The winos told me I had been fortunate to be in the park when the officers arrived. Otherwise my gear would have been seized and anything left loose would have been torn up. They said the police often did such things. Opinions differed as to what the police did with the things they took. Some said the officers went through things and took for themselves anything they wanted. Others thought the gear was searched to gather intelligence about the owner. The Fourth Amendment of the Constitution, of course, applies only to people who have homes. The third opinion was that the police just did this for fun and they disposed of the gear in some remote place.

I returned to the market on several days. All that the winos had told me about their arrests seemed to be true. The park patrol and the foot patrol came to the market and never bothered the winos except to say a few words, and as often as not these appeared to be congenial exchanges. Day after day the other officers came, parked their patrol car on Guadalupe, and conversed with the vendor who was supposed to be the sister-in-law of one of them. Mr. Two Dogs tried to insinuate himself in these conversations and volunteered many opinions, but clearly he was superfluous to the proceedings. The officers would arrest three winos and depart.

Once I was convinced of the winos case, I wrote a crank letter to *The Austin Grackle*. My letter brought a sharp reply. The vendors denied nothing. Instead they excused themselves on the grounds that the winos dealt drugs, looked disreputable, smelled bad, and offended potential customers.

All of these were precisely the complaints the established merchants had had against the original vendors.

THIRTEEN

Daniel

One evening at dusk a young man approached the pew and called Lizbeth by name. I did not recognize him and I did not know how he came to know my dog's name.

He explained that he had roomed with Jerry. Lizbeth was supposed to have been Jerry's dog. He adopted her when he lived with me at the shack on Avenue B, and when he moved out he woke me from a nap to say that he could not afford a pet deposit at his new apartment, but he would take Lizbeth to be destroyed if that was what I wanted.

Jerry now lived somewhere that Lizbeth and I passed often. He had pointed us out to this young man. In fact, the young man said, he had just come from Jerry's place. He had hoped to spend the night there, but Jerry had not come to the door. Whether Jerry was avoiding him or was sleeping, the young man did not know. Jerry is a sound sleeper.

The young man told me his name was Daniel. Lately he had

been staying at an apartment he had supposedly vacated. The manager had not changed the lock and Daniel had been letting himself in with a duplicate key. But at last Daniel had been discovered and he did not dare return.

Daniel said he was on the waiting list for admission to an AIDS hospice in Houston. He expected to be admitted within a matter of days. In the meantime he had no place to go.

I nodded. Daniel looked as if he had AIDS. I never knew it if I had met anyone before with full-blown AIDS. Daniel had the hollow cheeks and the emaciated look about the neck that I had seen in photographs of people with AIDS and otherwise only in photographs of concentration-camp survivors. I asked Daniel what the local AIDS agency had done for him. He said they were mostly burned-out on him.

Although I had donated what I could to the AIDS agency, I did not have much confidence in them. I could see, however, that Daniel was a hard case, a prickly pear.

Most agencies, and especially their volunteers who do so much of the real work, want cuddly, warm clients. In the case of AIDS, that means the volunteers are best prepared for people who will lie down and die quietly. Many people who apply to work with persons with AIDS envision themselves as ministering martyrs among the lepers. They imagine the work will involve many tender and touching moments as their patients struggle to express eternal gratitude before expiring gently. Such scenes are filmed through gauze and Vaseline.

But what if the client was not a model citizen before he became ill? What if having AIDS really pisses him off? What if suffering silently is not his cup of tea? What if he resents the hell out of having to have things done for him? What if he feels entitled to steal five dollars from Florence Nightingale's purse?

And even when the client is a saint, there is a great deal more to being of real service than fluffing pillows and holding hands.

I asked Daniel whether it really had come to the point that the agency would do no more for him. He said he was afraid that it was so.

They had discovered he had been trading his hard-won food stamps for marijuana. That was, I gathered, only the last straw. In the present crisis, the agency had given Daniel the name of a man who supposedly had a standing offer to put up people with AIDS. But the agency had made a point of saying they did not recommend Daniel call the man, but passed the name along for Daniel to do with as he wished.

Other than to make this rather peculiar referral, the agency would do no more. Having no better plan, Daniel called the number in spite of the agency's disclaimer. The man invited Daniel to stay with him and gave Daniel directions to a house in Hyde Park.

When Daniel got to the address, the man offered him a sofa bed, and Daniel, being by then very tired, lay down. He said he had almost fallen asleep when the man began to massage him. Daniel did not want this attention, but he was too weary to make an issue of it until the massage reached his crotch, whither it arrived with uncommon haste.

Daniel asked the man to stop, but the man had not. And thus Daniel left.

I recognized Daniel as a manipulative sort of person. That someone would open his home to people with AIDS in order to make passes at them seemed incredible.

But Daniel mentioned the man's profession—which was an uncommon one for men—and the neighborhood of the man's home. These rang a bell with me. Daniel had not written down the man's name and had forgotten it. But he had the slip of paper on which he had recorded the man's telephone number. I wanted to take the number to the telephone book at the convenience store across Twenty-ninth Street to see if I could confirm my suspicions. But as I questioned Daniel, he remembered the man's name in a flash. I knew the man.

I cannot say that Daniel's story was true, but only that, whether fiction or fact, it captured the salient features of the man's character better than any other single anecdote might. I believed Daniel then and all the more because he could see I could not give him any money.

What Daniel did want was to sleep on the pew as Lizbeth and I watched over him. He proposed to take a number of Valium and he perceived that the bench was not the safest place in the world. I sat on the curb beneath the pew. As the evening was growing cooler, I offered Daniel my sleeping bag. He threw it over himself and, after being reassured I would not leave him until morning, took some pills and promptly fell asleep.

Lizbeth was upset to lose her place on the pew. She paced for a while and then curled up under the pew, where she was hidden by the drape of the sleeping bag.

Daniel left his pill bottle standing on the pew near his head. Without disturbing the bottle I could read its label. The patient's name matched the one Daniel had given me. The doctor was one of two in town I knew to have a large AIDS practice, and even before the AIDS crisis he was known for prescribing drugs like Valium with a free hand. I saw Daniel had exceeded his prescribed dose, but not to an alarming degree. Eventually I nodded off to sleep, my back braced against the pew.

Lizbeth roused me three or four times when men approached the pew. The adult arcade, which was in the storefront next to Ramblin' Red's, stayed open all night, and any of its patrons might have inquired of us, since late at night the pew is usually occupied by hustlers or other available men who cannot or will not pay the two-dollar admission.

Occasionally when I worked late into the night, the staff of the arcade came out to investigate complaints of a possibly dangerous vagrant. But I enjoyed the favor of the clerks on the night shift at the arcade, for I had once seen a number of magazines fall from the pants leg of an inebriated shoplifter as he stumbled away from the arcade. I knew inventory of the display items was taken every shift and the clerks must make up any deficit as much as if the cash drawer were short, so I had returned the magazines.

We had nothing to fear from the staff of the arcade or its regular customers, but perhaps one of the men who approached us in the night had meant us harm. All of them were surprised when Lizbeth leapt from concealment to announce them.

Daniel woke shortly after dawn. He was to go to some agency that would give him a voucher for a bus ticket if the hospice was ready for him. I told him I would leave the sleeping bag under the steps at Sleazy Sue's in case he had no better place to stay that evening and I was, for some reason, elsewhere.

When Lizbeth and I returned to the pew that afternoon, Daniel was wrapped in the sleeping bag although it was an hour before sunset and still very warm. He had taken a chill and what is more he had not got anything to eat all day. Lizbeth and I had eaten as we came to things. Our reserves were exhausted.

I left Lizbeth with Daniel and my gear and went around to the Dumpsters to find what I could while there was light remaining.

These were bleak days at the Dumpsters. We ate orts from the dormitories. I did not think I could give anything of the sort to a person with AIDS. I stirred through the Dumpsters with little hope of finding canned goods or other sealed items such as I had taken in better times to the AIDS food bank. I found a few open things that I would have eaten myself. But I had a recollection that one of the more perilous opportunistic infections to which PWAs are subject is transmitted by cat shit, and few Dumpsters are entirely free of used cat litter. I found nothing I could give Daniel.

At the end of the line of the best Dumpsters I turned and retraced my steps. I sifted through the Dumpsters again, determined to make them yield something.

When I reached, save by one Dumpster, my starting point, a college woman came down the back stairs of one of the apartment buildings. She carried a paper bag that I believed she was going to discard. I returned to business, taking as little notice of her as I could for fear of alarming her. "Do you want something to eat?" she asked, startling me slightly. I had not realized she had approached me. She handed me the crisp brown bag. "I made some sandwiches," she said.

I was not speechless but nearly enough that I said nothing intelligible. I do not appear much in need of food. The woman meant to do a little good by feeding me, but had done much more than she meant by feeding Daniel. Unfortunately I tried to tell her so all at once and she understood not a word.

The sandwiches were freshly made and not her leftover lunch and she had put a nice apple in the bag. Daniel made quick work of the food and I could believe he had not eaten all day.

We spent the night at the pew as we had the night before. But the next night Daniel did not return and I assume he went to Houston.

FOURTEEN

Lizbeth on Death Row

I still had the down jacket Jack Frost had given me in Hollywood, and besides that I had made a poncho of a run-of-the-mill wool blanket I had found in a Dumpster. But the blanket would not cover my arms as I went through the Dumpsters and the down jacket was too warm. I wanted something with sleeves, for the only shirts I had were T-shirts.

Fortunately, the sororities observed the birthdays of their members, and a favored way of presenting a gift that season was to present the recipient with the end of a piece of yarn. The recipient had to trace the yarn to its other end, around and around the house, with several skeins spliced in.

The mess of yarn was discarded.

I collected the yarn and untangled it. When it seemed to me I would have enough yarn, I made a circular knitting pin of a length of television cable and the point guards of two ballpoint pens. This implement left a lot to be desired and my sweater went

slowly. As the fall winds grew crisper, I carried my knitting everywhere and worked on it whenever I had a spare moment.

While I knitted I liked to imagine I was knitting while the
heads of yuppies rolled past my feet.

As I knitted in the Renaissance Market one day, a woman approached me and asked if I could not use more yarn. As very commonly happens, she had undertaken a knitting project some years
ago and bought all the yarn for it, as is recommended because colors vary slightly from dye lot to dye lot. After a brilliant start, the
project had been laid aside to be completed someday. At last she
was willing to admit that she would never take up the project again
and would be just as happy to be rid of the yarn if I had a use for it.

I certainly did want the yarn. I wanted to make the sweater quite
long so it would not ride up and expose me when I stretched to
reach into a Dumpster. I had untangled the scraps of yarn into balls
according to color. I was knitting the sweater seamlessly, in narrow
horizontal stripes, arranging the colors more or less at random. I
was unsure I would have enough yarn. As I knitted, the balls got
smaller, and as they got smaller, they got smaller more quickly.

The woman said she came to the market every day to pick up
someone who worked nearby. If I were at the market the next day,
she would bring the yarn and I could have it.

The next day began windy and cold, bleak and gray. If not for
the yarn, I would have found a leeward place and stayed there. But
I led Lizbeth to the market and the weather improved as the day
progressed. True to her word, the woman brought me the yarn.
By then the clouds were much higher and the wind had died. I decided to stay in the market and knit.

The Christmas season was upon the market. It was nothing
like it had been in the old days. Vendors did not occupy as many
as a third of the marked-off spaces, but it was busy enough that
Lizbeth and I could not sit on the benches around the planters.

We sat instead on the sidewalk in the unused western part of the market. There a row of small trees had been circumscribed with six inches of curbing, and I could from time to time rest my back against the curb.

I had installed another snap on Lizbeth's leash, making one on each end. This had proved handy in many ways. In camp I could extend Lizbeth's range by attaching a strap or whatever I had to a tree and snapping her leash onto that. When we left camp, I had nothing to untie, but had only to unsnap the leash. I could fix her easily to Dumpsters when I needed both hands to go through the contents.

When I sat on the sidewalk at the market to knit, I put the leash around my waist and snapped the usually free end onto her collar. As I am uncommonly stout, this left Lizbeth only a little slack. When the weather was cool, of course, she did not want much slack. She got on my lap and curled up, and somehow I managed to knit. So it had been many days that we visited the market.

That day I had no sign of impending trouble, but suddenly Lizbeth jumped up with a snarl.

Students from the blind school were brought to the market to practice getting around in crowds. One of them had approached us from behind. If the student had been feeling the sidewalk with his cane he would have hit my leg with it. But instead he was waving the cane through the air about a foot from the ground, and so, with an accuracy a sighted person would have had difficulty matching on purpose, he poked Lizbeth in the face.

The student, who was about twenty years old, began shrieking curses immediately and demanded that Lizbeth be killed on the spot. I knew that some forms of blindness caused by brain damage can be accompanied by a personality disorder that results in the subject being especially demanding and impulsive. Whether the student had that particular disorder or not, I could see from the attendant's expression that the student's outburst was nothing unusual. The student repeatedly demanded to know why Lizbeth had attacked him. At last the student's energies were mostly spent. The attendant, a rotund distinguished looking middle-aged man with a carefully trimmed white beard, said firmly, "Because you won't keep your stick on the ground, you poked the dog in the face."

That shut him up. The student and his attendant went on, reached Guadalupe Street, and turned south. And that might have been the end of it.

I noticed that Mr. Two Dogs took off rather suddenly to the south, but whether he influenced the subsequent events I cannot say.

The student and his attendant returned after about twenty minutes. I held Lizbeth closely, thinking only they were returning the way they had come. But the attendant stopped to ask me whether Lizbeth had her shots. She had. From my experience as an attendant at the lunatic asylum, I could see the attendant had gone into cover-your-ass mode. He would not be approachable by reason and he could not be expected to exercise even a modicum of judgment. I asked the attendant to show me the bite. The student extended his hand. I could see a raw spot the size of a bit of glitter, between his large gold ring and his knuckle.

That Lizbeth, tied around my waist as she was, could have bitten him there was a physical impossibility. I pointed that out to the attendant. He shrugged. It was out of his hands. He had retreated behind policy and procedure. He was only following orders. I had seen other attendants adopt the same demeanor. I knew Lizbeth and I were in trouble.

I suppose it was barely possible that Lizbeth had reached the student's knuckle with a claw. But the tiny wound looked much more like something the student had done with his own long, filthy fingernail. He had said nothing of the wound when it supposedly occurred, and the little spot he showed me seemed too fresh to be twenty minutes old. I believe the attendant thought as I did, but seeing that the student would not shut up about the incident, justice be damned, the attendant would do whatever was necessary to avoid a nasty note in his personnel file.

As soon as they were out of sight I bundled up my knitting, and Lizbeth and I hurried to the pew at Ramblin' Red's. We were quite in the open there, but I thought it was far enough away that I would have some time to think. A long time later I came to know that the pew faced the street whereby the blind school expeditions always returned, although it was not the most obvious route from the market to the school.

The attendant and his student had left the market ahead of us, and Lizbeth and I were afoot. But no doubt the attendant remembered seeing us on the pew many times before and had reported that. In any event, the dogcatcher found us very quickly.

The dogcatcher's appearance was about as agreeable as his profession. He demanded to have Lizbeth. He said it was only a matter of observing her for ten days. He said she could be given her heartworm medication in the shelter. He said that in cases such as ours there was a process whereby the fees could be waived and I could reclaim her.

This last was a damned lie and I knew it.

I left my day pack on the bench and Lizbeth and I fled. It was hopeless, really. My only hope was to slide between buildings where the dogcatcher could not follow in his truck. If I could think fast enough and if the dogcatcher were not willing to go against the traffic on the one-way streets, perhaps we could evade him. But I was not thinking fast enough. I was not thinking at all.

I hoped to double back, perhaps to hide in the space under Sleazy Sue's until it would be safe to see if Billy would give us a ride out of town. I ducked between two buildings: the building that housed *The Austin Grackle* and the adjacent apartment building. There I was cornered, for the way was blocked by a stout iron fence that was firmly anchored to the buildings. I had seen the fence a thousand times and had I thought I would have known that it was there.

It is no exaggeration to say I was hysterical, and even now I can recall the scene only in the third person, as in nightmares one sees himself from without his body. When the third police car arrived, I had nearly cried myself out. Being unarmed, I saw I had no course but to give up Lizbeth. If I were arrested, I could do nothing to help her.

I held her in my lap and she licked the tears from my cheeks. I cried that she was all I had. And that was so. My books and papers and every irreplaceable thing except my day pack had been taken a few nights before when I had gone to visit Tim in jail.

Now every so often a man takes a gun to a crowded place and begins to kill as many of the people there, although they be strangers, as he can. Commentators call these senseless crimes and they say no one knows why a person would do such a thing. But I know.

When I got up I could hardly stand. I led Lizbeth to the dog-catcher's truck and let her into the cage myself.

As for the police, I suppose they perceived the naked sincerity of the scene. They did not detain me.

I GOT MY day pack from the bench and walked the considerable distance to the animal shelter. Of all the things the dogcatcher had told me, I thought it was possibly true that Lizbeth could get her medication there.

At the shelter I was told Lizbeth could receive the medication I brought as soon as the vet was in to order it, a formality I could consider as good as done.

The shelter was not, strictly speaking, a city facility. The building was on public land, but the shelter was operated under contract by the humane society. It was nothing more than the good-cop, bad-cop routine, with the society in the role of the good cop and the dogcatcher as the bad cop.

Yes, the possibility of Lizbeth's fees being waived did not exist. It was a lie and, so said the society, a lie the dogcatchers commonly told in spite of the society's repeated objections. Although Lizbeth was property, the law provided no pretense of due process in her seizure. There would be no hearing. It was not even necessary that the alleged victim produce a wound. Once a bite was alleged, the dog was seized. It was up to the dogcatcher, and no one would or could, according to the law, review his decision. (I learned later that this summary power of the dogcatcher was known to some landlords who would harass tenants they found undesirable by claiming to have been bitten when they came to inspect the property. The tenants' dog would be seized repeatedly until at last the tenants moved or the dog was killed. I can only suppose the landlords provided something to allay the dogcatcher's suspicions at being summoned to seize the same dog over and over.)

In all, Lizbeth's fees would amount to about a hundred dollars, provided I could substantiate my claim that she had been vaccinated—her tags were not sufficient evidence. The bulk of these fees was what the society charged for board, but it was pointless, so said the attendant, to discuss whether the society would waive their part because the law required them to collect the city's thirty-five-dollar fee for picking Lizbeth up. I did not quite see that it was pointless to discuss the difference between a hundred dollars and thirty-five dollars. Clearly this humane society would put Lizbeth to death before they would waive their portion of her fee.

I could not even hope that Lizbeth might be adopted by someone better able to provide for her—a faint hope at best, for she was a grown dog. According to the rules, Lizbeth was now a *bite dog*. If I could not redeem her, she would die. I would be allowed to see her only once; now or later. I decided I wanted to see her right away.

If I could not get the money I might get a gun, and if so I would want an idea of the layout of the place.

Lizbeth was in a cold concrete cell. She was pleased to see me and seemed not so much unhappy as perplexed. The attendant would not let me into the cell. I put my fingers through the chain-link fence so Lizbeth could lick them. Then I hurried away so she would not see me cry.

The attendant offered me a paper towel. Surely, she ventured, it was not so bad as I made out—why all the time she saw people collecting cans, couldn't I raise the money that way? I had ten days.

That was the world she lived in. Did she really think cans paid any better than a bottle of wine per day?

I was given Lizbeth's collar.

I could not help asking.

No, the society no longer used the vacuum chamber. Dogs were executed with sodium Pentothal, just like the prisoners on death row.

AFTER I LEFT the pound, I went to Billy's apartment complex. It was much nearer than camp and I could only maintain my composure a few moments at a time.

When Billy understood Lizbeth's situation, he began to excuse himself from contributing. I had not thought of it, but Billy had computed that Lizbeth's ten days would be up on the first of December, coinciding with Billy's payday. Billy said his next month's pay was spent already and I could see that everything that could be hocked had been.

The next morning I wrote letters. I thought I would write everyone who knew Lizbeth or knew of her. Unfortunately, my address book had been among the things recently stolen. I could write only three or four letters, but I was at it for a long time. I had to convey grim tidings and to beg, neither of which was easy for me.

Billy drove me to camp, or rather to Sleazy Sue's. He still had the price of a couple of drinks and we could talk in Sue's. Billy said he would try to find some money toward bailing Lizbeth out, but his tone indicated that he was wishing, not planning to do so. He told me again that he always thought it was a mistake for me to try to keep her. If I did not have Lizbeth, Billy said, I might have better luck getting assistance.

He had written her off and was thinking of reasons it was all for the best.

I could not follow this line of thought. I changed the subject slightly. I said, as I had often said to Billy, that I thought someone must have a bit of property out of town, a place with potable water where Lizbeth and I could camp and I could have a little tent so I could keep a typewriter. If only I could find that someone.

I was sure I could raise the money for a bag of dog food for Lizbeth and tobacco and a bottle of vitamins for me.

I needed someone to spot me eight months. That was how long it took to be paid for a short story once I finished it. If I could write for eight months I believed I would have a steady income.

Before, I discussed my hope of finding somewhere to camp as the only way I could think of to get off the streets and not as a reflection of my slight distaste for society. Once Lizbeth was seized, I hoped only to have her back and to go somewhere where we would never see another human being.

Oh yes, Billy remarked, he did know someone who had a place out of town. He had discussed my staying out there and the person had seemed agreeable. Billy said he would discuss it again with his friend, but the friend had already said I was welcome to stay on his property whenever I wished.

I wondered how long Billy had been sitting on this news. Why had he not mentioned this before? Had he thought I was kidding about wanting such a situation? If we had got out of town, I still would have had Lizbeth.

I urged Billy to speak to his friend again. If I saved Lizbeth, I would want to take her away at once.

I HAD COME to a decision. I was going to panhandle. Soon after Lizbeth and I lost our home, I had adopted the policy of taking whatever was offered to me and I had done so. But I had been resolved from the first never to beg, that is not to solicit cash on the streets.

I perceived a distinction between begging on the streets and hitchhiking, accepting the hospitality of Roy and others I hardly knew, and receiving gifts and open-ended loans from people I had known before. Whether there is any distinction in principle, as a practical matter I believed I did not present a sufficiently sympathetic image to beg successfully. Then too, in Austin panhandling is illegal. I had had to violate certain laws, by sleeping in the park, for example. But as I feared any arrest would be the end of Lizbeth, I had complied with such laws as I could.

Beyond these considerations, and perhaps above them, was a simple matter of taste. I preferred scavenging to begging. Begging was a desperate measure.

Only I could reclaim Lizbeth, and if I were arrested for begging that would be the end of her. But it also would be that if I did not raise the money to save her.

I had little difficulty extracting some poster paper and Magic Markers from the Dumpsters. I walked to the pound, which stood near the Colorado River in what had been the annual flood plane before the upstream dams were built. The entrance to the pound was a long gravel road. I stationed myself on it and made a sign. I scarcely know now what I wrote—SAVE LIZBETH in large letters and some more that was smaller. I stood with my sign from about noon until after dark. After sunset the road was quite dark. There were no streetlights. A young man stopped and gave me his watch. When the pound closed the watch was all I had collected. I was very discouraged.

I stashed the sign and walked back to camp, a distance not much less than three miles. I slept little and all of that was nightmares.

In the morning I had no better idea.

I thought of posting little notices at various places in the neighborhood, and then I meant to take a sleeping bag and to remain at the pound for the duration. The sleeping bag was one that had not been stolen because I left it under Sue's for Daniel, if he ever returned.

I made the notices on notebook paper and posted them at Sleazy Sue's and above the pew at Ramblin' Red's where Lizbeth and I usually sat. This took longer than it might have because I would break down at irregular intervals; I would be overcome with little warning.

I took another notice to *The Grackle* and began to tape it to a large window where fliers and notes were commonly posted. *The Grackle*'s business manager saw me and inquired about Lizbeth. I explained as well as I could. Of course most of *The Grackle*'s staff had seen Lizbeth taken away or had at least heard me when she was, but I did not know whether anyone had witnessed the dogcatcher's assurances that Lizbeth's fees could be waived. I told her the fees would come to about a hundred dollars. She went into *The Grackle* office. I had no intention of lingering around the office, but before I had finished taping up my notice, the editor came out and told me that he would give me the money to get Lizbeth out.

I never did understand whether he made this offer speaking for himself or on behalf of the paper or if they had passed the hat. I was grateful beyond words.

I had been submitting various things to *The Grackle* in long-hand. Among these were a couple of small items the editor thought he could use. I thought he mentioned the pieces to make the offer to help Lizbeth seem less baldly a handout.

I had no objection to a bald handout if it would free Lizbeth. I thanked the editor profusely and incoherently. But once I left *The Grackle*, I did not know what to do. I had only the editor's promise, and while I did not mistrust him, it was not the same as having a money order for the amount in my pocket. And even that would not have reassured me. Too many things might go wrong before I could get Lizbeth out.

I gave up the idea of begging at the pound. I wanted to mitigate the editor's contribution if I could, but if I were arrested, no contribution could save Lizbeth.

If I was not to beg, I did not know what I would do.

I spent a few hours on the pew at Ramblin' Red's. The proprietor at Red's asked about Lizbeth's situation. I explained all of it, including the editor's offer. I got the impression that Red's was prepared to help Lizbeth if *The Grackle* somehow did not. But no impression or assurance would really console me.

While I remained on the pew, less sincere people asked about Lizbeth. I could not withstand that. I soon gave up sitting there. My response to misfortune or injury is something like shame. This is a peculiar feeling in any event, but it is most puzzling when I seem to have been the victim of happenstance. If I had not been poor, if I had not stayed in the market that morning, if I had sat down to knit facing the other way—in a thousand ways I could have avoided Lizbeth's being seized. Yet there are always these tantalizing and wholly hypothetical alternatives in the aftermath of any accident. I did not see that I was at fault and I could not understand my feeling of shame. But I felt it.

Billy returned to Sleazy Sue's. Evidently he found a little more money or some new place to pass a hot check. Billy examined the watch I had been given the night before. It seemed to me to have some value and he thought so too. He suggested we pawn it.

I would have done better as a homeless person if I had been more familiar with pawn shops. I do not like pawn shops. I never pawned anything I found. One objection I had to the idea of pawning things I found in Dumpsters was the possibility that the item had been stolen before it was discarded, a possibility that seemed more likely when the item was in good condition and most pawnable.

Billy went into the shop with the watch. He was more presentable. They pay more if they think the item will be redeemed, or so Billy said. My share was ten dollars. Billy told me he had talked again to his friend who had the place out of town and I was expected whenever I might show up. I assured Billy I would want to get out of town on the first of December—as soon as I regained Lizbeth, if I could. I arranged to call Billy on the first, either when I had Lizbeth or when the issue was otherwise decided.

The following day was Thanksgiving. Sue's had set a free buffet. I do not remember much of it, for I was lost in my own concerns.

Friday was my birthday. I spent my proceeds from the watch getting my ID card renewed at the Department of Public Safety. My ID expired on my birthday and my impression of the Humane Society was that they might kill Lizbeth if my papers were not strictly in order.

On my way back from the DPS, I stopped at Lizbeth's veterinarian's office to obtain the written record of her vaccination—this would not free her or improve her status, but it would save the expense of revaccination if she were to be released. I had expected a duplicate of the certificate I had been given when she was vaccinated, but I got only a note from the receptionist. I was concerned that this would not be good enough.

Then I could do nothing except to stay out of trouble until the first of December. I spent the rest of my birthday in Sleazy Sue's. I had my complimentary birthday cocktail and a few more besides, because gentlemen would buy me drinks when they would not contribute the same funds to the cause.

I have never had a more somber birthday.

My dog was on death row. I was homeless. And that day I turned forty.

I SLEPT VERY little while Lizbeth was in the pound and not at all the night before the first of December.

I gathered my things from the camp at the Triangle. I packed the bedroll and the daypack. I no longer had much more than I could carry except for extra bedding I had found, which I stashed under Sue's. I was at the pew at Ramblin' Red's very soon after dawn.

The proprietor of Red's arrived early in his van and offered to take me at once to the pound. But the pound was not open and I did not have the money yet. Again I had the impression that he would save Lizbeth if something went wrong at *The Grackle*.

It was a very long morning.

I went around to *The Grackle* building at 10:00 A.M., which was the agreed hour. The new issue of *The Grackle* arrived. Indeed they had printed the two little pieces the editor had discussed with me. This was *The Grackle*'s homeless issue. *The Grackle* always ran a slogan, in very tiny type in its banner, which varied from week to week. I folded the paper and put it in the backpack. Only two years later did I look at the issue closely enough to notice the slogan: FREE LIZBETH.

The editor seemed to be tied up in one meeting after another. Late in the afternoon he was ready to go to the pound and I was beside myself by then.

He drove to a convenience store and extracted some money from a cash machine. He left me at the pound with a hundred dollars. Of course I would not mind walking uptown with Lizbeth once she was freed, but I felt queasy about being left at the pound before the matter was settled. The Humane Society might not accept the written note from the vet's receptionist or they might discover some additional fee at the last minute.

They did not take me to Lizbeth until all of the paperwork had been done and they had given me a license tag for her collar. The Humane Society's representative remarked on Lizbeth's medication, saying many more well-to-do dogs did not get it.

At last I was led to Lizbeth, who was in the same cold cell where I had last seen her. She began jumping vertically into the air and it was just as well all of my business with the pound had been concluded. As soon as I had Lizbeth's leash on her she made for the door.

The pound was surrounded by a grassy field and the moment we were out of the office, Lizbeth wanted to run and to jump and to roll in the grass and to play Piranha Fish, which I suppose did not enhance her reputation with the Humane Society workers if any of them witnessed it.

Lizbeth's celebration was somewhat subdued by the kennel cough she had acquired at the pound. She ran a fever for several days and had coughing fits whenever she got excited. Concern over this rather dampened my enjoyment of the reunion.

FIFTEEN

To Hollywood Again

My first thought once I had Lizbeth again was to get out of Austin as soon as possible.

By the time we reached the pew at Ramblin' Red's, the proprietor had gone for the day, but he had left a sack for Lizbeth containing several cans of dog food and a large rawhide bone.

Billy came to Sue's to drive me to his friend's place at the lake. He had to fortify himself with a couple of cocktails before we left, and when we got to the lake he had difficulty recalling the way to his friend's cabin. Because of the darkness, Billy was not sure at first he had found the right place. The friend was not there. I was very uneasy about not having met my host. But it was the first of the month and Billy was eager to get to the bars. He told me one of the back doors was missing a panel and I was supposed to let myself in that way.

Billy took off.

I decided not to attempt breaking and entering until the morning. I laid out our bedroll on the porch. It was the first good night's sleep I had since Lizbeth had been seized.

The first thing in the morning Lizbeth buried the rawhide bone. We were not so far from civilization as I had wished. The cabin was set on a lot of, perhaps, a half an acre, and all around were similar lots, many with nicer houses. Nonetheless I let Lizbeth off her leash. I was determined to enjoy whatever more time she and I would have together and to resist the impulse to keep her in a bell jar. I watched her bury the rawhide bone, thinking I could find it later.

Lizbeth's attitude toward rawhide bones has been marred by an unfortunate puppyhood experience. She had the largest rawhide bone I could find, which she kept, between chews, in a bucket near the back steps. We had about a week of rain. When Lizbeth looked for her bone again it was nothing more than a little scum; the bucket had filled with rainwater and the bone had dissolved.

Perhaps she thought it had been stolen.

After that she never played with a rawhide bone again, hiding them as soon as she could. They were, I gather, much too valuable to play with and liable to be stolen if not carefully concealed. At the cabin she concealed the bone too well and neither of us ever saw it again.

After a couple of days, our host arrived at last. He was not prepared to see us at his cabin, but Billy had not overstated our invitation. C.K. was happy to have me use the cabin because I had once written a piece that he had admired and because there was a cloud on his title to the property. C.K.'s family was trying to sell the property—or they had sold it, I could not make out which. He said the sheriff had a proven policy of neutrality regarding the conflicting claims; I would not have to confront lawmen bearing writs. But I could not rely on the law if the other claimants arrived, which

C.K. said would not happen unless the property were obviously unoccupied for a long time. As he was going to Austin for some time and possibly then to California for a longer time, our presence to secure his possession of the property was especially welcome. I hardly found this reassuring.

C.K. said he would return for his things before he left for California. But as he left he took almost everything in the place.

We weathered an ice storm in the cabin, but after two or three days the storm broke. In the first sunshine a well-dressed woman came to the cabin and called me out—or rather she called for Charles Krebbs Brookshire, which I supposed was C.K.'s name— and I responded. My story was essentially the truth—that I was a writer who had hoped to get some work done and C.K.'s cabin seemed to be the ideal place to do that.

The woman's complaint was that she owned several of the adjacent properties, including the one that was the source of C.K.'s water, and that C.K. had not made any arrangement with her for the water, but had helped himself as he had often done in the past. She was about to disconnect the hose that C.K. had rigged up, and if she found it installed again she would summon the sheriff without further discussion.

I feigned surprise, but I had seen C.K.'s arrangement for charging his water lines from the standpipe of the house on the adjacent property and I had suspected something was amiss. I did learn one horrifying fact from the woman—the water was just pumped up from the lake and was not treated. After the woman left I bundled up our things and led Lizbeth to the park known as Hippie Hollow—although it now has another official name—where there was a public phone. I reached Billy and learned from him that C.K. had left for California. Billy was surprisingly agreeable to coming to rescue Lizbeth and me again.

———

WE REMAINED IN Austin ten weeks more.

At first we camped again in the Triangle. Once the students left for Christmas, the Dumpster finds were few and far between. I had intestinal disturbances from just before Christmas until after New Year's.

Fortunately the season was mild by Austin standards. Although the foliage that gave us cover dropped, our place in the Triangle remained inconspicuous. When it was dry, and when my bowels did not require otherwise, we could remain in our bedding, amid the limbs of a fallen oak, until the sun was high and the morning chill dispelled. When the ice storms moved through, we sat on the pew, wrapped in a sleeping bag, day and night for the two or three days the storms remained.

After New Year's we were evicted from the Triangle by the park patrol. This time we had not been singled out, for I had watched the work progressing slowly toward us from the south. Evidently city crews were clearing brush all along Shoal Creek and Lamar Boulevard, and in the process they removed the homeless, discovering a number of camps, some rather fancy—at least one was neatly framed with two-by-fours and walled with plastic sheeting.

Across a side street from the Triangle was a large grassy area with a stand of bamboo on the far side. I had thought of moving my camp there, but through the Christmas season the Optimist's Club had occupied the lot with their Christmas-tree stand and blocked the way to the bamboo. After we were evicted from the Triangle, Lizbeth and I began to sleep there. I thought it very likely that the bamboo would be cleared too and so I did not really establish a camp in it. I kept most of our things under Sue's.

The proprietor at Ramblin' Red's thought the bamboo would remain. He and his spouse owned some rental property on the east side of the bamboo. He recalled that the issue of removing the bamboo had occurred before and it had remained to serve as a barrier to the traffic noise from Lamar Boulevard. I was unsure.

For the most part we went to the bamboo after dark and left it at dawn. In this Lizbeth was very useful for it was often too dark for me to find our place in the bamboo by my own senses.

I received a very little fan mail. One of the fan letters was from Jack Walden, who was having some success writing and illustrating. When he learned of my situation he suggested that I send him a story in longhand, which he would type and submit. I wrote out the story and sent it to him. He also wrote that if Lizbeth and I were to find ourselves in Los Angeles we could stay with him while I got some work out. This last seemed so agreeable a solution that I could hardly contain my excitement. I wrote again to be sure that his was a serious offer. In response I received a letter from Carl. Apparently Carl had some kind of rooming house in Hollywood in which Jack Walden lived, and they were agreed that I might have one of the vacant rooms there while I attempted to put a career together.

When I understood this I had difficulty restraining myself from hitting the road at once. Since Lizbeth had been seized I had wanted to get as far away from Austin as I could. But the memory of my first hitchhiking trip to California helped me to restrain my first impulse.

At last I heard that the story I sent to Jack Walden had sold; I could expect payment soon after I reached Hollywood, if I were to come. Some months before I had taken on a student who had a lucrative career but who wished to learn to write for publication. He was so happy to be published that he sent the proceeds of his first story to me. When I had that money in hand, I could see no reason to delay our departure.

One Sunday late in February, at dawn, Lizbeth and I walked to Pease Park so I could wash up in the men's room. As we returned I let Lizbeth off her leash to chase the pigeons. The pigeons of course evaded her quite easily and swooped in low spirals just ahead of her. She seemed to enjoy the chase. It made a pretty picture.

When we returned to the bamboo I thought I might have a bit more sleep before I called Billy. But I discovered my small bankroll was missing. As soon as I was sure it had not slipped out of my pocket in the bedding, I could only think it had dropped out of my pants when I had sat on the toilet in the rest room.

No one had been in the rest room when I was, but someone surely had been there since. I almost did not go back to the park to look. I was sure the money was gone.

Nonetheless we did go back. We were not yet near the rest room when Lizbeth pulled me off the path. I thought she had done all of her dog business, but I soon saw the point. She pulled me right to the bankroll, where it had fallen in a clump of grass. I had seen dogs trained to do such things, but of course Lizbeth had no such training.

We had stepped off the trail at this place the first time because a runner with a loose dog was coming along. I must have put my hand in my pocket then and dropped the money. That Lizbeth found it again seemed very auspicious.

That afternoon I called Billy. We planned for him to take Lizbeth and me to the highway the next day. But Billy had not been paying much attention to the weather forecasts. An ice storm moved through and I could not leave until Wednesday.

Wednesday we went out of the way for a cocktail at Sue's. Billy considered this a tradition of my departures. I supplied myself with tobacco at Ramblin' Red's and bought dog food.

I took a backpack, a bedroll made of a shower curtain and a sleeping bag, and a rollbag with another sleeping bag and the blanket I sometimes wore. The rest of my gear I discarded. I was resolved to remain in California whatever happened.

LIZBETH AND I did not reach the interstate until Friday evening, so late that I thought it best for us to turn in. We were by the road before the dew rose, and the first car that came along stopped for us.

The ride lasted little more than an hour. As we approached Junction, the driver said he was going into Junction and asked where I wanted out. I told him I wanted to stay on the highway and the exit to Junction would be the place. When we left the highway at the Junction exit I saw at least six other hitchhikers, one with a large, long-haired black dog. But the driver did not let me out. He said he would take me through town. I was relieved because I did not want to hitchhike with so much competition.

I wondered at the significance of Junction's name. I did not notice any railways. Another highway intersected the interstate there, but the town antedated the interstate system. Junction sits at the confluence of the north and the south forks of the Llano River, but to call this a junction seemed peculiar. I saw the deer industry was a considerable part of the economy. One locker had a pile of antlers as large as a two-hundred-dollar Christmas tree.

The numbers of hitchhikers I saw at the first Junction exit inspired the thought that we would be stuck in Junction, much as we were in El Paso when we came east. Between Junction and El Paso are 450 miles of road and not much else. Some stretches in Arizona and California appear more forbidding, but they are much shorter. If a ride did not work out the driver would have to put up with the rider for many hours or be responsible for putting him out, if not in an absolute desert, then near enough to come to the same thing as prospects for survival go. I do not know if drivers make these calculations.

As I stood by the last Junction ramp, the sun set in the south.

We crossed the frontage road and I found a cactus-free spot of the right size along the fence line. I attached the various makeshift extensions to Lizbeth's leash and tied the free end to a fence post. I prepared our bed in the last few moments of twilight. I encouraged Lizbeth to eat some dog food, but she was not hungry. She wanted only to get under the covers. The sky was clear. The night was cold already.

I sat up to smoke what I thought to be my last cigarette of the day. I saw in silhouette against the last brown light of twilight a man with his thumb out, standing where we had been standing. After a while I called to him and he came over to us. Lizbeth was excited to have company and I suppose she seemed fiercer than usual. But eventually I convinced him to extend his hand so she could lick it.

I could hardly see him, the night had become so dark, but I perceived he wore a short-sleeved sports shirt. He had no coat and no bag. He shuddered.

His name was Mike. He was not drunk and did not seem crazy. As Lizbeth and I would not fit in a zipped sleeping bag I had laid the bags open as if they were blankets. There was room for Mike if he wanted to stay the night with us.

Mike resisted this suggestion at first. He said he would get a ride before it got much colder. But his bravado evaporated quickly once he discovered he was shivering too hard to light a cigarette. He started to say he would be back if he did not get a ride soon, but he seemed to realize how ridiculous he sounded. "Shit," he said, "it's so dark they won't even see me."

Lizbeth had crawled back under the covers and the hardest part of rearranging the bedding was dislodging her. After I had spread out the bedding, Lizbeth and I crawled back in. Mike held back a moment. Then he pulled off his boots and dropped his pants and got under the covers too.

We talked, as the hour was early. Mike's story was that he was the only one working in a household of many young people and had finally had enough of it. A domestic dispute would explain his taking to the road with no gear. If it were so, his temper might return and he might decide not to leave after all.

When I suggested this, he said the house he left was in San Antonio. He had hitchhiked all day and not thought of its getting cold at night.

He asked me if there were a Salvation Army in Junction. I did not know. He said he might try to get a coat in the morning. Otherwise he had no plans. He would go to L.A. or San Diego however the rides worked out. He did not really care. He would be starting from scratch wherever he went. We agreed to stop talking and to try to sleep.

Having offered Mike the protection of my bedroll for the night, I felt it would be ignoble to make a pass at him. I was afraid that if he refused me he would feel obliged also to leave. I might have chanced that if he had been been properly dressed to withstand the cold. Yet high resolve had little chance against my proximity to his young virility and his proximity to my warmth. As a tacit compromise, first I, then he, masturbated barracks-style—that is, each as the other pretended to be asleep. Perhaps this compromise was best, for although whenever I woke I found his arms around me, the following day he offered up various, apparently gratuitous, homophobic remarks.

About 2:00 A.M. I was awakened by distant gunfire. From the hoots and hollers I deduced the gunfire was only the natives saluting Saturday night. I fell asleep again.

I woke first in the morning. Lizbeth stayed abed. I walked east toward the underpass, looking back to see if Lizbeth had noticed I was up. I went to a restaurant at the intersection and got two carry-out coffees. I would never have got back without spilling the coffee if Lizbeth had come. As I got near the bedroll, Lizbeth got up to greet me. Mike remained a lump in the covers. He had put on his pants. I spoke, getting nothing coherent from him until I mentioned the coffee. He sat up. I saw his face in light for the first time. Mike was such a ringer for John Travolta—the younger,

TV John Travolta—that any other description would be pointless. Stupidly I remarked on the resemblance immediately.

"That's what everybody says," Mike said. He was not flattered. No one is when the obvious is pronounced. Mike said he would get us a ride in no time.

I doubted anyone would pick up two men and a dog. Mike alone could get a ride easily, and so I advised him. He would hear nothing of it.

Sunday morning passed without a nibble. We got no ride, but were not passed by many prospects. We saw many convoys of concrete I-beams, which reminded me of the unfinished interstate in Phoenix, a bit of natural foreshadowing. We saw also BART (Bay Area Rapid Transit) cars on their way to San Francisco. They already bore their logos. I believe even Mike was discouraged by ten o'clock. He asked me if I had any money. Naturally I lied and said I was broke. He went to the store for cigarettes, saying I should take any ride I might get while he was gone. I did continue to try to get a ride until I saw him returning. I was not sure he would be back. He had bought a pack of cigarettes for each of us. By noon we were hungry and the water bottle wanted recharging. I left the gear with Mike and went to the store. That was taking a chance, but Mike had won a measure of my confidence.

At the store I bought some bologna and bread and took on water from the rest-room tap. So far as I could tell, Mike never moved off the bags while I was gone. When I offered him a sandwich, Mike said he thought I had said I was broke.

"I lied," I said. I looked him in the eye and could see this stratagem and my frankness about it was appreciated. No one after all needs a fool for a partner.

During lunch we discussed the situation further. I again doubted the wisdom of trying to travel together. But Mike insisted that things would work out. Sure enough, shortly after lunch Mike stopped a pickup. But the pickup was far down the road before it stopped. Lizbeth and I with the gear were slow to catch up. I expected the driver to take off with Mike. The driver told me later he saw only Mike and would not have stopped if he had seen me and the dog. But Mike had insisted on waiting for us.

The truck bore a very ponderous machine. Lizbeth rode with it and I feared for her should the load shift.

We were very crowded in the cab of the pickup, mostly for the ice chest. Fortunately the driver drank little. He was a tall lean man, perhaps not yet thirty. He was dressed as a drugstore cowboy. And he did not remove his black hat. The machine in the back, so he said, was an electric motor. It was a prototype of a motor with a winding that improved efficiency beyond any achieved before. This sounded suspiciously like perpetual motion. I questioned the driver. The prototype, far from being perpetual motion, only improved efficiency by a few points. Even so slight an improvement, however, was worth millions for the energy it would save.

The driver said the prototype worked at the inventor's laboratory in Montana, but evidently the machine was damaged in transit and had not performed properly at a demonstration in Florida. Unfortunately, the inventor, for whom our driver worked, was an eccentric who never left his laboratory. The machine had to be returned to him for repair; he would not come to it. Moreover, the inventor's fortune was made. He saw his machine as a public benevolence in a world starved for energy. He expected the world to come to him for it and saw no reason to disturb himself to prove the worth of his gift. Our driver's fortune, however, was not made. His employer paid him well, but that was not like being rich. Rich was what our driver hoped to be, for he was to have a large share of the proceeds if he marketed the invention.

In any event we were welcome to ride so long as we wished, to Montana if we chose.

I knew I wanted out in Phoenix. Mike, however, was unsure. If he were to go to San Diego, he should get out in Tucson; if to

L.A., then Phoenix. He had said one place was as good as another, yet he fancied the idea of Montana.

At the first stop our driver removed his hat very briefly to wipe the sweat off his head—a thing he could do because he was prematurely bald. The hat was vanity. Mike and I tried to kid him out of wearing it on the road—for he would surely be more comfortable without it, and now that we knew his secret there was no point in his wearing it. The driver kept his hat on.

When Mike went to the rest room the driver asked me about him. Mike did not have a wallet, an ID, a belt, or a coat. That he might be an escaped prisoner had occurred to me too. I said we met only the night before.

We passed into Arizona about dawn. I was happy when we put Tucson behind us. Mike said he would continue with the driver as far as Flagstaff, but I could see he had decided to go to Montana. I was again invited to come to Montana too, and had I no better plan I might have accepted.

I was let out in Phoenix.

The interstate had been completed through town and the corner where we had stood the year before was no longer on the main route. Although it was still early, I recognized that I needed sleep. I found a gutted building; evidently it had been a bar, but its patio seemed an agreeable place and we bedded down there.

We walked most of the following morning through the streets of Phoenix as I attempted to find a suitable ramp onto the interstate. When I found one, I discovered large, verbose, hand-painted signs affixed to the lampposts, all on the theme WILL WORK FOR FOOD. I thought this inauspicious.

We were there until the end of the workday. A businessman gave us a ride out of town—to Avondale or Goodyear. If we had stopped here the year before, the ramp was much changed and the post with hitchhikers' graffiti was removed. We slept by the

ramp. The mesquite thorns were everywhere and I did not entirely avoid stepping on them. About nine the following morning
we were picked up by a family of the area's aboriginal people.
They were husband and wife and two grown daughters in a fully
loaded sky-blue pickup. Lizbeth and I could barely fit in a corner
of the bed. They were going no farther than Burnt Well, which I
recognized as the rest stop we were at the year before.

At Burnt Well, I secured Lizbeth and went into the men's room
to shave and wash. When I came out, the women I had ridden with
had laid blankets in the main pavilion and were setting out silver
necklaces for sale. I overheard that the cheaper pieces were about
seventy-five dollars. They even had a credit card stamping machine.

The man was stationed with the ice chests and picnic baskets
at a shaded table, some distance from the main pavilion, and there
he drank beer so long as I observed him. In the early afternoon a
man approached us afoot. He spoke cockney once-removed; perhaps he was Australian. He said he was traveling west and after
he had finished his lunch he would pick me up if I were still there.
He seemed fond of Lizbeth.

When he stopped to pick us up, he was driving a recreational
vehicle, evidently custom-made. It was boxlike, utterly without
streamlining. The driver's seat was a hard, padded plywood bench,
as was the passenger's seat, although the latter was sideways. The
vehicle had a kitchen and a bedroom. Nothing was well-suited for
movement. Curtains fluttered, all the furniture had sharp edges,
and in a tight curve, clothes on their hangers flew out of the closet.

My driver was not talkative, but I learned he would stop at a
flea market in Quartzite. He told me Quartzite had begun as a
recreational-vehicle park. A few old people had parked there year
after year until they formed the core of a community. News of
Quartzite had spread on the RV grapevine and more people parked
there. Now Quartzite had a population of a million in season. The

arrival of a McDonald's seemed to old-timers a discouraging sign of institutionalization. And so it is when a few people have a good thing going and have not the sense to keep quiet about it.

We were soon at Quartzite, near the California boarder. Indeed I saw acres of RV park and the dread Golden Arches.

The driver let us off at a crossover and said if we were at the on ramp when he had done his business in Quartzite he would take us to Blythe. The on ramp at Quartzite was very desolate. Our best chance was the driver keeping his word.

I sat down short of the NO PEDESTRIANS sign and looked for the sunscreen in my bags. Presently a highway patrol car stopped. That was the first sign of law enforcement I saw in my travels in Arizona. I tied Lizbeth to the signpost and tried to remember to keep my hands visible. My first impulse in such situations is to put them in my pockets or behind my back.

The officer was apologetic. "You're on this side of the sign and I have no problem with that," he said. He wanted only to ID me, a reasonable request, as the denizens of Quartzite seemed frail. The officer gave me a warning ticket, which said I had been in the roadway, but he admitted the infraction was a figment to make a record of the transaction. I observed the traffic in and out of Quartzite for a couple of hours. I do not know if the history of Quartzite as the driver told it is so, but all I saw confirmed it. Besides the officer, I saw only white people over sixty.

As I watched them pass in their RVs I realized they were Kerouac's contemporaries. Here was the beat generation, ending their days on the road. I was stunned by the irony and shuddered in spite of the heat.

Fortunately the previous driver did return and, except to stop to conceal his fruit before we reached the California inspection station, our trip to Blythe was uneventful.

THE LAST OF the light revealed that Blythe was green. The air in Blythe was clammy. The waters of the Colorado are sprinkled liberally into the air around Blythe, creating a cloying coolness like that produced by evaporative coolers. The driver, oblivious to the risk of being rear-ended, let us off on the exit ramp. I had seen signs that said Blythe had three exits. The driver had asked which exit I wanted and I said I wanted out at the last. So far as I knew the driver had complied with this request.

The evidence was that some hitchhikers had been at this ramp for many days. There were many clumps of rusting cans; the labels I could read bore the generic markings of surplus commodities. The third day we were at the ramp a woman of advanced middle age, who had passed us many times, stopped and gave me a large sack. A handout is not a bridal shower and I usually did not examine what I was given in the donor's presence, for I meant to create the impression that I was grateful for whatever I got.

By then I was hungry, for I had only pocket change left. When the woman was gone I looked into the sack. It contained three boxes of dog treats, a small bag of dry dog food, and two cans of dog food. Lizbeth, of course, had not missed a meal on this trip, and I still had ten pounds of her food in my bag.

It is too easy to despair of a spot after a short time and to waste time and energy seeking another spot that proves no better. But the fourth night we were in Blythe I was convinced we were at the eastern ramp in Blythe and that we would have to walk through town to reach the last ramp.

We walked what seemed a very long way that night. Blythe appeared to be the nearest town to a military base. We passed many clubs and restaurants. At one of these, some ladies who were leaving stopped to give us a bag of chicken. At last I found highway markers; the strip we walked along was the interstate's business route. After midnight we reached the third Blythe exit. Like many Western towns, Blythe has not considered the needs of pedestrians very well and several times Lizbeth and I were in the street, a situation made worse by the drunken young people cruising about in their Jeeps.

The entrance ramp did not seem promising when we reached it. It was short and rose steeply. Drivers hit the accelerator when they turned onto the ramp and floored it until they were far into the desert.

All that, I thought, would wait until morning.

Along the ramp was about five yards of round rocks bordered by oleanders. I thought we would hide in the oleanders to camp. But in the oleanders the ground fell off steeply and I sought a level spot in vain. I spent a few hours dozing and sliding down the rocks, but Lizbeth found a ledge her size over my head and had a restful nap.

I am not sure I slept at all. In any event I was up before dawn. When there was light enough that we could be seen, I stuck my thumb out. We got a ride almost immediately in a rusted van. It had captain's chairs and cutout windows, but the interior was thoroughly trashed. There were many other passengers but only one who knew any English. The ride lasted until we reached a rest stop in the middle of the desert. Then the one who spoke English explained I would have to pay money. I gathered these were new arrivals or otherwise they would have known not every white man has money. I had only three or four quarters, which I meant to use to make phone calls once I arrived in L.A.

At least there was water at the rest stop—so I consoled myself as I led Lizbeth to the highway. Water, and certainly no cop to object to my hitchhiking on the highway. In fact, the spot seemed so desolate that people would think twice before passing us by.

The sand was so fine that it blew along the ground, infiltrating my bags and my shoes. Cacti were everywhere. It is a wonder anything survives in such a place, but all that does has stickers or stingers.

We had another ride soon.

Two men occupied the front seat and three of us and the dog were squeezed into the back. I learned that all of us in the back were hitchhikers. One of the other hitchhikers was a very old man and the other was very drunk. I never did know if the front-seat passenger had been a hitchhiker too, but he and the driver were now partners and they planned to take Hollywood by storm.

When we ran low on gas, the driver pulled into a little desert town and conned a church out of a tank of gas. His story was, I think, that his mother was ill and he was rushing to her side. Who the rest of us were supposed to be I am not sure. Of course the deacon knew it was all lies, but I imagine a tank of gas seemed a small price to pay to have the lot of us peacefully on our way.

I do not remember where the old man got out. Near La Puente, the drunk came to life and demanded to be let out. His English was poor, but I gathered he meant to get out several hundred miles earlier—or he had not meant to travel at all. Apparently he had no idea where he was and did not remember getting into the car. He was let out at the first exit after he awoke. He was furious. But there was nothing to be done for it and we still could not discover where it was he wanted to be.

When we reached L.A., the driver assured me he would drop me off in the heart of Hollywood. But first we were going to whiz by Long Beach. I do not know why I did not insist on being let out, but I was very tired and the prospect of not having far to walk was very tempting.

Once we were in Long Beach I began to understand the driver and the passenger had no plan. We went first to a modest neighborhood where the driver went into a house, ostensibly to solicit lodging from some acquaintance. I thought his true object was to conclude a drug deal. Whatever his mission, he returned disappointed. Then we went to the Queen Mary.

I know not the point of this side trip. But I was to stay with the car in a restaurant parking lot, somehow to prevent its being towed if that seemed likely, while the two of them went to view the Queen Mary and the Spruce Goose. I had mentioned wanting to throw Lizbeth in the Pacific Ocean as I had promised her the previous year when we were stranded in the desert and they suggested I do that. But the Pacific here was a little brackish inlet and not the blue surf I had seen in Santa Monica. When they returned they still had not developed a plan. Between them they mentioned almost every place in California I had ever heard of as a possible destination and none was accepted or finally rejected. I was relieved that the car did seem to be returning to Los Angeles.

They were no nearer a decision when the driver pulled off the freeway and told me to get out. He seemed to be perfectly arbitrary in this. We had been much closer to Hollywood many times. I was let out east of downtown.

The sun was low and red in the haze. Lacking landmarks, I used it to judge west. Lizbeth and I set out on the streets of L.A. This was by far the most difficult part of our journey.

We had been let out in a Latin neighborhood—so I call it for I did not discover whether these were Chicanos or more recent arrivals. We walked west, and before the sky was dead black—for there are no stars in the sky over Los Angeles, or at most Sirius and Venus—we had walked through a warehouse area, a bit of some Chinatown if not the Chinatown, downtown L.A., and a neighborhood of nice older homes, duplexes, and apartments in some hills.

I supposed from the hills that I had overcompensated for the season and vectored us to the north of our destination. I began looking for ways of descending the hills. I found many cliffs at the ends of culs-de-sac and at last I found a narrow, steep stair. The stair ended at Sunset Boulevard in Silverlake. This I thought was a neat piece of dead reckoning for we had not been much, if any, out of our way. But I could hardly be smug; we had so much farther to go. Fortunately the portable toilets for the L.A. marathon were still on the streets. The streets seemed unusually quiet. We walked and rested, walked and rested. I would think we had walked miles only to discover the street numbers had advanced by only a few hundred.

As we crossed the Hollywood Freeway on Santa Monica Boulevard, I realized the address I had been given was within a few blocks.

I had been here before.

When I found the address it was a little door between storefronts. I rang the bell and Carl came down to let me in.

All the rest is in a fog of fatigue. Carl fed me and let me shower. He led me through what seemed at the time a maze to a small room where he said I might sleep. He offered me a futon, for the room was quite bare. But I said that could wait until morning.

The window looked onto Santa Monica Boulevard. The service station where I had waited for Roy to rescue us, as we were leaving town the year before, was right across the street.

Pondering this irony, with Lizbeth at my feet, I fell asleep.

WE WERE THEN off the streets for about four months. I called the voter registrar the first thing Monday morning. One of the things that bothers me most about being homeless is being disfranchised. Even Third World countries have somehow mastered the technology required to permit all adults to vote. Tinhorn oligarchies do not fear the poor, but the United States does. I had always registered and voted when I had an address.

But in Los Angeles I had an ulterior motive. I meant to remain in California, and my attempt to rent a mailbox the year before had taught me the importance of getting my local documents in order. The voter's registration I could get without money. When I had the money, I got a California ID at the Department of Motor Vehicles. I had tags with our Hollywood address made for Lizbeth, and I applied for a library card.

People who have seen only the boulevards and the avenues of Hollywood may not realize that many of the smaller streets between have a very residential character, with lawns and gardens. Much of Hollywood is impoverished, but like other poor areas in Los Angeles, the slums do not look like the slums of Eastern cities. Large old houses and even small cottages are subdivided and subdivided again into apartments. But they look like houses and they are invariably brightly painted. Sometimes a second or even a third house has been installed on a lot, but there is still room for some grass and shrubs.

I took Lizbeth on as many errands as I could. We often took a zigzag course to explore the side streets as we went. We encountered a number of dead ends. In many places the Hollywood Freeway has cut streets off. The studios still maintain several compounds in the area, and the most ordinary-looking street will sometimes come to an end at one of their gates. We made slow progress because Lizbeth found everything smellworthy. She loved to smell Hollywood more than any other place we have been.

Dawn in Los Angeles is brisk, even well into the summer, and we always especially enjoyed the morning walk, for the cool air would bring back a bit of her puppyhood friskiness. Hollywood is at its best in the early hours of the morning. A street-corner musician gave Lizbeth the name Proud Midnight, and indeed she did prance proudly as we walked.

I had spent but a few homeless days in Hollywood, and those I had spent camped in the fire zone. While I was at Carl's, I observed the condition of the homeless in the area.

What I noticed first was the Dumpsters. The down jacket Jack Frost had given me had finally come to the end of its useful life, and quite a bit past it by the standards of less desperate people. I bundled the jacket with the trash I had accumulated on my journey from Austin and went down the backstairs to the

Dumpster. It was locked. When I inquired upstairs, I was shown its key, which was kept on a large ring on a nail in the roomers' kitchen.

In Austin I had encountered only two or three locked Dumpsters. I had assumed they were meant to keep scavengers like me out of them. Surely that was the reason the Dumpster at the plasma center was locked: to prevent anyone from coming to grief with the used venipuncture sets. In the guise of The Unknown Scrounger—for I had worn a paper bag over my head when I delivered the canned goods I found to the drop point in Sue's—I had written *The Austin Grackle* concerning scattered medical waste and the failure of some labs to red-bag their biologically contaminated garbage. One of the columnists at *The Grackle* had then run an item on the subject. Whether the plasma center had used a locked Dumpster before the item ran, I do not know. But I was all in favor of medical waste being deposited out of reach of can scroungers and divers who might not realize the nature of the material until it was too late.

A Dumpster at a pizza shop in Austin was locked, I thought, out of pure meanness.

As a survey of the alley behind Carl's place made clear, L.A. Dumpsters are locked to prevent unauthorized dumping. The alley was often so full of trash and garbage that vehicles could pass only with difficulty.

In Los Angeles, jobbers get together and rent large storefronts that are then divided into stalls. This is what is meant by *flea market* in Los Angeles. Evidently only a few of these businesses provided themselves with trash service, and those who did had to lock their Dumpsters in order to have the use of them. Occasionally what I supposed was a city crew came with a large truck and cleared the alley, but the alley would revert to its previous condition within a few hours.

I planned never to have to scavenge again. But that almost all of the Dumpsters were locked was yet another reason for me to think scavenging would be impractical in L.A.

Across the alley from Carl's place was a small parking lot. There a group of homeless men had established a camp. In the central plaza of L.A. I had seen groups of homeless families, almost all of whom were black. The homeless people I observed in Santa Monica were mostly young and white and equipped with good backpacks and other nice gear. But this camp in a seedier part of Hollywood consisted only of men. I was told they were mostly Central Americans and mostly illegals. Many of them were young and able-bodied and went in the morning to the informal labor market that formed around a paint store, a block west on the boulevard.

They had no shelter in the parking lot. The camp consisted only of some flattened cardboard boxes they sat or lay on and, sometimes, a discarded mattress or sofa. The number of men in camp varied from five to fifteen. They exposed themselves to urinate whenever they felt the need, but so, in this neighborhood, did other men who seemed not to be homeless. That they defecated in the alley at night I would discover in the morning, for Lizbeth would point out the evidence. How they ate, I do not know. They drank and always had a bottle of wine to pass around, but on the whole I would say, for their numbers, they drank much less than the drinking groups I had observed in Austin. Weekdays, during business hours, the young men were gone from the camp. I believe they did work or did seek work regularly.

Although on one morning I found the boulevard blocked because the Immigration and Naturalization Service was conducting a raid on the informal labor market, and although the owners of the parking lot often had the furnishings and cardboard removed, I did not see any official interference with the group.

Gangs came at night to spray-paint the walls around the parking lot, and painters came in the morning to paint over the graffiti, but neither the gangs nor the painters seemed to bother the homeless camp.

SIXTEEN

In the Bamboo

Carl was a short, rotund, ruddy man, perhaps in his fifties. He had operated a bathhouse in Hollywood that had catered to the leather crowd until it was razed by fire. Although I did not know it while I was his guest, Carl had been quite an activist in the early days of the gay movement of Los Angeles. He had a crusty and sarcastic facade, but he was in fact a generous and kindhearted man whose interest in helping me, and others who came to his door, derived of nothing more than a desire to see gay people do well.

Jack Walden was a tall, lean man with a gray crewcut, who was in his mid-forties. He was illustrating and writing for a number of gay magazines, and he hoped to gain from me some pointers on writing. In that, I failed him while I was in Hollywood. I thought his career was sufficiently advanced that he would not appreciate my most thoroughgoing criticism. Yet that was exactly what he wanted, and after I left I gave it to him by correspondence.

The rooming house was rather like a dormitory, for the shower was one way down the hall and the toilet and lavatory were the other way. There was much towel-clad traffic in the hall, although Jack preferred to go nude. A gay dormitory in Hollywood may sound like a sexual shooting gallery, but for me it was more like a monastery. I found myself missing the little convivial encounters in the rest room of Pease Park.

Jack advanced me the price of a manual typewriter I found in a Hollywood thrift shop. I was very fond of it, and all the more because it still bore property tags from United Artists and MGM. I became, for me, terrifically prolific. Some weeks I turned out four or five short stories, and they all sold, although in most cases I would not realize payment for six or eight months.

On the other hand, as I became acquainted with the rent structure of Los Angeles, I discovered that even if I maintained such productivity for six or eight months, at which time I might have a steady income, I could not afford even the smallest apartment of my own. Indeed, I could not afford to pay what Carl's paying roomers were supposed to be paying, and they all assured me there were no cheaper accommodations to be had in all of Los Angeles. Nonetheless I tried to establish every sort of connection with California and Los Angeles that I could. To build some ties to the community, and because it was an interest of mine anyway, I began to go to Plummer Park in West Hollywood on Wednesday nights to attend meetings of ACT UP, the AIDS Coalition to Unleash Power.

At first I looked around these meetings for people who had the emaciated look that Daniel had and that from news photos I expected to see in people with AIDS. It seemed to me very peculiar that no one in ACT UP would have AIDS. Moreover, some of the educational presentations suggested that the problems of AIDS in the 1990s would be increasingly the problems of managing a chronic, rather than a terminal, disorder. I began to imagine that

ACT UP was composed of healthy do-gooders who had a wildly optimistic view of medicine's ability to manage AIDS.

I attended a meeting at which the expense of AZT, the principal antiviral drug then in use against AIDS, was the subject of much discussion. Many of the people present revealed that they wanted the drug for themselves. But at just this time AZT was first being prescribed for people infected with HIV who had not developed AIDS. I supposed that in addition to the healthy optimistic do-gooders, ACT UP had also some members who had the latent virus.

Only at the last did I come to know that many of the young men at the meetings, who looked healthier than I had looked on the best day of my life, had full-blown AIDS, as it is called, and some of them had been hospitalized and near death many times. The talk of learning to manage AIDS as a chronic disorder was not altogether wishful thinking, and the evidence was sitting in the chairs around mine.

ONE DAY, QUITE out of the blue, Tim arrived at Carl's place.

When I had seen Tim at Billy's as I recovered from phlebitis, Tim had seemed like a new person, entirely calm and reasonable. Moreover his supposed attraction to me had manifested itself more consistently. Billy, though he professed to have no romantic or physical interest in either Tim or me, threw a temper-tantrum whenever he found we had got naked in his living room.

After I recovered I had visited Tim in jail several times and found him the picture of equanimity. When I talked with Tim in jail we had discussed—idly I thought—many possibilities, among them that we might find an apartment to share when he was released or that we might travel to California together. When he was released from jail Tim learned from Billy that I had gone to California. Tim concluded that I meant for him to join me in

California. As I was finding no romantic or sexual prospects in Hollywood, I might have thought to send for Tim if I had secured an independent situation. But at the time his arrival was the last thing I expected. I had not even sent him my address, but he had browbeat Billy to reveal it.

When I had visited him in jail Tim had told me he was receiving a rather strong antipsychotic drug, which he agreed to take to demonstrate to the authorities that he was cooperative and that he ought to be released sooner, rather than later. In spite of my experience in mental health, I failed to think that Tim might be getting the medication because he needed it or that the positive changes in his behavior might be due to the medication. I was not to escape the consequences of this bit of stupidity.

The first night he was in Hollywood, Tim slept with me. He rolled a condom onto me as if he were filled with delighted anticipation. Yet shortly after I penetrated him, although he obviously remained physically aroused, he changed his mind. This was the old Tim.

However sick Tim got, he retained the ability to be perfectly charming and ingratiating when it was to his advantage. By the time I woke in the morning, Tim had made a place for himself in his own right at Carl's, in Carl's bed. Tim then told me, in the way that the soap opera villain explains his wicked plans to his intended victims, that in establishing a beachhead for him in Hollywood I had served my purpose, that if I remained at Carl's I would be in his way, and that he proposed to drive me out.

His abrupt and extreme changes of mood had returned. Sometimes he would come to my room saying he wished to make up and offering me sexual services that I did not always have the wisdom or fortitude to refuse. Other times he came nude into the TV room, lay on one of the sofas, and began masturbating, only to accuse me of making him uncomfortable by staring.

He would tell another roomer that I was sexually obsessed

with that roomer, and then he would return to me to say that the other roomer was tired of receiving my longing glances. As in any dormitory situation, from time to time money or other valuable objects would be missed by one or another of the tenants. When that happened Tim would let slip that he had seen something like whatever was missing in my possession, but then he would assert that of course I was above suspicion.

By playing both ends against the middle, Tim managed to create a lot of disharmony at Carl's place while creating the impression that I was the culprit. I was made very uncomfortable, and even some who could see what Tim was up to could not always avoid being taken in by one or another of his stories. At the same time, Tim seemed sincerely to believe that I was persecuting him, and two or three times got worked up enough that he physically attacked me.

I do not know whether Tim would have succeeded in his plan of dislodging me. Carl's landlord appeared one day, discovered Lizbeth, and then there was no question of our remaining where we were. Several of Carl's lodgers, who had experience in the system, told me that because I'd been careful to document my residence in California I was now eligible for emergency housing. This would not be a cot in a homeless shelter, but a room in a decent, if not luxurious, hotel. Of course I would have to get rid of Lizbeth. This was no solution, because I could have stayed at Carl's at least awhile longer if I were willing to get rid of Lizbeth.

After the Fourth of July, I got one of Carl's boarders to take me to the library to return some books, and then to a ramp on I-10.

WE HAD MANY short rides and in a couple of days we reached a rest stop east of Riverside. There we were picked up by a young man in a red Volkswagen beetle. He asked me to assure him that I was not a serial killer before he let me in the car. He seemed very serious in making this inquiry and was much relieved when I told him I was not a serial killer. Shawn's story was that he was going to pick up his son from his ex-wife's home in Phoenix, and then they were going to have a vacation together that would include a visit to the Six Flags amusement park near Dallas. I cannot account for the similarity of stories and various other similarities among several people who gave me rides, but I can only say that it is not a trick of memory, but is confirmed by my few contemporary notes and letters that survive.

The Volkswagen did well until we reached Phoenix. Then the battery could not hold, or could not get a charge. We pushed the Volkswagen to several service stations in north Phoenix, but as the hour was late, no one on duty could do any more for us than to give us a jump. A jump would start the engine and then we could go a few blocks before the car was dead again.

Shawn said he wanted to conserve his money for his vacation, but clearly he would have to get the car fixed. He said he would get some bids in the morning, have the car fixed, pick up his son, and then the three of us would proceed to Texas. Several parts of this story did not quite add up. For one, as we had approached Phoenix, Shawn had revealed that he did not know precisely where his ex-wife and his son were. If he were going to Dallas, his most direct route it seemed to me, for again I did not have a map, would take me far out of my way. And then there was that wherever we stopped for a jump in Phoenix, Shawn asked about the availability of speed.

For once the lessons of experience were not lost on me, and Lizbeth and I jumped ship.

We were in north Phoenix, by the Flagstaff Highway, all of the next day, and the next night we walked through town. Once we were at a suitable ramp on I-10, it was yet another day and night before we got a ride out of Phoenix. We were picked up by two gentlemen in a pickup who took us to a rest stop I had not known existed, between Phoenix and Tucson. I had scarcely filled our water bottles and smoked a cigarette before two other gentlemen offered me and another hitchhiker a ride in their pickup.

This ride was supposed to go to Tucson, but we were put out somewhere considerably short of Tucson. The other hitchhiker walked on. But Lizbeth and I stayed the night where we were. I could detect no signs of civilization around this ramp and all the next morning we saw only three cars. But late in the afternoon a man whose station wagon was filled with tubs of crushed aluminum cans gave us a ride to the fancy truck stop south of Tucson.

There I met a boy of fifteen or sixteen years who had a hand-held citizens band radio. He said he was using the radio to hitchhike around the country and this was his summer vacation. Yet he had absolutely no gear and I suspected he was a local who did his traveling in fantasy. He assured me he would soon find a ride for me with his radio. Nothing came of this, except that I learned from the boy's radio what name the truckers gave to the camp followers at the truck stops, which was "lot lizards." This struck me as immensely amusing at the time, and for several days I would break out giggling whenever I thought of it.

Lizbeth and I had a ride with a businessman in a very nice new car the following morning. We were let out across the highway from a new development whose architecture was so advanced that I can only describe it as otherworldly. Moreover, the development was waterscaped, evidently with wastewater, so extensively that Venice might seem arid by comparison. Finding potable water in this place, however, proved challenging, for the shopping center and the service stations and the motel had been planned to be all of a piece, and the plan left no room for such accidents as unattended water taps.

In July, of course, Arizona was far worse than it had been in other seasons, and on the trip to the development for water we consumed almost as much water as we got. I did not know what to do. Clearly we could not stand in the sun where we might be seen, for the sun was too intense. We sat in the shade of the crossover for many hours.

A Cadillac DeVille stopped a few yards past us. I could not believe this was a ride, for the driver could not have seen us. An enormous black woman, as stout as I, got out of the passenger side and relieved herself. I averted my eyes and planned not to look back until I heard the car drive away. But when she was done with her business and back in the car, she rolled down the window and called to me.

She questioned me closely. I offered her my IDs. She asked if I had a weapon and I told her there was a folding knife in my pack, which she might keep with her if she wished. She said that would not be necessary, but as I could see, my bags would have to go in the trunk anyway. And so I could see, for half the backseat was taken up with a box of provisions. Now I suppose any serial killer might have passed her examination as well as I did, but at last she said for us to get in.

The driver was an enormously muscular young black man and I never did know if he was her son, her servant, or her companion. At all events he did as she said, and if he ever disagreed with her judgments or opinions he never revealed it. He got out and helped me pack my bags into the trunk, and we were off.

The woman said she had been visiting friends in Los Angeles and was returning to her home in Georgia. She proposed to let me out on I-10 at whatever place seemed to me best to make connections to Austin. The ride proceeded without incident, but as we were all of an imposing physical presence, and an unlikely combination to boot, we seemed to inspire anxiety among the locals wherever we stopped.

At dawn the following morning, Lizbeth and I were let out at Kerrville, Texas. Two days later we had got only so far as Fredricksburg. It was summer and the fire ants were at large. I tried to call

Billy in Austin, but he had moved and his number had been changed. I never heard of him again. Eventually I reached a friend who was willing to pick us up in Fredricksburg.

LIZBETH AND I went first to the stand of bamboo where we had slept before we left Austin. It was still there. Just as I had been told at Ramblin' Red's, the project to remove the brush and the homeless the brush concealed had not reached the bamboo. I surveyed it as I had not before.

I discovered Tim had camped in it, for I had told him while he was in jail of the places I had found to sleep. Evidently when he had been released from jail he had worked at a fast-food restaurant until he got the money for his bus ticket to L.A. His uniforms were among the things he had left in the camp. He had packed up everything in plastic garbage bags, but the growing bamboo had pierced the bags and everything had been ruined by mildew, including his expensive motorcycle leathers.

As he had taunted me that he would force me to return to Austin, he had said he would give me the bicycle he had stashed there. He planned to be a star in Hollywood and would never want the bicycle again. I found a bicycle in the bamboo and I supposed it was the one he meant.

There were several well-marked trails and old camps in the bamboo. I left the old camps intact and contributed Tim's gear to one of them, for I meant for them to be decoys. I carved a nine-by-four-foot room out of the wall of bamboo and was pleased to discover that the entrance was invisible from even a few feet away.

By all rights I should have felt perfectly hopeless. The trip to Hollywood was a better chance than I could expect to have ever again. But as a boy I had read *The Swiss Family Robinson* over and over—I loved the idea of it so. Putting the camp together in the bamboo was just such an enterprise. I found shower curtains and learned to layer them to keep the rain off our heads. I rigged several of them on bamboo poles so they could be lowered down the bamboo walls; I was planning against the winter winds, although it was July. I camouflaged the shower curtains overhead to prevent their being seen by aircraft.

I installed cushions and a foam mattress on them. I put in makeshift bookshelves. I found some large fresh dry cells and wired them to a radio so I did not have to change the batteries every hour as I listened to the news. When I satisfied myself that light in my camp would not call attention to us at night, I discovered how to make lamps that would burn on cooking oil, a commodity that was always available in abundance in the Dumpsters.

In spite of the obvious trails, it was very rare that anyone else entered the bamboo at all. I could see no reason I might not bathe in the bamboo, and I set out vessels to catch rainwater for this purpose. I always had some little project. I had come to believe that Lizbeth and I would die homeless. And that seemed to me too bad. But then, why shouldn't I try to make us as comfortable as I could, wherever I could? I had put us to considerable discomfort several times in my attempts to struggle against homelessness. For a time I would just accept it and make the best of it.

Of course this was a policy easier to effect while we were out of public view in the bamboo, than it would have been if we were still sleeping in the open in Adams Park.

The first month in the bamboo was an adventure and a vacation. Curious as it sounds, I needed a vacation. I had worked very hard in Hollywood, and one of the principal problems of self-employment is that after eight hours or ten or twelve, no boss comes by to say that you might as well knock off for the day. We went around in the coolness of the morning to the Dumpsters and returned to the bamboo to eat—although because of the rats, raccoons, and possums I was careful never to bring food into our sleeping quarters. I puttered around camp, installing whatever improvement I had thought of, and in the heat of the day we lay in comfort and I read. I wrote long letters and began to make a few sketches, which have become the present book. I could read at night by the light of my improvised lamp. And if I read too late and overslept the next morning, I had nothing to fear.

This was as good as homeless life gets, and that could not last.

ON THE SIXTEENTH of August, precisely a month after we had returned, I was a little surprised to hear someone moving through the bamboo, but I was not alarmed because people had been in the bamboo before. I became increasingly concerned as I realized this was no one passing through, but whoever it was was making a systematic search. He was carefully exploring each of the culs-de-sac and the false trails I had built. We would be discovered, there was no doubt.

The last screen to the entrance of our sleeping area parted.

"Well, there you are!"

It was Tim.

When I went to check my mail at *The Grackle* that afternoon there was a letter from Jack Walden warning me that after I had left Hollywood Tim had turned his spite against one roomer after another until the roomers en masse had confronted Carl and given him an ultimatum, the result of which was that Tim had been cast bodily into the street. I should be on the alert, Jack wrote, for Tim had made some remarks that suggested he was heading back to Austin.

But as Tim told it, he had just become bored with Hollywood. Tim told me he intended to make my life so miserable that I would abandon the bamboo and he would have the nice camp I built. In making me miserable, he succeeded.

He had no intention of working as hard as would be required to hack another place out of the bamboo. Instead he camped a little farther up the hillside where the bamboo was sparse. As he had learned from me to check the Dumpsters, he soon found a dozen shower curtains and a roll of duct tape. With these he erected a wall tent, which might have been a lighthouse for its general visibility. I consoled myself that while his tent might increase the chances of our detection by the civil authorities, against anyone else it would be an effective decoy.

Tim had a morbid fear of the creatures that moved through the bamboo at night. But though I advised him otherwise, he kept loads of poorly packed food in his tent, with the result that one possum, which was especially smelly even for a possum, called on Tim nearly every night. Besides keeping my camp clean, I did have Lizbeth to discourage the idle curiosity of critters. Tim considered Lizbeth the source of my courage, and as I kept her on a very long lead in camp—one that would reach Tim's tent— he was always trying to entice her with tidbits to stay with him through the night. She went, of course, for the tidbits, but the only nights she stayed I suspect Tim detained her. He would call back to me, "Now, see how you like it when the possums come." The possums never came, but I did watch the rats scurry across the shower curtain overhead, if not with pleasure, then without concern.

Before long, creatures began to visit Tim that did not exist in the bamboo or anywhere else. He sat up for hours at a time, shrieking.

He went through my camp whenever I was away, and once he had grasped the principle of my two little oil lamps, he built a half-dozen lamps on a much larger scale. These he burned throughout the night. I wondered why the fire department did not come, for from any distance at all, his lamps created the impression that the bamboo was afire. The lamps did not keep the creatures away, and the shrieking went on night after night.

Tim found a scrub suit in the Dumpsters, and of course he did not have difficulty finding student apparel that fit him. He began to go to the hospital at which his companion had died, where evidently he had learned something of the routine. He sometimes appeared as a visitor and other times he dressed as an orderly— or so he told me. He pilfered patients' belongings, made off with dinner trays, grabbed the purses left unattended for a moment by distraught visitors. Whether he thought of this on his own or had run across my unfinished novel as he went through my desk at Carl's, I do not know. I do know we had never discussed institutional parasitism. I do not even know that he went to the hospital, as he said he did, but only that he was stealing somewhere. He consistently had more cash than he could have retrieved from Dumpsters and I doubted he was hustling.

As in Hollywood he would sometimes want to make up and would offer me sexual services. I had perhaps grown no wiser, but I no longer needed much fortitude to refuse Tim because while I was living in the bamboo I could make myself reasonably presentable and when I went to Sleazy Sue's, in spite of having Lizbeth with me, I was having an unparalleled streak of luck in receiving invitations to spend the night with one of the other patrons. As in Hollywood, Tim tried to find a place to masturbate so that he could accuse me of staring at him. For the thickness of the bamboo around my camp, he could not find such a place. After I ran him out of my sleeping area a few times, Tim began to go around naked much of the time. Whether this was to entice me or to tease me or had nothing to do with me, I do not know, but as I went about my business I would sometimes find Tim in the middle of a trail, squatting on his heels, masturbating.

From these episodes, and what had come before, I began to think that Tim really could not distinguish feelings of sexual arousal from feelings of rage and that he was bound, once he aroused himself sufficiently, to lose his facade of sanity. As he made it easy for me to observe his physical state, I began to think I could guess Tim's state of mind by observing the state of his penis. I did not take this theory too seriously, for in psychological matters researchers too often find whatever best confirms their hypotheses. But I did think, though Tim could maintain his composure well enough to get around in public, that he could not perform satisfactorily as a hustler.

Tim claimed to be having an affair with a police officer, and perhaps he had once realized his fantasy of having sex with one. But I very much doubted that any real policeman, having made it safely to the end of his shift, would think it very recreational to maintain an affair with Tim.

In September he went to the hospital less often, or so he said. He began breaking into cars, and he reported he did not even have to break into many, because freshmen from the sticks had not yet learned to lock theirs.

When he found a pair of white overalls, he began to leave camp some days in them. He said he masqueraded as a maintenance man at the very large apartment complexes. He had a large ring of keys that he carried on these expeditions. The keys would not fit any of the locks, of course, but people who saw them would assume he was authorized to be wherever he was.

He would pound loudly at the door of an apartment. If there was no answer he would try the door. Often it would be unlocked or could be forced without drawing undue attention. If someone came to the door, Tim would say he had come about the sink. A few times there were problems with the sink, and once or twice the occupants of the apartment left while Tim was supposed to be inspecting the problem. They saw the keys, but they did not notice that he had no tools. He could always escape by saying he was going to the hardware store to get parts.

Again whether he got money by this scheme as he described it or by some other, several times he came by fifty or eighty or a hundred dollars that I think he could not have got legitimately.

He also confided in me that he had a holy mission. He would not quite admit to being the Second Coming of Christ, but if not that, he was anointed by God for something nearly as cataclysmic. After many hours of intensive study as a Seventh-Day Adventist he had gained the power of infallibly interpreting scripture, and as he studied the Book of Revelation he came to realize that many passages alluded to him personally and to his mission.

Some nights in the bamboo he had evil thoughts. He pored over his Bible for a week or two, telling me he was getting nearer and nearer to determining the source of these thoughts. At last he announced that he knew, with biblical certainty, that I was Satan's agent and that I was planting the evil thoughts in his head. He said it was a matter of fact that his holy mission could not reach fruition while I lived. That I had gone to Hollywood just before he did and had returned to the bamboo just before he did proved that Satan was giving me advance notice of Tim's movements.

I believed Tim had followed me to California, and that he had followed me back. If I abandoned my camp to him, I did not think he would be satisfied with it, any more than he had been satisfied to be left in his situation in Hollywood. I thought he would follow me wherever I went.

I could not appeal to the law.

I said nothing, but I decided that as soon as I could think of a way of disposing the body I would have to kill Tim. In the meantime I began to scatter my orts around his tent to encourage his nighttime visitors. This last proved to be useless, for Tim had by now been given the power to understand and be understood by animals. He and Mr. Possum began to have long and inane conversations that lasted late into the night.

Tim's body weighed about 150 pounds. I knew I could not carry it far if I left it in one piece. The soil in the bamboo was not deep, and there was no hope of burying him in the limestone rock beneath it. Perhaps I could dismember him and carry him a piece at a time to the Dumpsters. I knew when the Dumpsters were emptied and I could slip the parts into them just before the trucks came. We were coming to the rainy season. If we had a flash flood, I might stave in his skull with a rock and send his body into the creek. His body would be discovered, but no one would question the matter. Every time it floods, a few fools are washed away. I was the only person in the world who cared whether Tim lived or died and I was all in favor of the latter.

On Saturday, October 7, several different groups of fraternity boys came to the bamboo and hacked a considerable amount of the stand away. I thought perhaps they meant to remove the bamboo altogether. But it was only that they were having various parties with South Seas themes and they wanted the bamboo for decoration. They took bamboo from what I thought of as the back of the stand and they hacked it away until they reached Tim's tent.

Tim was at home. The boys apologized profusely. They were near enough to my camp that I could hear them clearly, but my camp was still well concealed. I was convinced that they had no intention of dispossessing any homeless person. Tim remained of at least two minds on the subject of the boys' intentions, but as I made my Dumpster rounds I did verify that they made use of the bamboo according to their story.

The cops came the night of October 16. I had removed my shoes and retired. But Tim's lamps were ablaze as usual. Lizbeth growled, but I managed to keep her from barking. After they rousted Tim, the cops were very surprised when he informed them that there was still a man and a dog in the bamboo. Indeed, they had shone their flashlights into the entrance of my camp, but they still had not seen it. Once Tim told them of my camp, they still could not find it until he showed them the way.

I was given time to shorten Lizbeth's lead, but not time to get my shoes. They made me walk up the hill, barefoot on the freshly cut bamboo stumps. At the back fence of one of the houses at the summit I was questioned. But every question put to me, Tim answered before I could respond. He was of course very eager to please the male officer. At last we were released and given an hour to get out of the bamboo. My feet were all bloody when I got back to Lizbeth.

The proprietor of Ramblin' Red's, who had some of the nearby property, got the rest of the story. The cut the fraternity boys had made in the bamboo exposed Tim's tent to the view of one of the grander houses at the top of the hill. As chance would have it, a woman who lived in this house had an active imagination, and as a prominent physician's wife she had the influence to have her view of reality heard and treated as solemn fact by the authorities.

Tim's tent, which was no more than seven feet by four feet, became to the doctor's wife a half-dozen six-man tents. And Tim, who was the only one of us she could have seen, became a well-armed paramilitary organization. Whether he was supposed to be a fascist or a communist, I do not know, but when the police turned us up we were escorted to the fence of her house so that she might see for herself who we were. By then, however, she could not be satisfied with fact. She insisted the army was still in the bamboo. A week after we were evicted from the bamboo, she had not shut up, and so the city had to send in the bulldozers. All the bamboo was destroyed, and as anyone who has ever tried to remove bamboo will know, this was no mean task.

I PACKED SLOWLY and then I sat on the curb on the street that ran by the bamboo.

Tim said he was going to a homeless camp he had discovered to the south. When I was sure he had gone that way, I took my things to Sleazy Sue's. Sue's had closed in early September. We slept under the building for a couple of nights, but then there seemed to be no reason we should not sleep in the main entryway. The entryway was a five-by-eight room that showed only a door-sized arch to the alley.

I was at a loss for many days.

SEVENTEEN

A Roof over Our Heads

On Halloween 1989 I saw Tiny, who had owned Sue's. He suggested that I camp on Sue's porch and I admitted that I had already been doing so. Tiny said his lease on the building was paid through November and I could stay on the porch at least until then if I wished. That was the first I knew that Tiny did not own the building as well as the business that had been there. His offer seemed a tremendous boon, for although the nights were not yet very cold, the fall rains had set in.

I visited the barren ground where the bamboo had been. I could not even tell precisely where our camp had been. Lizbeth sniffed around a bit, but I do not think her nose told her more than my eyes told me.

The Austin Grackle ran a free display ad, soliciting a cheap or free typewriter for me. The result of this was an old upright Royal delivered to Ramblin' Red's. One of the regular contributors at

The Grackle left some typing paper, Wite-Out, and steno pads for me at the office.

I found a stout cardboard box that would hold the typewriter and my supplies. When it did not rain I got the box from under Sue's and took it to the pew at Ramblin' Reds. I forget now what I was working on, but remember only that I was frequently interrupted by the principal neighborhood drunk.

Vandals had smashed the pew after I had left for Hollywood. But when I returned, the proprietor of Red's, who had preserved the pieces, had it reconstructed, refinished, and reinstalled. The drunk perceived that I had something to do with the pew's disappearing and reappearing and for some reason resented me.

To avoid him, I tried to work on the porch at Sue's on Monday, the sixth of November. In the afternoon a police car pulled into the lot and a policewoman got out. She demanded my identification as soon as she was sure Lizbeth was restrained. I pulled my ID card out of my wallet and flipped it at her feet. This was exactly as other officers had instructed me to do so that I would not have to come near them, but it infuriated this one. I thought it was standard operating procedure, but she took it as an affront and I never could quite explain to her why I had surrendered my identification as I had.

She asked me what I was doing on the property. I told her I had the permission of the owner—by which I meant Tiny. That she contradicted, and I said at any rate I had the permission of the man who had the lease on the property. She retired with my ID to an old blue Cadillac at the far end of the parking area. I cannot say that I had ever noticed this car before. Much of the paint was worn off or rusted through and the plastic parts of the fenders were broken or missing. Indeed I did not recognize it as a Cadillac.

The officer had a discussion with the driver of the car and in a few minutes the car drew near the porch. The driver was a very old and frail-looking man and the passenger was a blue-haired woman of about his age, but better preserved. This was Lefty Smith and his wife. Smith chewed on the stub of a cigar that had gone out as I explained to him that Tiny had told me I could stay on the porch until his lease ran out at the end of November. Smith's hearing was much impaired and about half of what I said had to be repeated to him by his wife. Even so he seemed to get only parts of what was said.

He said that he owned the property and that Tiny's lease was several months in arrears. His manner was gruff and abrupt. I supposed Lizbeth and I would have to move on. Smith said the property had been sealed by the bankruptcy court, otherwise he would have taken possession of it by now. But at last he said he could see no harm in my remaining for a time, provided I did not allow companions to join me and provided I was sober. I assured him I could easily meet his conditions and he dismissed the officer.

I learned that Smith's policy was to be petty and mean, but to be so through intermediaries such as the police officer. Whenever someone applied to him directly he was perfectly accommodating, so long as it cost him nothing out of pocket.

He and his wife often stopped and spoke to me as I typed on the pew at Ramblin' Red's. Eventually I learned that he owned the strip center as well as Sue's.

Lefty had an overpowering fear of dogs. Some others have been afraid of Lizbeth when her behavior could be called ambiguous. But around Lefty, she was as docile as she was with children. I wondered if she did not recognize infirmity as well as she recognized childhood—I suppose that passes credibility. At any rate she was always on her best behavior when Lefty was around and he was always deathly afraid of her.

On the ninth, a heavy-duty pickup came to Sue's while I sat on the pew at Ramblin' Red's. The truck pulled up on the sidewalk at the gate of the patio and soon a group of three or four young men were loading liquor from the bar into the truck. I recognized a couple of the young men as bar workers, but as staff tends to rotate from bar to bar, I was not sure which bar they were working for. One of the young men looked a lot like Clint, whom I had left in the shack on Avenue B when Lizbeth and I first set out for California, and whom I had not seen since the previous summer at Shipe Playground. I could not trust my eyes at that distance. I found it hard to believe that Clint would be working for a bar, but if it were he I thought he would not reckon it a favor for me to hail him while the others were around.

Tiny came around the next day. He suggested I might be more comfortable on the patio and gave me the key to the patio gate. I believe he might have done so sooner if he had got rid of the liquor sooner. The patio key did not, of course, admit me to the bar, but the high fence around the patio would have concealed any effort to break into it. Now, of course, I knew there was no court seal on the bar. That was just what Tiny had told Lefty to keep him at bay. Tiny had filed for personal bankruptcy a few months before, and no doubt the papers connected with that had convinced Lefty of Tiny's story. The bar was in fact, but not in law, bankrupt.

I had heard from some of Sue's former employees that the bar was far in arrears in rendering to the IRS the taxes that had been withheld from paychecks. Unfortunately, in such a situation the IRS holds the employees responsible as much as the employer, and many of them were in serious trouble, although they had done nothing wrong.

I stashed my gear on the patio, and Lizbeth and I went Dumpster diving. When we returned I found that a car was parked on the sidewalk at the patio gate. There were two men in suits in the car and so I sat on the pew at Ramblin' Red's to see what might develop. One of the men got out of the car. Although I could not recognize Clint from the same distance, I could see the man was a Treasury agent. I cannot say precisely what a T-man looks like, but I know one when I see one. I was afraid the IRS was going to seize Sue's and with it my gear on the patio.

I tied Lizbeth to the bench and went into Ramblin' Red's to ask if anyone knew what was going on. The proprietor and one of the staff stepped out of the shop and the three of us gawked at the Treasury men. The proprietor refined upon my observation. "Secret Service," he said. Mrs. Lyndon Johnson was having her hair done at the beauty parlor that was next door to Sue's.

SUE'S PATIO SEEMED a wonderful place to be. Lizbeth could be let off her leash. I could leave her locked on the patio with some confidence that no one would interfere with her. Parts of the patio had been roofed, and with but a little difficulty I placed my bedroll where there were no leaks. The patio bar, where the keg beer had been served, also remained dry and I set my typewriter on it. Happily this was near enough a street lamp that I could work at night. The pay phone had not been removed and was in working order, although I never made much use of it.

The first night, someone, I imagine it was the drunk, tried to climb the fence into the patio, but Lizbeth convinced him to climb back before I was fully awake. I suppose he had been sleeping on the patio before. Despite occasional similar intrusions, I enjoyed my privacy on the patio second only to my ability to work there. This privacy was not the sort of privacy one misses while in a dormitory or a barracks, but was a kind of privacy that is more to do with having a right to be somewhere. And, I will have to admit, it had something to do with my having some ability to exclude others.

Since our camp had been busted, I had been afraid of Tim's showing up again. If I was where I had no right to be, I would have no right to prevent him from being a few feet away. But I could count on Tiny to back me up if I wanted to keep Tim off the patio, and this was a great relief to my mind.

I discovered that the water was still on in the little taco stand attached to the bar, which had reopened briefly before the bar closed. The stand and the bar had once been separate properties, though they had a common wall, and the meters and accounts remained separate. I ran hoses from a spigot outside the restaurant to the patio and thus managed to shower. By then I had not had a real shower or bath in several months and I hardly minded that the water was cold. I showered every day for about a week—removing the hoses when I was done to avoid calling attention to the arrangement.

I worked as hard as I was able. The thought of what might happen at the end of the month terrified me so, I simply refused to think of it. We had an unusually long spell of cold, wet weather that put an end to my daily showers and slowed my work because my fingers hurt too much for me to make them hit the keys. When the wind was strong, my papers got wet and I was afraid to uncover the typewriter.

Lefty discovered I was inhabiting the patio. I was afraid he would suspect the bankruptcy action was not as he had been led to believe. I did not like to deceive him and I did not like to be caught between him and Tiny. But Lefty, though he could not bear to part with the price of a new car, was a very rich man; he had leased the bar to Tiny for about twenty years, during which time he had recovered his investment in the property more than thirty times over. If he had been very eager to repossess the property immediately, he could have consulted an attorney, but he had been unwilling to go to that expense.

I did my best to volunteer nothing that would compromise Tiny. I played stupid for the first time in my life, and I felt stupid for not having seen before how smart a strategy that can be. A little stupidity went a long way, for Lefty always clung to his snap judgments, and once he was convinced I was a dimwit, he never changed his opinion.

On the twenty-second, Tiny gave me the key to the bar. He told me he had no intention of vacating the bar until January and he thought he might get Lefty to keep me on as a watchman after that. That did not seem very promising to me. I could not see how the building could ever be anything except a bar, but that the property was not zoned for a bar was one of the reasons, after years of battling the neighborhood association, Tiny had given up on the business. Without a speck of insulation, the building required several thousand dollars a month to air-condition—a cost that might be borne by a popular gay bar with an established clientele, but one that no restaurant, or any other business I could think of, could withstand. I thought Lefty, who took pride in being a sharp businessman, would realize he could do nothing with the building except raze it.

But it was true that so long as the building was vacant, Lefty would need a watchman if he did not want the place reduced to rubble.

The weather had become so bad that I could not work on the patio. As a bar, Sue's had been dim, and the few windows that were not boarded over were nailed shut and darkly tinted. I had light to work for only a few hours of the brightest days. The gas was still on in the bar, but there was only one small space heater, which did little physically to heat the place, though it was cheery to look at.

On a dry day I found a mattress and springs by a Dumpster and dragged them to the bar. At night I laid these in front of the heater. For a while I concealed my bed in the daytime, for I did not want to make the situation entirely clear to Lefty or to whoever else might come into the building.

On the third of December I was in Ramblin' Red's, talking to the staff and warming myself, when I noticed Clint was in the store. I had not seen him come in. I had not spoken to him since the summer of the year before. I told him to drop by Sue's sometime that we might discuss old times.

I was a little surprised to be awakened by Clint's knocking on the door at first light the next day—if only because he was not, to my memory, an early riser. Lizbeth was overjoyed to see him.

It had been Clint moving the liquor out of Sue's. He did not work for the bar that bought the liquor, but had done it to settle a bar tab. This seemed peculiar to me because I had never known Clint to drink more than half a beer at a sitting and I could not imagine him in a bar.

Clint told me he was living in a very small house, about eight blocks away, with an Indian student named Gupta. Whatever the truth of that was, I eventually discovered that Clint actually spent much of that winter on the streets, sleeping in boiler rooms of apartment buildings on the coldest nights. Clint began dropping by the bar every two or three days.

Even before the gas was turned off, the bar became extremely cold at night. I had been working in a small room that adjoined the patio because I had discovered it had the best light. At one time the room had been the patio bar and there was a long flap that had opened to provide service to the patio. I removed the nails that had sealed the flap, and on warm days I opened it for even more light. The room was about seven by eight by five. Eventually I noticed that with the flap down and the door closed, the room was the warmest place in the bar, for in so small a space Lizbeth's body heat and mine had some chance to accumulate. I moved the bed into the small room.

When Clint stayed the night, as he did more and more often, he slept on the two-foot width of floor that was left beside the bed. As the door opened inward, finding our places at night was rather like working a slotted number-square puzzle.

Lefty discovered that I was occupying the bar. He saw that the furnishings were being removed bit by bit. He could not have continued to believe any of the court-seal nonsense, but evidently he and Tiny had reached some kind of understanding, although as they came to the end of a twenty-year business arrangement that had profited them both handsomely, they seemed to me to argue needlessly over nickels and dimes.

Lefty especially approved of my taking up in the small room, for this kept my bedding and writing effects out of the way. He had begun to cast about for new tenants, although he said he would not show the place until he received the key from Tiny. He wanted Tiny to make a copy of the key for him—after all, I had one. But Tiny confided to me that he believed this was a matter of symbolic importance to Lefty. Once Lefty had the key he would consider the building and everything in it his property again.

On the twenty-first of December, Lefty brought me what he called Christmas dinner—it was obviously from his wife's kitchen: turkey and all the trimmings. I thought it most politic to remain too stupid to notice the date. He returned on Christmas Day with two more dinners, these from a community dinner for senior citizens and boxed in plastic foam.

We had in these days some of the coldest weather Austin has ever had. One night the low was two degrees Fahrenheit officially—I set out the refrigerator thermometers Tiny had left in the beer coolers and they read something below zero on the patio—and the highs were generally in the twenties. Lizbeth and I stayed bundled up in the little room day and night—there was no question of working. I am doubtful we would have survived in the open.

I had received a few tips for packing up glassware and such for the various bars that were absorbing Sue's equipment. And one evening that it had been warm enough I had gone around to the Dumpsters, and a woman, seeing me digging in one, had given me twenty dollars. For Christmas I gave myself an oil lamp. I bought the scented lamp oil for it at a yuppie hardware store nearby and continued to buy the expensive oil for a long time before I discovered the store had kerosene. A friend of Tiny's gave me a propane lantern, and until I broke the chimney I had plenty of light to work at night. I burned the propane lantern for heat on some of the coldest nights and so managed to keep the temperature in the room at thirty-five degrees.

At the first of the year, Tiny came around with a hired truck and men he had found at the informal labor market—which the city has since disbanded on the theory that the sight of so many people looking for work might create, in the minds of people attending events at the city's new convention center, an unfortunate and accurate impression of the Austin economy.

As Lefty watched and whined at the removal of almost every fixture, Tiny and his men removed the things that Tiny reckoned to be his. He said he would come back to check the premises that evening, and if he was satisfied, he would mail his key to Lefty. Of course Tiny never sent the key and he told me he never would, just to spite Lefty.

Then Sue's was gone and the place was Lefty's vacant building.

Without gas, electric power or running water, for the water in the taco stand was soon shut off, the bar was little better than a cave. In some respects it was worse, for Lefty felt he had claim on as much of my time and labor as he wanted. I was essentially a serf. But I had a mailing address and at night, by kerosene lamp, I could write whenever Lefty had not exhausted me. I managed to register to vote—and the registration stood up to a challenge from an old political enemy—but though I wrote the Secretary of Commerce I could not get counted by the census of 1990.

A cave would have offered more privacy. Lefty insisted that, no matter the weather, I had to keep the building open during all daylight hours, lest he lose a prospective tenant, and in the summer, since the windows were sealed, I had to keep the doors open at night as well to keep us from baking. The nights the doors stayed open, Lizbeth proved her worth, for the winos in the neighborhood continued to think there was a huge stock of liquor in the bar.

I suppose by some standards I was no longer homeless once I reached the bar, but it seemed to me only an improved camp.

Clint stayed at the bar more and more often until at last he had moved in, although his presence had to be concealed from Lefty.

We remained in the bar until September 1991, surviving on what I could glean from the Dumpsters, my occasional checks from writing, and what Clint could make at odd jobs. Without a shower, a car, or telephone and with only an abandoned bar for an address, Clint could not find a job. At times our income was good enough that we could have paid the rent and bills in a small apartment. But we could never get ahead enough to afford all of the various deposits. Although I deceived Lefty that I was alone with the dog in the bar, I deceived him in nothing that affected his ability to rent the property. At times, however, he would accuse me of telling prospective tenants of the property's defects. He falsely accused me of telling people the building had been a gay bar, for he wished to conceal the fact and had not realized Sue's was locally famous. He asked me over and over what I had done with various furnishings, although it would always be something that he had seen Tiny put on the truck. For the defect in his hearing he could not deal with prospective tenants without an interpreter, and he accused me of misrepresenting things when I served him that capacity. The roof had several small leaks when I had moved in, but Lefty would not pay to have them fixed. When, as small leaks will, the small leaks became large leaks, he accused me of punching holes in the roof so that he could not rent the building. He often threatened to board up the bar and send me packing, and he discounted every claim I entered that the services of a watchman are worth something.

He decided the patio concealed the building from the view of prospective tenants. He ordered me to demolish the patio fence and the various awnings and roofed parts. That required a week of heavy labor from me, and at the end of it he gave me a check for five dollars.

He remained in fear that someone might park on his property, and I was another week at building barricades and painting signs to prevent it. He was very pleased and wrote me a two-dollar check with every indication that he sincerely thought himself generous. That someone might park in the lot of his strip center without going into one of the stores was a thing against which he was eternally vigilant. Before I arrived he had ordered several cars towed, some of which had belonged to legitimate customers, and for that reason his tenants pleaded with him to leave the parking situation in their hands.

But he could not. Almost every day he came to the bar and honked. Then I had to sit in his car with him for three or four hours while we observed the lot for illicit parkers. Unfortunately his powers of observation were not good and he frequently annoyed customers, and sometimes more than annoyed them. The parking aside, he enjoyed watching people go into the shops and he would try to guess how much each of them spent. Whenever one of the stores in his center experienced a little rush he said the store was getting too prosperous at his expense and he would have to raise the store's rent when the lease came up for renewal.

In truth, parking was a problem in the area. Yuppies who went to the yuppie bakery across the street from Lefty's property parked their BMWs and Volvos where they pleased. I wondered that people who so much relied on the concept of property had so little regard for it. Many of them thought I was insane when I insisted they remove their cars from Lefty's lot, but if I winked at one of them, there would soon be ten cars in the lot—and when that occurred, invariably Lefty would drive by and tell me that if it happened again he would put me on the street.

I cannot be bitter at Lefty—for he had come to the end of his long life having learned nothing but how to squeeze a dime, and that seems to me to be sad enough. After we left, he tried boarding up the building as he had always said he would do if he evicted me, but as was bound to happen to any such structure in that neighborhood, it began to be demolished a board at a time. That must have hit Lefty very hard.

On my own account, I do not believe I could have got out of the bar on favorable terms. But just as it seemed most certain that Lefty would act on his suspicions of me—after many months of applications—Clint was accepted as a normal subject in a drug study with one of the several firms in Austin that conducts these studies for pharmaceutical companies. This firm always schedules many more subjects for a study than the study requires, to be sure enough of them will show up, and Clint's time was taken in getting worked up for several studies, without pay, before he finally managed to get in one. Once he was admitted to the paying part of a study, he was subjected to scores of blood draws and he had to remain at the firm's facility day and night, where the diet was so poor by comparison to Dumpster fare that he lost weight. In the time Clint had to spend applying for various studies and undergoing various tests, he might have made more money at minimum wage, if he could have found work without an address. But the drug study did pay off in a lump sum. With the proceeds, Clint obtained for us a very small apartment within a block of the shack on Avenue B that I had left as this narrative opened.

As I write these last few words we still must rely on the Dumpsters from time to time, and we often do not know from one day to the next where the rent will come from.

I found an XT personal computer in a Dumpster and it seems possible I will soon be able to provide myself a regular income. But it is far from certain. Any little difficulty with my health—or that of the machine—could put us on the streets again.

I certainly would be there if Clint had not worked to pay all the bills and rent some months and did not every month bring in some money from trading in rocks and minerals and doing odd jobs. I feel as if I am a struggling swimmer who has got his head above water but who remains far from shore.

Lizbeth is now eight years old and loves her comfort as much as ever. When we pass the shack on Avenue B, she gives no sign of recognizing her puppyhood home. She had, however, remembered Clint, and she is now as much his dog as mine.

AFTERWORD

In the more than twenty years since I parted with the galleys of the first edition of this book, it has had its career, and I have had mine. At first, of course, we were close companions and I traveled widely with it and its various editions. There might have been even more of that if I had allowed Lizbeth to fly as baggage, but I would not do that. Instead she remained with our companion, called "Clint" in the book and here, in a rented house with a fenced yard she could excavate at will.

I was exceptionally bad at reading my work aloud; I wrote for the page and could not get my mouth around many of the sentences I had written. I do not suppose I made an especially pleasant appearance. I often thought that if I had been very good at that sort of thing, I would have undertaken to be an actor or lecturer—or perhaps merely a personality, not a writer. I had thought that modern poetry had largely become performance art, but as I traveled and participated in group readings it seemed the same was true of prose.

Several times I was met with mysterious and vague skepticism. I found those who had not met me tended to think I had written the book but that the events had not happened, while those who had met me thought the events *had* happened, but that someone else had written the book. In the years since, I have learned something of the situation of outsider art in general and outsider literature in particular. At the time, I had no idea what was happening to me. I knew from the beginning that the book was *suis generis*, and I have no argument with those who prefer to call it a fluke. At any rate, unlike someone who gets caught up in being the outsider flavor of the month, I knew this book could not lead to a sequel or a series.

After the book's publication, I cast about for something else to do, but many of the factors that had led to my being homeless in the first place had not changed. Lizbeth, Clint, and I faced many new perils and had many more adventures, and the book went its own way. Every semester I still receive a few inquiries from students, which I answer, so far as I am able. Their questions taught me much, and with the students' help, I have become an expert on my own book. Traveling back in time to meet one's former self is a staple of science fiction, but barring some great revision in physics that I do not foresee, revisiting this book is as near to that experience as I will ever come. Often that encounter is embarrassing; occasionally it is delightful. But it is clear that the once-was-me is me no longer, but the book remains what it is and what it was.

Reviewers have been kind enough to provide me with lists of my antecedents. I had never heard of *Travels with Charley* when I wrote my title. *Travels with My Aunt* was the title that suggested mine to me. I had not read it either and somewhat confused it with *Auntie Mame*, which is not so far-fetched an error, considering the parallels in the characters of the aunts and their naïf nephews. I also had not read the London parts of *Down and Out in Paris and London.* When I did, I found those parts much more pertinent than the Paris parts. I encountered the Paris parts in anthologies for students, and I suppose editors thought that squalor and poverty would be less distressing to students if set where people speak French.

Many of the homeless (tramp, hobo, vagabond) books were written by people who were only masquerading as homeless. Whether those writers thought of themselves as journalists or participant observers, or something else, they certainly had the right approach for learning something about homeless people. I would have made a more informative book about homelessness and homeless people if I had set out to investigate them. But in fact, my object was never to learn more about homelessness, but was always to learn how to cease to be homeless. After the book came out, I was shown diverse homeless situations from the camps under New York City's West Side Highway to Copenhagen's Christiana (now so well established that it is more commune than homeless camp), but my subject was my experience, not homelessness per se.

My adventures were considerably more adventurous for lack of cell phones and wireless communication. There were many missed connections, wrong turns, and mistakes that could have been ameliorated—if not eliminated entirely—if I had had a prepaid cell phone that I could have refilled with the small amounts of cash I could reasonably have come by. If the social sites and free Web pages that exist today had existed then, I cannot help but wonder what my memoir would have been, or whether it would have even existed at all. I do not believe the material facts of homelessness have changed, or are likely to so far as I can see, but writing a memoir can clearly never again be quite the way it was.

I did indeed write the book myself. Some of the first draft was printed in *The Threepenny Review,* which created the impression that the book was heavily edited. It was, but heavily edited by me. I can always use plenty of copyediting, for I often write from mental composition and think ahead of myself as I write, omitting prepositions and pronouns, dropping tense endings, and making careless errors that I would correct immediately if I read them. I rarely catch these errors because when I attempt to read my own copy, I see it as I intended it. I had an extensive, Tristram Shandy–like first draft with lengthy digressions and a wide-ranging subject matter. When I focused on my experiences most related to being homeless, I cut perhaps 90 percent of the extraneous material. And I suppose the best 10 percent of anyone's stuff is likely to be pretty good.

The events did indeed happen to me. There are some disagreements among the participants and observers, such as those involved in the event that led to Lizbeth's impoundment. I am told I misstated the various regulations for public assistance. The few differences there illustrate the difference between journalism and memoir. The journalist should seek out every side of the story, research the regulations, be certain that every point of view is represented—especially where there are contradictions. This is generally a good approach, especially when the differing accounts are well matched, but there is the drawback that absurd or idiosyncratic views may be disproportionately represented. Nonetheless, that is the journalistic approach to truth.

The memoirist, on the other hand, owes only a single honest account, not every account at once. I wrote what I was told when I applied for assistance; a journalist perhaps might have found that the published regulations differed. I wrote my side of the story. I expect readers understand that. No one should be surprised that autobiographical writing tends to take a charitable view of its subject; I trust readers can account for that. I do not expect, and no one else should, that other parties in crises and conflicts would agree with me in every detail. While the points of view and opinions of the events I wrote about would naturally differ in the accounts of others involved, there were no fictional incidents and no composite characters. This is the truth of experience, the truth of memoir.

Around 2005, a number of phony memoirs were exposed, which in turn led to a number of articles recalling earlier literary frauds. I think it only fair to the authors to point out that several of the books had first been proposed as novels, and some of them would have been good reads as such. I had a very minor role in one of the exposés. This seemed to explain a number of odd questions, winks, and nudges I received when I was interviewed or questioned less formally about my book. Apparently many literary people suspect that an outsider memoir is not entirely on the up-and-up. On the other hand, I was often uncomfortable and mystified when strangers seemed to know so much about me—especially since I often have trouble recognizing acquaintances from long ago and am seldom sure if they are strangers or someone I'm supposed to know. Many awkward moments like this reminded me that I had written a memoir, and it was much too late to reconsider whether so much self-revelation was a good thing.

I resist being identified as an expert on homelessness. I am not. I flatter myself that if I had intended a study of homelessness, I would have done a better job of it. The experience, of course, is a valuable part of understanding the problem, but experience is necessarily limited. Charts and graphs cannot answer the questions of experience, but neither can the limited perspective of experience answer the broad questions.

The chapter on Dumpster diving has been widely anthologized. I have learned that it has been claimed by recyclers, Freegans, diggers, anti-consumerists, and various other groups and interests, some of which preceded me. I intended it to be something of a protest of an economic system that produces waste and excess on the one hand and want and privation on the other. My essay was based on the facts of my life. My model was Jonathan Swift's "A

Modest Proposal" (which I had recently reread in a Dumpster copy of the *Norton Anthology of English Literature,* where my Dumpster essay now also resides). Although his proposal was fantastic, I did not intend to write a field guide to garbage, but I noticed that Swift's Proposal benefited for the detail of his plan. Swift had to imagine his details; I had only to record the facts of how I lived. I did not mean to advocate that anyone try to live as I did any more than Swift meant for anyone to undertake to enact his proposal. I meant to encourage reform, which was also Swift's intent.

From Swift I also took the dispassionate tone and elevated register which is now especially pronounced in Swift although no doubt he was elegant even by the standards of his own age. Irony, as they say, is a two-edged sword.

Swift was much better at it and only a few readers took his essay at face value, but nearly everyone thought I was teaching urban survival.

Many have noticed my dispassionate tone throughout the book. I am naturally very reserved to the point of Stoicism, and besides, I was determined not to whine. Lately it occurred to me that there might be an underlying cause for my attitude, but I am not qualified (if anyone is) to make a reasonable diagnosis after so many years. I am at a stage in life where it hardly matters. I acknowledge I am indebted to Jim Parsons for his portrayal of Sheldon Cooper; I now understand so much better what has always been wrong with me.

The circulatory problems in my left leg, first described in this book, recurred with a vengeance. Perhaps the problem was exacerbated by the long airline flights I took in connection with the book. At any rate, I am now all but crippled and can get around only a few yards at a time with a walker.

We do not live where eating from Dumpsters is practical, but Clint sometimes picks up a computer or something of the sort, which I gut for parts. Clint also recycled copper from discards and items he found in creeks until the prevalence of copper thieves made sales a nightmare of paperwork.

Lizbeth survived until September of 1998. She had declined rapidly that summer, but had some good days to the very last, and died quietly at my feet one night. Her remains were not committed to a Dumpster. We have since had another dog who has died just as I write this. She was a very different dog, they all are different you know, but she underscored to me how exceptional Lizbeth had been. Because of my age and condition I think it would be unfair for me to have another dog.

I did not say what became of many of the people and businesses in the book. In many cases I do not know. My memoir was a work of nonfiction, and I simply do not know what became of many of those who gave me lifts or who talked to me on the streets. If the events occurred today, many of them might have friended me on a social Web site, but nothing of the sort could happen then.

Billy was Robert David Crane. I saw him once or twice after the book came out. Because of his romantic obsession with Clint, it was impossible for me to maintain contact with Bobby without causing trouble. I cannot explain the beauty and the beast thing with Cliff and me, but Bobby thought it must have been that I was poisoning Cliff's mind against him. Bobby seemed to be very ill whenever I saw him, but he survived until 2011.

Rufus is Russell Wade Ballew. After the book came out, I received a letter from a third party I did not know soliciting contributions for Rusty's commissary account in a California institution. I do not know whether that letter was true in the claim that Rusty was incarcerated in California. Rusty was arrested and sentenced for a crime involving a minor in Bozeman, Montana, in 1994, and again for a probation violation in 2010. I have not heard from him directly and was mildly astonished to learn of his whereabouts.

I returned to Tucson for a charity reading and discovered an entirely different and more agreeable part of town that reminded me more than a little of Austin in the late Seventies and was much pleasanter than parts of Tucson I saw the first time. Beaders and other craftspersons squatted on the sidewalks and offered their wares. There was an organic grocery, an independent bookstore, and so forth, all within a few blocks. On the other hand, Benson, which had seemed nice in a quaint way, had experienced a burst of development that had obscured or replaced places I might have recognized.

Jack Frost produced as John Summers and his true name was Vaughn Kincey. He died in his home in North Hollywood in 2010. He last made news with a claim, rejected by the courts, that Michael Jackson had stolen his idea for a black-cast version of Cinderella. I think Kincey himself believed this claim, and he did have many contacts within Jackson's entourage. Kincey had been in adult entertainment since most of the industry was underground, and was a hustler to the last.

I learned no more about the fiery car crash when Lizbeth and I camped along San Gabriel Canyon Road, north of Azusa. There must have been contemporary reports, but online archives do not go back that far. I have learned that this road is no stranger to spectacular crashes. At least some of the perceptions of peril I had at the time appear to have been well-founded.

I do not know Tim's ultimate fate, but I suspect the worst. Tim had, by chance I think, discovered me in the bar when Clint and I were camping in it. I had told Clint about Tim and in particular that Tim had informed on me when we were camped in the bamboo. Clint had a word with Tim outside the bar. I do not know what was said, but I never saw Tim again. Tim was involved with the Davidians (or so he claimed) when we camped in the bamboo, but it was a fractious group (hence the "Branch" in Branch Davidians). At any rate he seems to have still been living after the conflagration of the compound near Waco, whether he was ever associated with that faction or not.

Billy (Robert Crane) told me Tim had managed to succeed in his dream of dating a cop, but later Clint reported that Tim was camped farther north on Shoal Creek. When, a few years later, I had a chance to inspect the camp that Clint indicated, it was trashed or torn up by storms. I found a few objects that convinced me Tim had been there, but I cannot now recall what the objects were. His camp was near a very well-established and extensive camp created by a man who had been there for many years. I suppose if Tim had been annoying, that man may have run Tim off, or worse. It has been fifteen years since I found Tim's destroyed camp, and I have discovered nothing more of him since.

The bar I called Sleazy Sue's was known as Sally's Apartment when it closed. It had been founded as The Apartment by B.K. "Bunch" Brittain (whom I have called Tiny) in the late Sixties. For several years the management of the bar was let to Houston-based interests who had a bar there called "Dirty Sally's" and so renamed The Apartment. In a college town, history seldom goes back further than four years, so when Bunch terminated his arrangement with the Houston group, the name became Sally's Apartment in deference to customers who had never known it as anything but Sally's. The Apartment had not been the first gay bar in Austin, but it soon became the longest lived. Bunch founded and often presided over the Austin Tavern Guild and was a force for good in the early days of the gay community. Bunch was very flattered by the book. He had heart problems for many years and moved to New Orleans where there was an experimental treatment program that he thought might do him some good. We spoke many times, at length, by telephone. He died in March of 1995. I wrote a small eulogy in the form of a letter to the editor and was honored that it was inserted in the program of his memorial service.

Ramblin' Red's was Oat Willie's on 29th Street. Such shops are now, and at the time of my book, generally called "smoke shops" in observance of Texas laws designed to put them out of business. There is more history to Oat Willie's than I can recount here, but it is the successor of The Austin Underground City Hall, and gained its name and mascot from underground cartoonist Gilbert Shelton (*Wonder Wart-hog, the Fabulous Furry Freak Brothers*) who was a partner in the original venture. The proprietor is Doug Brown, who was very helpful in many ways when I was camped in the area.

The Grackle was *The Austin Chronicle,* now best known nationally as the founder and sponsor of South by Southwest (SXSW), an annual showcase and convention that has expanded from music into electronic games and motion pictures. I took the name (with her permission) from Sarah Bird's fiction. It turned out that her fictional Grackle was based on a different Austin publication. I thought it would be mildly amusing to perpetuate the Grackle name, but I have since had inquiries from historians of the underground press who have turned up no information about *The Grackle* aside from Sarah's books and mine. There was a Grackle bookstore for a while; it might have had a newsletter. Otherwise there never was a real publication with the name.

Of Don, Daniel, Mr. Two Dogs, other homeless people I mentioned and people who gave me rides I know no more than what I have written.

Jack Walden is F. Valentine Hooven III, an illustrator himself, who has produced several works about early gay cartoons and cartoonists including *Tom of Finland: His Life and Times* (Stonewall Inn Editions). Carl is Ken Bartley.

During the time I stayed in Ken's place near Santa Monica Boulevard and Western Avenue I was told Ken once had a bathhouse and I could see he was somewhat involved in a community clinic. Later I learned Ken had been an early activist in the gay community, including at the Gay Community Services Center as early as 1972. Ken's health led him to retire to work in his family's bakery after I left Los Angeles and, I suppose, his rooming house closed. I somehow gained the impression that the building subsequently was razed in the riots of 1992, but present-day photographs seem to suggest the building survived and has been extensively refurbished. When I was in the area, many buildings still bore alien-ese inscriptions from a time when the motion picture *Alien Nation* was made in the area. I cannot find a present-day photograph in which any of these markings survive.

Steven Saylor, who collected my drafts, sent parts of it around, and acted as my literary agent, is a very successful mystery novelist whose best-known books are set in ancient Rome.

After Clint, Lizbeth, and I removed from the bar I was never again much in that neighborhood. We had our ups and downs, but had them elsewhere. After the book came out, Doug Brown at Oat Willie's told Clint that Lefty was looking for me. Lefty had learned of the book, but somehow thought I might be persuaded to return to watch his building for free. As I had thought, soon after I left vandals began to demolish the building, bit by bit, which must have hit Lefty very hard. Because of a lack of parking, subsequent enterprises (various restaurants and drive-throughs) were confined to the footprint of the original building. After Lefty died I heard from several of his neighbors who had recognized him in my book. They all commended me for disguising his name and disguised it shall remain.

Clint counts our relationship as beginning the day we met, making it twenty-six years last year 2012. That suggests to me that so far as he is concerned, he foresaw that our fates were entwined from the first day. Being a little slower, I tend to count it from when he first moved in with me in the shack on Avenue B and to deduct the time we were separated by homelessness, making it more like twenty-three years. In any event, he did not sign on to be a public person and so remains "Clint."

My main regret is that I did not remove from Texas for good when I had the means to do so.

Lars Eighner
Austin, Texas
2013